The Baseball Bat

The Baseball Bat

*From Trees to the Major Leagues,
19th Century to Today*

STEPHEN M. BRATKOVICH

McFarland & Company, Inc., Publishers
Jefferson, North Carolina

All author royalties will be donated to charities

LIBRARY OF CONGRESS CATALOGUING-IN-PUBLICATION DATA

Names: Bratkovich, Stephen, author.
Title: The baseball bat : from trees to the major leagues, 19th century to today / Stephen M. Bratkovich.
Description: Jefferson, North Carolina : McFarland & Company, Inc., Publishers, 2020 | Includes bibliographical references and index.
Identifiers: LCCN 2020025391 | ISBN 9781476679280 (paperback : acid free paper) ∞
ISBN 9781476638539 (ebook)
Subjects: LCSH: Baseball bats—History.
Classification: LCC GV879.7 .B73 2020 | DDC 796.357028/4—dc23
LC record available at https://lccn.loc.gov/2020025391

BRITISH LIBRARY CATALOGUING DATA ARE AVAILABLE

ISBN (print) 978-1-4766-7928-0
ISBN (ebook) 978-1-4766-3853-9

Front cover: Boston Red Sox left fielder Ted Williams at bat
(National Baseball Hall of Fame and Museum, Cooperstown, New York)

Printed in the United States of America

*McFarland & Company, Inc., Publishers
Box 611, Jefferson, North Carolina 28640
www.mcfarlandpub.com*

To Colton and Brooks

Acknowledgments

Like baseball, it takes a team effort to accomplish goals. I certainly had an excellent one in compiling this book. I couldn't have done it alone!

Daughters Amy Erickson and Emily Bratkovich were extremely helpful as my "coaches" for this project. Backing-up my files, locating and editing photographs, obtaining necessary permissions to use certain materials, and a host of other unenviable tasks, I thank you immensely!

Collin Miller, Charles Blinn, and Mark Turgeon "came off the bench" and provided excellent duty. They gave me encouragement and advice along the way plus interviewing bat and billet owners and employees, drafting specific chapters, typing endnotes, and much more.

Many bat manufacturers opened their doors and welcomed "the rookie" with open arms. Private tours, photographs, answers to endless questions, and book chapter reviews were just a few of their many contributions.

Other individuals, too numerous to name, provided valuable assistance in "running the bases." Fact-checking player statistics, reviewing Major League Baseball rules, suggesting book revisions, and providing valuable expertise are a sampling of their duties.

Last, but certainly not least on my "thank you" list, is my wife, Janet. She was with me from the beginning of this project until I mailed the final draft to McFarland. She was enormously helpful in many ways including constant encouragement and wise suggestions amidst my long "extra inning" effort to finish this book. Also, Janet proofread every word of every chapter, including endnotes and bibliography. She made sure I "rounded third and headed safely for home." I Love You!

Table of Contents

Introduction

Whose woods these are I think I know.
His house is in the village though;
He will not see me stopping here
To watch his woods fill up with snow.
—Robert Frost[1]

Throughout my life, I've loved the game of baseball. As a young kid, I remember the games of catch first with my father and then with my younger brother. My dad would throw me fly balls and I would sometimes catch them "basket style" like Willie Mays or Roberto Clemente.

My brother and I would "pitch games" to each other, alternating between pitcher and catcher (although we were both destined to become infielders). In these make-believe games, the catcher served as the infallible umpire, calling balls and strikes, sometimes to the chagrin of the hurler.

I was a happy and proud fourth grader on October 13, 1960, when my heroes, the Pittsburgh Pirates, defeated the New York Yankees, to win the World Series. I listened to Bill Mazeroski's walk-off homer while waiting for the school bus in my teacher's classroom. Boy, my classmates and I were excited when Maz's hit sailed over the left-center, ivy-covered wall at Forbes Field.

Like many kids of my generation, my first foray into organized baseball was with my Little League team. We won the local championship in 1964, my first taste of competitive victory. I batted cleanup that year although I went homerless. I used a 30-inch Hillerich & Bradsby, 125LL, Louisville Slugger, crafted from white ash.

I have no idea of the *weight* of the bat I used in Little League. Such matters meant little to a 12-year-old. The number of ounces or half-ounces of a bat was a foreign language to us. If a bat was too heavy, my teammates and I would simply "choke up." If the heavy bat still didn't feel right, we looked for another. We hoped our search of the equipment bag revealed

1

the perfect "lumber." If a bat was too light, we also looked for a heavier one in our slim stockpile. The bat selection process was similar as I aged and advanced to older leagues.

From Little League, I moved on to Pony League and then to American Legion baseball. My dreams of playing Major League Baseball ended somewhere along this baseball continuum. The deal was sealed for good when I didn't "earn" a uniform for my freshman baseball team at a Big-Ten university. (The old baseball saying of "good glove, no hit" applied to me.)

Other than adult softball teams, I played limited ball past the age of 21 or so. Consequently, I became a full-time fan when my playing days were over.

In college I studied forest science, learning about trees that grow throughout this great country. I also discovered that tree-covered land has traditionally been called "forestland" or "forests." Then, as now in the 21st century, this land is known as "forests" in the western U.S. and as "woods," "woodlands," or "woodlots" in the east. Typically, these latter terms are used by a landowner who is an individual or other non-corporate entity, i.e., family, trust, estate, or family partnership. (The language in Robert Frost poems illustrates well the eastern version.)

College-trained "foresters" and many groups and agencies like the U.S. Forest Service use the term "forests" to describe all tree-covered land.[2] "Forests" is used throughout this book to refer to a tree-covered area regardless of geographic location.

After graduation, I had a fulfilling career with a couple of universities plus the U.S. Forest Service and a non-profit organization. Job assignments later in life gave me the opportunity to specialize in an area of forest science called wood products. Products like lumber, plywood, and paper come from trees, but this fact is often overlooked by a technology-laden society. Wooden baseball bats at the professional level are another product made from trees that are taken for granted by baseball enthusiasts and others.

I'm both a forester/wood scientist and a baseball fan, but I've never been mistaken for a historian or a guru on the subject of baseball. For me, baseball is a sport I can observe and enjoy. You wouldn't get an argument from me if I was even called an *enthusiast* of baseball. The intersection of baseball and forestry/wood science was the major genesis for this book.

Another genesis (the "a-ha" moment) occurred while watching a baseball game. A couple years ago in October, I was visiting a college friend who now lives in Chicago and works for an advertising firm. Stan (not his real name) was a business major, unlike me, but we met in a freshman class and developed a friendship that lasted a lifetime. Stan was not a sports or baseball fan, but we did have one thing in common: growing up in a rural area of Pennsylvania.

During my stay with Stan, the World Series was occurring, so spending a few nights with a non-baseball-loving individual was agony (visiting Stan during the baseball season climax—the World Series—is a separate story). When Stan nonchalantly asked one evening, "Do you want to watch some television?" I jumped at the chance and enthusiastically said, "Yes, but only if you do." However, I was secretly hoping he wanted to watch, and would flip through the channels and stumble across the game.

Fortunately for my national pastime "fix," this is exactly what happened. When Stan came across the game, he stopped channel surfing and said, "I bet you'd like this." So we proceeded to watch the second game of the Fall Classic.

During the game, Stan peppered me with questions like: "What's that white dot on the handles of some bats?" "My dad, who worked at a local sawmill for a few years, wondered why the trees in Pennsylvania were used for bats?" "You said ash trees used to be the primary bat wood but why not anymore?" "The only bat I had as a kid was printed with 'Louisville Something' [Louisville Slugger] on it—are they still making bats?" And on and on. When the game ended, I was exhausted from responding to all of Stan's queries.

After returning home, I asked some of my knowledgeable baseball friends a few of Stan's questions about baseball bats. In addition, I posed some of my own which are no-brainers for foresters with a wood science background. My questions included topics such as the anatomical differences between ash and maple and why this is critical in making a baseball bat, the reasoning behind the traditional shift in trademark location on maple bats, tree scarcity (or not) in the U.S., and the forest pest impact on Major League Baseball (MLB). To my surprise, many questions were either answered incorrectly or met with a blank stare. Consequently, my ambition has shifted from simply *enjoying* the game of baseball to one of *explaining* an important tool (bats) of the MLB game.

This book is focused on wooden baseball bats and the trees that produce them. The timeline starts with the early history of baseball, baseball bats at the major league level, bat manufacturers from the 19th into the 21st century, the evolution of a species change in MLB wooden bats, wood properties that influence the bat manufacturing process, the controversial

Introduction

issue of bat breakage in MLB, the forests that sustain MLB bats, threats to North American trees (particularly ash and maple) from the Emerald Ash Borer and Asian Longhorned Beetle, and much more.

So, sit back, grab a cup of coffee (or your favorite beverage) and enjoy running the bases with me!

1

Major League Origins

[Baseball is] a game whose very origins remain shrouded
in mystery, folklore, and misinformation.—Tim Wiles[1]

I never really thought too much about the origins of the game of baseball when I played—who invented it, where did it begin, changes to the
game over the years, and the like. Even though this book is about major
league baseball bats, it is appropriate to look briefly at the early years of
the game to put the subject of this book (bats) into proper perspective.

John Thorn, from upstate New York, is one of the leading experts on
baseball and the official historian of Major League Baseball. In his 2011
book, *Baseball in the Garden of Eden,* Thorn writes, "In no field of American endeavor is invention more rampant than in baseball, whose whole
history is a lie from beginning to end."[2]

So where did the game of baseball begin—a relatively slow-paced
game that continues to intrigue and inspire young and old but sometimes
finds a way to break our hearts?[3] If we simply want to find a game that
looks similar to 21st century baseball, then the hunt for the birth of baseball will likely lead to the early 19th century. In 1845, the Knickerbocker
Base Ball Club of New York City, modified existing rules and issued them
under their name. Whereas Alexander Cartwright got the fame and a
plaque in Cooperstown, other Knickerbockers—("Doc" Adams, William
Wheaton, and William Tucker)—had a better claim to "inventing" America's national pastime. (Adams also supervised the turning of bats for the
Knicks.)

A fourth gentleman, Louis Fenn Wadsworth, according to Thorn's
book, also played a bigger role in baseball's origins than Cartwright.[4] Although existing clubs had been playing the game since the early 1830s, the
Knickerbockers wrote down 20 rules to govern their club's intra-squad
play and distributed copies to their members.

The Knickerbocker rules were often called the "New York Game" to
distinguish them from other variants. Included in the rules were three

strikes and a batter is out, fair and foul territory, and elimination of intentionally hitting (soaking) a runner with a ball.[5]

Pinpointing the origins of baseball is a more complicated matter than just codifying the rules of a game we today call baseball. To put the issue into perspective, bat and ball games played by youngsters have likely been around as long as we've had youngsters. Whether these games were played with a simple stick, small limb, or merely a hand as the "bat" is open to argument. To complicate matters, these bat and ball games are of great variety, antiquity, and geographic diversity. Their origin and development often gets tangled up in the same evolutionary briar patch from which baseball emerged.

For most baseball enthusiasts, the "true" origin of the game is a moot point. However, baseball scholars and researchers are always finding new documentation and references as to the beginning of the game. It is extremely difficult, perhaps impossible, to pinpoint a single sport or game that evolved into *baseball* as known in the 21st century.

In the Beginning

Based on ancient temple descriptions (paintings) and other archeologist/anthropologists' research findings, "batting the ball" games can be traced to between 1460 and 1500 BC. There are even indications that a stick-and-ball game was played around the year 2400 BC in Egypt (as noted above, either a small tree or shrub, or some unknown material was likely used as a bat or striking instrument). Religious rites as well as simply playing for fun were the reasons this long-ago game was played. But without four bases and other important elements of the game that we all know, it's difficult for 21st century fans to call these ancient activities "baseball."[6]

Nevertheless, as Josh Leventhal points out in *A History of Baseball in 100 Objects*, most people today would look at a 14th-century Flemish illustration and say, "Hey, those kids are playing baseball!" The image dates to about 1301 and is depicted on a calendar that was likely produced in a monastery in what is today northwest Belgium.[7] David Block has the illustration on the cover of *Baseball Before We Knew It*, and the bat is quite recognizable to all that have played the game.[8]

According to Leventhal, the calendar illustration is most likely an early form of a game called *stoolball*. Stoolball had many variations and was played in England beginning around the 11th century. Basically, a pitcher threw a ball at a target, such as a stool or stump. Another player tried to keep the pitched ball from striking the target by hitting the ball away with a bat or stick. Stoolball was often an Easter activity, perhaps invented by milkmaids, who used their milking stools for bases.[9]

There are many documents and pictures from England between the late Middle Ages and the Renaissance Period that trace stoolball's development. Also, other countries from centuries ago have drawings and such that show baseball had many precursors. Baseball scholar John Thorn uncovered a depiction by a Flemish painter (1565) that appears to show "a man with a bat, a fielder at a base, a runner, and spectators as well as participants in waiting." And a German doctor in 1600 wrote about a Prague game that used a ball, club, and running back and forth between bases.[10]

The first printed reference to *base-ball* appears to be from England in 1744. *A Little Pretty Pocket-Book* contained rhymes with woodcut illustrations of children enjoying an assortment of outdoor activities. Pages were devoted to various bat-and-ball games including stoolball, trap-ball and cricket. One of the rhymes centers on *base-ball* and ends with a child running "home with joy." No bat is depicted in the illustration accompanying the rhyme. Unfortunately, the original 1744 publication no longer survives. The earliest reprinted edition available today is from 1760.[11]

Inasmuch as the first *printed* reference to baseball dates to 1744, the first *written* mention of the game is from 1755 in England. An Englishman and meticulous diarist, 18-year-old William Bray of Surrey, penned that he played *base ball* on Easter Monday in 1755 (the name *baseball* has been known throughout history as *base, base-ball, base ball,* and other variations). Bray didn't elaborate on how he performed that day, but his diary entry was an exciting discovery in the search for the origins of our national pastime.[12]

The earliest written reference to baseball from the U.S., thanks to John Thorn's research, is likely from a 1791 Pittsfield, Massachusetts, Meeting House bylaw. The bylaw as quoted in Josh Leventhal's excellent book (page 21), states:

> Be it ordained by the said Inhabitants that no Person, an Inhabitant of said Town, shall be permitted to play any Game called Wicket, Cricket, Baseball, Batball, Football, Cat, Fives or any other Game or Games with Balls within the Distance of Eighty Yards from said Meeting House—And every such Person who shall play at any of the said Games or other Games with Balls within the Distance aforesaid, shall for any Instance thereof, forfeit the Sum of five shillings to be recovered by Action of Debt brought before any Justice of the Peace to the Use of the Person who shall sue and prosecute therefor [sic] [emphasis added].

The Baseball Bat

The direct mention of baseball in the bylaws of the waning years of 18th century Massachusetts is likely not the same sport called baseball in the 21st century. However, the sport is clearly one that involved a bat and ball.

Nevertheless, the bylaw is significant for two reasons. First, it distinguishes baseball from other games. Second, it shows that baseball was common enough in western Massachusetts in the late 1700s that the game was a threat to Pittsfield's windows.[13]

The version of baseball played in the Bay State was known initially as round ball, and then after 1858 as the "Massachusetts Game."[14] Baseball in the "Big Apple" was often called the "New York Game." However, the New York version triumphed over its rival to the north, not so much that it was a better game, but largely due to superior press coverage.[15] Regardless, the New York version has survived over the years; the Massachusetts game has gone the way of dinosaurs and wooly mammoths.

A couple hundred years prior to the Massachusetts bylaw, the game of cricket originated in England. When British colonists came to the new world, they brought cricket along. The game became popular in the American colonies, so popular in fact that cricket became one of the first team sports in America. Even Ben Franklin got into the act in 1754, when he brought from England the official rules of the sport of cricket. Wicket is an informal variation of cricket and was played by George Washington at Valley Forge in 1778.[16]

Beth Hise argues in her book, *Swinging Away: How Cricket and Baseball Connect,* that the game of baseball originated in England.[17] Her theory is that baseball is rooted in English folk tradition such as the game of *cricket.* Hise notes that cricket and baseball have much in common.[18] For instance, both are bat and ball games, and both are summer sports (although the modern baseball season for most fans doesn't swing into high gear until the MLB playoffs and the World Series in October). Both cricket and baseball have similar rhythms in that events on the field dictate the speed of play; there is no time clock. Hise believes baseball and cricket are "blood brothers, separated at birth but genetically linked." She even noticed something that most folks never contemplated. In her interesting book comparing the two games, she explains[19]:

> I peered uncomprehendingly at baseball for ages until I suddenly realised [sic] there was a wicket—the strike zone. It's just invisible, that's all. Once I saw that, I saw everything. The techniques may be different but the duel is the same: pitcher v batter, bowler v batsman, the one trying to outdo the other using pace and/or duplicity.

Since there are so many traits that the sports share, it seemed natural for baseball and cricket to share similar grounds and players starting in the 1840s in America. In fact, Harry Wright (HOF 1953), a prominent baseball player for the New York Knickerbockers, also was a cricket instructor for the St. George Cricket Club in New York. Wright's brother, George (HOF 1937), played professional baseball and "first-class" cricket, making him the first and only person to play both sports at the highest level.[20] Albert G. Spalding, future Hall of Famer (1939) and sporting goods magnate, was a member of the 1889 Chicago Cricket Club. Indeed, players moved between the two bat-and-ball games, bringing features of cricket, the older game, to baseball.[21]

Block's *Baseball Before We Knew It* (Appendix 6) has an excellent undated line drawing from a 1941 publication illustrating old and "new" cricket bats. Also, the illustration depicts other bats used in bat-and-ball games.

Another example of a possible English origin to baseball is *rounders* (not the Matt Damon movie, for film aficionados!). Rounders was a baseball-style game played by British primary school children for many decades. In the 21st century, the game is played by adults as well.

Rounders dates back to the Tudor period (1485–1603) in England and Wales.[22] The game involves a bat, a ball, and players running the bases. Although rounders originally required one-handed hitting of an underhand-pitched ball, it evolved into two-handed hitting after 1888.[23] English-born American sportswriter and baseball statistician Henry Chadwick played both cricket and rounders as a young boy in England. Chadwick was born

Henry Chadwick proposed the "rounders theory" as the origin of baseball (National Baseball Hall of Fame [HOF] and Museum, Cooperstown, N.Y.).

in 1834 and came to the USA when he was 12 years old.[24] Among his many sports-related accomplishments, Chadwick was on the baseball rules committee in the late 1800s and devised the box score. When pondering baseball's birth, he looked to the games of his youth. Seeing so many similarities between these games and baseball, he pointed to rounders as the origin of our national past-time. In fact, many took Chadwick's lead and viewed "rounders" as baseball's official "origin." Chadwick, for all of his baseball achievements, was elected to the Hall of Fame in 1938 and was considered by many to be the Father of Baseball.[25]

In the early 20th century, the question of the origin of baseball came to a head. One prominent person who did not believe (or refused to believe) Chadwick's "rounders theory" was Albert Spalding.[26] By the early 1900s, Spalding was a successful sporting goods entrepreneur. As a former star player who won 204 games and lost only 53 in five seasons with the Boston Red Stockings, player-manager-president with the Chicago White Stockings, and a key figure in the founding of the National League, Spalding wanted baseball to have an American birth. He saw baseball as a direct reflection of American progress and undoubtedly agreed with Mark Twain, who called the game "the very symbol, the outward and visible expression of the drive and push and rush and struggle of the raging, tearing, booming 19th century."[27]

As a young man, Spalding agreed with the rounders theory, but he concluded later in life that the English game was very different from baseball.[28] In describing Spalding, Hise wrote:

> Spalding was a remarkable and driven man whose towering ambitions simply would not allow that the game that gave him a profession, then a sporting goods empire, baseball franchise and national and international recognition, could have come from a foreign children's game (he called rounders "that asinine pastime").[29]

Spalding argued that baseball was derived from the American game of "One Old Cat,"[30] a bat-and-ball activity known as a *safe haven* game. The safe haven, or base, is where the runner attempts to go after hitting the pitched ball; often a smooth, round stick was used as the "bat." While in contact with the base, the runner is safe from the fielding team and in a position to score runs. In One Old Cat, the offensive and defensive teams switch roles when the fielding team puts the batting team out.[31]

In 1905, Spalding assembled a special commission (it is believed by some that Spalding hand-picked members who supported his "American origin theory"). The Commission's purpose was to find the true origin of baseball. Headed by former National League president Abraham G. Mills, the group became known as the Mills Commission. During the Commission's tenure, a man came forth who claimed that in 1839, Abner Doubleday, in the village of Cooperstown, New York, modified the local game of town ball (not rounders), and called the new game *baseball.* Doubleday was an American Civil War hero who died over a decade before the Commission started its work, and could not verify the story. Since the game Doubleday supposedly invented was strictly American, the Commission quickly embraced the idea of an American origin to baseball.[32]

Interestingly, the Commission chose to ignore, among other things, that Doubleday was actually in West Point, and not Cooperstown, in 1839. Also, Doubleday's diaries and personal correspondence never mentioned baseball. Regardless, the Mills Commission report, released in 1908, concluded "the first scheme for playing [baseball], according to the best evidence available to date, was devised by Abner Doubleday at Cooperstown, N.Y., in 1839."[33]

The Mills Commission report with the Doubleday "baseball invention" claim was almost immediately debunked after release to the public. Not only did the report cause controversy, most folks didn't care about the "true origin" of baseball. Indeed, historians to this day uncover new facts and continue to poke holes in the Doubleday "creation myth."[34]

For example, David Block, in his thoroughly researched book *Baseball Before We Knew It,* quoted the Hall of Fame in 2005: "Doubleday didn't invent baseball, baseball invented Doubleday." Block also stated that *base-ball* predated *rounders* in England by almost a century. He maintained that the rounders theory as the birth of baseball is just a "tired old axiom" that should be "put to rest."[35]

According to Block, the game of baseball is of English origin (originally a children's game) with aspects of *many* games, including "town-ball [combination of similar bat-and-ball contests], round ball [Massachusetts or New England] game; not 'rounders' per se] and base ball [sic]."[36] He documented this conclusion through historical *evidence* rather than individual "recollections" or similar sources.

In addition to the views of Chadwick (*rounders*), Spalding (*cat-games*), and Block (collection of games such as *town ball* and *round ball,* all of English decent), another idea can be added. Thorn posits that in addition to simply a *cat game* (the version with less than four bases), features of the U.S. National Pastime came from *town ball, round ball,* and *baseball.* So, which theory, or combination of theories, is the final answer to the dilemma?[37]

The question of baseball's origin doesn't seem to go away. In 2011,

The Mills Commission released its baseball origins conclusions in 1908. Both Ty Cobb (left; 1905–1928) and Joe Jackson (1908–1920) were early in their careers when the report went public (Library of Congress).

MLB Commissioner Bud Selig created a 12-member commission to examine the issue in a scientific manner. John Thorn, MLB historian, chaired the commission.[38] The commission chose to organize scholarly articles, primary documents, and educated speculation rather than publish a single final report. This decision is sound since there will always be new evidence to examine on the origins of baseball in North America and around the world (i.e., Japan, South Korea, and Australia). No single report on the subject can be considered "final" since a new analysis will undoubtedly be issued in the future. One thing is clear, however—the issue of baseball's origins has a complicated history—some things pure myth, others pure exaggeration or outright lies, and others yet to be discovered.

2

The Bats—
They Keep Changing!

Aladdin had his wonderful lamp, King Arthur had Excalibur, and Ted Williams had his bat.—Boston sportswriter Harold Kaese[1]

Introduction

Over the centuries, baseball bat shapes have undergone all kinds of contortions; Bat diameters have expanded and contracted and lengths have varied. Even bat wood species have transitioned from hickory and the traditional ash to maple, which dominates today in major league baseball (MLB).

Though baseball and its people have changed, the use of wood to make bats has not. In fact, at the highest level of baseball the object used to strike the ball is fashioned from a tree.[2]

The book *Baseball as America,* issued jointly by the National Baseball Hall of Fame and Museum and the National Geographic Society, argues that professional baseball has stuck with a wooden bat for numerous reasons, including safety, competitiveness, and the preservation of tradition.[3]

Sizes, Shapes, and Species of Wood

During the mid–1840s, when the Knickerbockers were playing the game under their rules, all players were responsible for their own bats. This "bring your own bat" to the game resulted in many different sizes, shapes, and species of wood being used.[4]

The earliest bats were quite primitive, akin more to a club than what we think of as a bat in the 21st century. Some bats came from tree limbs, and some began their life as axe handles. Early bats were often flat—like cricket bats—and most were handmade from various trees such as sycamore, cherry, spruce, chestnut, poplar, and basswood. For a short time, the cricket-favored willow was the preferred choice.[5] Ash, maple, and pine were also favorite woods of batters in the earliest days of the game.[6]

By trial and error, ash and hickory emerged as the most popular woods for bat-making in the 1870s and 1880s.[7] Hickory is heavier than ash and led to some massive bats. The dead ball era (prior to 1920) could have been known, also, as the "heavy bat" era. As an example, Hall of Famer Edd Roush led the National League in batting average in 1917 and 1919 while patrolling the outfield for the Cincinnati Reds and swinging a 48-ounce hickory bat. In addition, Roush hit over .350 in 1921, '22, and '23, all with his heavy weapon.[8]

Even though hickory is a very dense, strong wood, ash eventually held the advantage since it has an unusually high strength-to-weight ratio. Physicist Robert Adair, in his book *The Physics of Baseball*, wrote, "Ash was celebrated in medieval times as the only proper wood from which to construct the lances of knights-errant; an ash lance was light enough to carry and wield and strong enough to impale the opposition."[9] Roger Maris used a 33-ounce ash bat to hit 61 home runs in one season; a hickory bat of the same dimensions would weigh about 42 ounces.[10]

In 1884, the year the modern fountain pen was invented, the first Louisville, Kentucky-manufactured bat was made.[11] From the beginning, the Hillerich firm, later to become Hillerich & Bradsby, tried different tree species for bat-making. Eventually, the company settled on white ash (northern range of species) as the best.[12] For roughly a century, white ash (*Fraxinus americana*) dominated the bat market for all manufacturers and players. Within the first few minutes of Ken Burns's 18-hour documentary series *Baseball*, narrator John Chancellor intones, "The bat is made of turned ash, less than 42 inches long, not more than 2¾ inches in diameter."[13]

But players and entrepreneurs kept tinkering with bat dimensions and types of wood. In the late 1880s, many bat manufacturers were seeking new sources of raw material. The durable wood used for wagon tongues—which connects a wagon's wheel base to the draft animals—was considered fine material, and as Americans became less dependent on the horse and buggy, more of them became available.[14] Even newspaper ads advertised for wagon-tongue wood. As an example, A. G. Spalding & Brothers purchased wagon tongues from the general population with the specific intent of "turning [shaping the tongues] into bats." In one ad,

Spalding noted that he wanted to buy 100,000 old wagon tongues for use in his company's *Wagon Tongue Brand* of baseball bats. Spalding warned that he only wanted "straight grained, well-seasoned, second growth ash."[15] Another Spalding advertisement, available at the Baseball Hall of Fame and Museum, is from near the turn of the 20th century and features wagon-tongue ash, as well as willow and maple bats.[16]

At least one historian speculates that an early form of European baseball might not have included a bat at all. David Block, in the Our Game blog, writes, "The question of when a bat was first introduced to the pastime remains a mystery. It is certainly possible, if not probable, that, at its outset, the game of baseball [in Europe] did not employ a bat, and that a bare hand was used to strike the pitched ball." Block muses that the difference in baseball in Europe and the United States might be due to different social underpinnings. In England, baseball was played primarily by girls and young women, whereas in America, baseball became a sport for boys and men. The American version of the game—faster, rougher, and on a larger scale—might have accompanied the adoption of the bat, perhaps perceived in England as too unlady-like.[17]

Regardless of when a bat was first introduced in Europe, the vast Atlantic Ocean did not negate the appeal of baseball in the New World. The sport grew, and with the expanding interest in baseball came many modifications in bat dimensions. While some players were making the switch to wagon-tongue wood, another revelation appeared to them: A ball could be hit much more solidly with a round bat. This observation led to the adoption of a round bat as the standard that exists to this day.

David Magee and Philip Shirley explain in their book *Sweet Spot* that the design of a bat, including a round barrel, was not a given in the early days of the game:

> Some players used square bats for bunting, while others played with square-handled bats. Others preferred thick handles, resulting in a bat that was nearly uniform in width from handle to barrel. Players selected their bat of choice often based on little more than a hunch; if they happened to connect solidly in a game with one, they often used that one bat until someone convinced them otherwise. The bat, in other words, was still evolving by trial and error.[18]

Henry "Heinie" Groh spent 16 seasons in the major leagues, mostly with the New York Giants and Cincinnati Reds. He debuted in 1912 with the Giants and wrapped up his career with a one-year stint in Pittsburgh. Groh was a good hitter, posted a lifetime batting average of .292, and hit .474 in the 1922 World Series against the New York Yankees. He batted over .300 four times in a five-year span and was a part of five pennant winners, including two World Series championships. However, Groh is best remembered not for these or other accomplishments but for his famed "bottle bat," which had about a 17-inch barrel that tapered sharply to a thin, roughly 17-inch handle. Groh had small hands, and because thin handles were not commonly made in the early twentieth century, Groh devised a bat he could get his fingers around. The advantage was that Groh's long barrel gave him a greater hitting zone. Although Groh's unique bat didn't catch on with many of his contemporaries, the "bottle bat" worked for him.[19]

Heinie Groh and his famous "bottle bat" (National Baseball Hall of Fame and Museum, Cooperstown, N.Y.).

As the 20th century gave way to the 21st, more and more major league players switched to hard (sugar) maple. When the 2017 season began, about 75 percent of major league batters swung maple (*Acer saccharum*). Ash bats had dramatically fallen to 10–15 percent of the big league market.[20] Also, the number of firms supplying bats to MLB skyrocketed from the days of Pete Browning and Heinie Groh to 32 different licensed manufacturers for the 2017 season.

Rules

As the game spread in America, more and more men were organized into clubs, or teams, for the purpose of playing baseball. In 1857, clubs gathered in lower Manhattan to discuss rules and competition between one another (a year later a permanent body was formed: the National Association of Base Ball Players).[21] One of the rules adopted stated that a bat "must be round, and must not exceed two and half inches in diameter in the thickest part. It must be made of wood, and may be of any length to suit the striker."[22] Prior to this bat rule, a player could lug a piano leg to the plate if he wished.

However, flat bats were legalized by the National League in 1885 and became ideal for bunting.[23] In 1893, the 1857 rule requiring a round bat was reinstated.[24] Soft woods (like pine) and bats that were sawed off at the end were banned as well.[25]

In 1868, a rule setting the maximum length at 40 inches was established. A year later, the length was extended to 42 inches. In 1895, the National League allowed the bat diameter to expand to two and three-quarters inches.[26] As of the 2018 MLB season, the maximum length remains at 42 inches, and the diameter is capped at 2.61 inches.[27]

A bat altered by scooping out an ounce or so of wood from the end of the barrel is known as a cupped bat. Cupped bats were originally manufactured in the late 1930s by the Hanna Manufacturing Company of Athens, Georgia, but weren't legalized in MLB until 1975. Cupping results in a lighter bat and shifts the center of gravity farther down the barrel.[28] Jose Cardenal signed the first contract with Louisville Slugger for a cupped bat. Because the handle was not too thin and the barrel not too heavy, Cardenal said, as quoted in *Good Wood*, "It's just a very well-balanced bat. You put it in your hands and you can feel it."[29] Many major leaguers in the 21st century use a cupped bat. The 2018 MLB rule book limits the "cup" to one and one-quarter inches in depth and between one (minimum) and two (maximum) inches in diameter.[30]

The bat handle rules can be traced all the way back to the late 1800s, according to baseball historian John Thorn. In 1885, a rule was put into place by the National League that limited twine on the handle end of the bat to 18 inches. The next year, the rule was modified to account for gritty stuff like rosin and dirt (formally called a "granulated substance" in the rulebook).[31] As in the previous year's rule, 18 inches was the maximum length these substances could be applied to the bat handle.[32] Peter Morris (citing a *Washington Post* article) wrote in *A Game of Inches* that by 1948, baseball rules prohibited applying a foreign substance on a bat beyond 18 inches.[33] The rule language may seem trivial to some, but both pine tar and rosin were not specifically named, leading to some consternation.

During the 1975 season, the Yankees' Thurman Munson singled home a run against the Minnesota Twins. According to *A Game of Inches*, the Twins argued to umpire Art Frantz that the bat Munson used "had pine tar rather far up the handle." When the umpiring crew inspected the bat, they did, indeed, find that pine tar exceeded the 18-inch limit. Consequently, Munson was ruled out and the run was taken off the board. At the time, the batter was automatically out if an illegal bat was used (the umpiring crew deemed the bat illegal because pine tar extended past the 18-inch limit).[34]

In 1976, the rule was updated, albeit for a different purpose if one believes all, or part, of the reasoning. Team owners (again the Minnesota Twins were involved) apparently discovered that pine tar on bat handles was the leading culprit for the increasing number of soiled baseballs being thrown out of play by umpires. Led by Calvin Griffith of the Twins (formerly the Washington Senators), the owners, with an eye on saving money, pushed for a more specific rule that mentioned the sticky substance by name. According to Fillip Bondy's book *The Pine Tar Game*, the updated rule stated:

> The bat handle, for not more than eighteen inches from its end, may be covered or treated with any material or substance to improve the grip. Any such material, including pine tar, which extends past the eighteen inch limitation, in the umpire's judgment, shall cause the bat to be removed from the game. No such material shall improve the reaction or distance factor of the bat.[35]

The new language was tested on July 24, 1983, when George Brett of the Kansas City Royals connected with a two-run homer off Goose Gossage of the Yankees in the top of the ninth inning with two out and New York clinging to a one-run lead. Yankees manager Billy Martin popped out of the dugout and insisted to the umpires that Brett had used an illegal bat, since the pine tar on the handle extended well beyond 18 inches. After much discussion and arguing, including screaming and cursing by both teams, the umpires agreed with Martin, and Brett was called out, nullifying the home run that had put the Royals ahead. Several days later, after a lengthy review, American League President Lee MacPhail sided with Brett and the Royals. MacPhail cited his interpretation of rules 1.10 and 6.06, the "spirit" of the rules and the game, and an AL regulation that stated, "the use of pine tar [beyond] the 18 inch rule will not be cause for exemption or suspension..." MacPhail called for a make-up of the game's conclusion, replayed from the point of Brett's home run. Since the 1976 rule (1.10) said nothing about a player using a pine tar bat like Brett's being called out, the home run was ruled legal, although 1976 rule 6.06(a) states that a batter is out if "he hits an illegally batted ball."[36]

After that famous "Pine Tar Game," a clarifying note was added to the rule book. It states that if an umpire discovers a bat that has any material or substance beyond 18 inches from its end *after* it has been used in play, the batter will not be ruled out or ejected from the game. Furthermore, the

Copyrighted, 1895, and published by   Geo. D. Ide, 17 Exchange Place, Boston.

HUGH DUFFY,
CENTRE FIELDER OF BOSTON BASE BALL CLUB,
AND
CHAMPION BATSMAN OF THE WORLD.

Hugh Duffy hit .440 in 1894. The shape of his bat was characteristic of the time (Library of Congress).

rule book states, that action on the field will not be nullified and protests will not be allowed. A new numbering system was implemented in 2015; for the 2018 season, the complete updated rule is 3.02(c).[37]

Bats in MLB

The first baseball bats in America, even before the formation of the Knickerbockers, were heavy, thick, and barely tapered. To a baker, as well as to baseball players and fans, the bats looked like long rolling pins.[38]

Deadball Era (prior to 1920)

This era was called "deadball" primarily because of the baseball. According to Lawrence Ritter:

> The game was played differently then simply because the ball was different. It looked just like today's baseball, but when it was hit, no matter how hard, it did not carry long distances.... With such a dead ball, batters didn't swing with all their might.... They practiced bunting and place hitting ... they punch[ed] line drives ... and lap[ed] hard ground balls.[39]

Also, the extremely heavy bats favored in the first decade of the 20th century were made primarily of hickory, a very dense wood.[40] However, some players used ash as their lumber of choice since ash had the reputation as the best wood for a baseball bat.

Wee Willie Keeler, standing only 5'4" and weighing a mere 140 pounds, used a bat characteristic of the time regarding weight. Keeler's bat often weighed 46 ounces (although because of his small stature, the length was a Little League–size 30 inches). In 1897, he batted .424 and set a National League record with a 45-game hitting streak (according to the Society for American Baseball Research (SABR) Bioproject site, Keeler's streak stretched from the last game in 1896 through 44 games to begin the 1897 season). Keeler, who batted .341 between 1892 and 1910, espoused the hitting philosophy of the day: "Hit 'em where they ain't."[41]

Another MLB star who exemplified the Deadball Era was Ty Cobb, the 12-time American League batting champion (Note: There's a discrepancy with some sources as to whether Cobb won 11 or 12 titles. Baseball-reference.com lists 12 [accessed May 8, 2020]). When Cobb was 11 years old, one of his first bats was crafted for him with scrap wood by his next-door neighbor, a coffin maker. Supposedly, the wood used was black mountain ash.[42] Local names for different trees can vary, and since the only tree currently called a "mountain ash" is a smallish ornamental tree that isn't really an ash at all, the guess is that Cobb's "coffin-wood" bat was actually white ash (or perhaps green ash), native to his home state of Georgia. Regardless, Cobb brought his lucky bat in a cloth bag to the big leagues in 1905.[43]

In the majors, Cobb wielded a 34½-inch bat that weighed a hefty 40 ounces (although he used a lighter bat near the end of his career). He spread his hands a few inches apart on the handle, which made the heavy bat easier to control as well as providing stability to slap at the ball. Cobb explained in 1910, as quoted in the Charles Leerhsen book *Ty Cobb: A Terrible Beauty*, "The great hitters of our time grab their batting sticks a foot or more from the handle and, instead of swinging, aim to meet the ball flush.... I stick to the sure system of just meeting the ball with a half-way grip."[44]

In the early 20th century, Cobb wasn't the only superstar to swing a heavy bat or use a "split-grip" at the plate. Honus Wagner, who won eight National League batting average titles with the Pittsburgh Pirates between 1900 and 1911, also held his hands apart on the handle and wielded a bat that weighed up to 38 ounces. Although Wagner's bat was two ounces lighter than Cobb's, his "stick" was a tad longer, measuring 35 inches in length.[45]

Another Hall of Famer, Edd Roush, who started his 18-year big-league career in 1913, explained that his 48-ounce hickory bat with a thick handle was important to his success.[46] As quoted in *Good Wood*, Roush said, "I only take a half swing at the ball, and the weight of the bat rather than my swing is what drives it."[47]

Live-ball Era (approximately 1920 to 1940)

The Deadball Era ended for a host of reasons, including the elimination of the spitball and other trick pitches (1920), the use of more (and cleaner) baseballs per game (1921), and the center of the baseball featuring a rubber-coated cork core instead of a pure rubber core (introduced in 1910).[48] Not only was the heavy hickory bat gradually replaced by the lighter ash as the preferred tree species for MLB bats, but two other major shifts occurred.

First, a trend of tapered bat handles began. Rogers Hornsby is often overlooked as the player who popularized the practice of using a thin-handled bat. Hornsby realized that a thin handle enabled him to get the bat head through the hitting zone more quickly. He hit 36 home runs in his first five full seasons (1916–1920) but changed his ways in the roaring '20s. Hornsby ripped 21 homers in 1921 while also leading the National League in batting average (.397), hits (235), doubles (44), triples (18), runs (131), and RBI (126). He followed up that spectacular season by clubbing a league-leading 42 home runs in 1922 while batting .401 and driving in 152 runs. For six consecutive seasons starting in 1920, Hornsby led his league in batting average, on-base percentage, and slugging average.[49] With Hornsby's success at the plate, coupled with the rise of another superstar, the trend toward tapered handles began in earnest.

Although Babe Ruth swung a heavy bat (up to 47 ounces), especially in his early playing days, he realized that a thin handle (patterned after Hornsby) and big barrel gave him more of an opportunity to swing from his heels.[50] (Ruth sometimes used bats heavier than 50 ounces, but mostly in spring training.[51]) Since Ruth was paid to hit home runs rather than advance runners one base at a time, he wanted a large barrel on his bat so he could clobber the "lively" ball. He once said, "There's nothing that feels as sweet as a good, solid smash."[52] A thick bat handle—favored by many Deadball Era stars—did little for what Ruth wanted to accomplish at the plate.

The 714th and last home run Ruth ever hit was in 1935 with the Boston Braves, when he was experimenting with, in his mind, a lightweight, 36-ounce bat. Ruth's blast was the first time a baseball cleared the right field roof at Pittsburgh's Forbes Field.[53]

Author Charles Leerhsen pointed out major differences between slugger Ruth and Deadball place-hitter Cobb:

> [Ruth] held [the] bat very differently than Cobb gripped his much thicker club—all the way down at the knob end—and swung it differently, too, with a decisive uppercut motion, and with such force that if his spikes stuck in the clay around home plate, he could, and sometimes did, wrench his back. When he made contact with ... the "jackrabbit ball," the results were electrifying.[54]

Some deadball stars frowned on the home run since the game they played depended on place hitting, advancing the runner, bunting, and speed. It's important to recognize that baseball started out as a meadows game. Once it was realized that people would dole out money to watch the game, fences were erected to eliminate non-payers. To preserve baseball's character, it was not uncommon to build the fences far away to keep them out of play. Consequently, batters—with the encouragement of coaches, managers, and owners—attempted to hit line drives, not out-of-the-park home runs.[55]

Early in Babe Ruth's years as a slugger, he and Ty Cobb (right) disagreed on batting philosophies, but eventually they saw the merits of each other's style (National Baseball Hall of Fame and Museum, Cooperstown, N.Y.).

To shed a perspective on distant outfield fences, consider the original Braves Field in Boston. The left-field foul line was an incredible 402.5 feet from home plate, and the right-field line measured 375 feet (though various books and websites list the ballpark's Opening Day distance between 369 and 402 feet). Center field measured a whopping 461 feet, with right-center a gigantic 542 feet from home plate. A 10-foot wall rimmed the park. When Cobb saw the new Braves Field in 1915, he exclaimed, "Nobody will ever hit a baseball out of *this* park." Cobb's prediction was a bit sarcastic, but it did take two years before a home run sailed over the wall.[56]

Cobb was one of the deadball players who initially believed Ruth's swing-for-the-fences mentality was the wrong way to play baseball.[57] Many managers, writers, and fans argued that Ruth's bombastic show lessened the game and wasn't effective baseball strategy. They preferred the more chess-like game played since the late 1800s.[58] However, Cobb finally relented and said Ruth's style was a legitimate, alternative, and crowd-pleasing way to play the game and should be encouraged.[59] Consequently, and with the blessings of two of the all-time greats of the game (Ruth and Cobb), thinner-handled bats changed the game for the next century.

Bat Speed Era (approximately 1940 to 2000)

Another milestone in the history of MLB bats occurred when Ted Williams came to the majors. Williams, a rookie in 1939, batted .327, smacked 31 home runs and led the American League in RBI with 145.[60] Williams said many times that hitting a baseball properly is the most difficult thing to do in all of sports, and succeeding three times out of 10 is a great performance.[61] If so, Williams did very well at the task. He posted a lifetime .344 batting average in a career that spanned from 1939 to 1960.[62]

Early in Williams' career, he established a mark in batting average that is talked about today. September 28, 1941, was the last day of the season for Williams and his Boston Red Sox. He walked to the bat rack in the Sox dugout and selected his custom-made lumber. The bat was a 33-ounce hunk of white ash with a length of 35 inches.

For the day, Williams banged out six hits in a double-header against the Philadelphia Athletics, upping his season-ending batting average to .406.[63] It was the first time in over a decade that a major league player had hit more than .400. Through the 2019 season, it was the last time the elusive .400 average has been topped in the majors.

The Williams' bat was manufactured by the Hillerich & Bradsby Company of Louisville, Kentucky. The white ash originated from a tree growing along the New York–Pennsylvania border.[64]

Williams' bat length and choice of ash wood were comparable to many players of the Deadball Era. However, the "Splendid Splinter's" bat

25

Ted Williams believed in bat speed and "light lumber" (National Baseball Hall of Fame and Museum, Cooperstown, N.Y.).

was much lighter than the earlier players' (some hitters swung bats more than 45 ounces, and Babe Ruth occasionally wielded a hickory bat in excess of 50 ounces). When Williams felt tired or exhausted, the bat weight would drop even more, slightly below 33 ounces. Williams' secret for hitting a ball was the speed he generated with a light bat.

2. The Bats—They Keep Changing!

Williams' theory was that a lighter bat could still produce plenty of power because a hitter generates more bat speed. One story that Williams told in his own book, *My Turn at Bat*, was that as a minor-leaguer in 1938, he felt tired near the end of the season. By chance, Williams picked up a teammate's light bat and liked the feel of it. Williams wrote, "It had a bigger barrel than mine, but lighter by two ounces at least." Williams got the approval of his teammate to use the bat that night with the bases loaded. Against a left-handed pitcher, Williams wrote, "I got behind two strikes. I choked up on the bat, thinking that I would just try to meet the ball.... The pitch was low and away, just on the corner of the plate. *Unnh.* I give this bat a little flip and gee, the ball flew over the center-field fence." A 410-foot grand slam, and Williams' theory of a light bat was solidified.[65] As the old saying goes: The rest is history.

Williams was meticulous (some might say paranoid) about the weight of his bats. He urged the Red Sox to install a scale in the clubhouse so he could precisely weigh his bats, saving a trip to the post office.[66] One time, as legend has it, J. A. Hillerich, Jr., laid out six bats on a motel bed in front of Williams. Hillerich asked Williams to close his eyes and pick out the heavy bat, which was only a half-ounce heavier than the other five, a difference likely imperceptible to most humans, but not to the Splendid Splinter. Williams wrote in *My Turn at Bat*, "I picked it out [the heavy bat] twice in a row."[67]

Williams was meticulous about more than just the weight of his bats. He once got a new shipment of bats from the Hillerich & Bradsby factory. Displeased with the handles, he returned the set of Louisville Sluggers with a short note that said, "Grip doesn't feel just right." Upon receipt at Hillerich & Bradsby, employees used calipers to measure the bat handles. Williams was right; the handles were five-thousandths of an inch thinner than he had ordered![68]

Ted Williams was a perfectionist as a hitter beyond just the feel, heft, and end-to-end distance of his bats. As Magee and Shirley wrote in their book, *Sweet Spot*:

> He wanted the very best bat, from the best wood, with the perfect weight and length. He wanted to know what made a bat as good as it could be and spent time with the craftsmen who made [his] Louisville Sluggers to understand how to maximize their potential. In fact, he once called his first visit to Hillerich & Bradsby's Louisville Slugger bat factory "one of the greatest things I ever did in my life."[69]

Williams always seemed to be looking for the slightest edge over pitchers. He was known by bat factory employees at Hillerich & Bradsby as the player who climbed over piles of lumber, looking for the perfect piece, which included 10 growth rings or fewer per inch. When he found it, he showed the lumber to one of the craftsmen and demanded that *his* bat be made from this particular chunk of wood. Williams wanted the best tools of the trade, and he got them. "Everybody said I got the best bats in the league," he said.[70]

Williams wasn't the only MLB player to demand a particular piece or type of wood. The man who signed Williams on a scouting trip to California in the 1930s was also very particular about his lumber. Eddie Collins, then the general manager of the Boston Red Sox, had enjoyed a 25-year playing career beginning in 1906 and spanning the Deadball Era and the roaring '20s.[71] He hit third and played second base for both Philadelphia and Chicago in the American League, collecting over 3,300 hits and leading the Athletics to three World Series championships. But Collins was remembered by Louisville Slugger employees for probing through stacks of wood for just the right cut.[72]

Collins wanted all of his bats made from the heart of the tree. Since heartwood is darker than the lighter-colored sapwood, his bats often were reddish or dark brown on one side and white on the other. Input—or special requests—from major leaguers to bat-makers is encouraged as long as the contribution conforms to the rules of the game. Williams and Collins were two prolific hitters who stood out for their finicky, but legal, demands.[73]

Heavy bats made a short-lived comeback in the 1960s with a few marquee players. Roberto Clemente sometimes swung a 39-ouncer, and Orlando Cepeda and Dick Allen hefted bats that weighed 40 ounces or more.[74] Clemente often took a couple of bats to the on-deck circle, making his final selection on feel, intuition, and the tendencies of the pitcher.

Tim McCarver toiled in MLB for over three decades (1959–1980) and was twice an All-Star with the St. Louis Cardinals.[75] McCarver wrote in 1998 that a few sluggers in his playing days still used a heavy bat even though conventional wisdom was the opposite.

> [Dick] Allen was extraordinarily strong ... [b]ut possibly he could have been even better with a lighter bat. Batters can't have a short, quick stroke if they use a heavy bat. If waiting and then using your quick hands are the two elements of sound hitting, then why would you use a heavy bat? If you have a heavy bat, you have to start sooner. Lighter bats make it easier for you to speed up the bat head, so you can wait longer—and by waiting longer you pick up the ball better and then use your quick hands.[76]

In spite of a few star players swinging heavy lumber, like Allen, Cepeda, and Clemente, lighter bats were in MLB to stay. For example,

Hank Aaron primarily used a 31–32-ounce bat, and Rod Carew won seven batting average titles swinging a 32-ouncer.[77] Joe Morgan carried a lightweight, 30-ounce bat to the plate.[78] Even David Ortiz swung a 32-ounce bat early in his career, and later switched to 31½ ounces.[79] More recent stars like Bryce Harper (31–33 ounces), Mike Trout (average of 31¾ ounces), Kris Bryant (31 ounces), and Joe Mauer (31–33 ounces) swing light lumber.[80]

In 1920, most bats used by major leaguers were typically no lighter than 36 ounces. At the beginning of the 21st century, bat racks in MLB held few bats heavier than 36 ounces. Of course, the range of weight, length, wood type, shape, handle diameter, and other bat factors vary from player to player.[81]

Maple-Bat Era (approximately 2000 to present)

When Derek Jeter broke into the big leagues in 1995, he used a 32-ounce, white ash Louisville Slugger with a length of 34 inches.[82] The Jeter bat is one of many examples of the dominance of ash as the preferred wood for bat-making through the 20th century. However, wood enthusiasts and bat gurus continued to experiment with new innovations, including looking for a new wood that would give the batter an advantage. One such innovation was hard maple (as opposed to the less dense "soft" maple).

Joe Carter of the Toronto Blue Jays was the first MLB player to use a maple bat in a game, in 1997. He was also the first to hit a homer with one.[83] Carter said, "When you first use them, it's a totally different feel from a normal [ash] bat. I mean, totally different. After you use them, you don't want to go back."[84]

Maple has long been a fixture in the sporting world because of its hardness and durability. Many of the hardwood floors used for basketball courts are made from maple. The different shades of maple (called "grades") give many courts a distinct appearance. Of the 30 National Basketball Association courts, 29 are made from maple (the Boston Celtics' court is oak).[85]

Sixty years and over 100,000 games after Williams had his .406 batting average, Barry Bonds also etched his name in the record books. On an early autumn day (October 5, 2001), Bonds' San Francisco Giants squared off against their fierce rival, the Los Angeles Dodgers. The setting was the Giants' home stadium of Pacific Bell Park. Chan Ho Park was the starting Dodgers pitcher who would face Bonds head-on.

The Baseball Bat

Entering the game, Bonds was tied with St. Louis Cardinals slugger Mark McGwire for the MLB all-time season home run record of 70. In Bonds' 1st-inning plate appearance, history was made. Bonds launched a deep drive to right field that easily cleared the outfield wall and set off a celebration (the blast was estimated at over 440 feet). Bonds had his 71st "dinger" and now stood alone as the single-season home run king. After 162 games of the regular season, Bonds had a total of 73 round-trippers.

Like Williams' ash bat, the maple for Bonds' bat came from a tree growing in the same geographical region of North America. Also, the Bonds bat was a lightweight 32 ounces with a length of 34 inches. Unlike Williams, Bonds had a half-cup barrel on his bat. One reason for cupping the barrel end of the bat is players' belief that bat speed is enhanced.

Another difference from Williams and other stars of previous eras was Bonds' choice of lumber. Bonds selected sugar maple, often called hard maple. His bat was personally crafted in a small wood-working shop in Canada. Although Bonds wasn't the first big leaguer to use, or even homer, with a maple bat, the switch away from ash as the favorite bat-making tree species was soon underway.

Two years prior to Bonds' record-setting home run year, he made the full-time switch from ash to a maple bat. In addition to the home run record Bonds established in 2001, his slugging average was .863 (performance-enhancing drugs will be ignored regarding Bonds and other players). After Bonds' power display, maple bats surged in popularity in the major leagues. Many players surmised that maple added home runs to their totals (although an exit velocity study demonstrated otherwise).[86] As of the 2017 season, the vast majority of big leaguers strode to the plate carrying a maple bat.[87] Ash was a distant second-most popular, followed by the up-and-coming yellow birch (*Betula alleghaniensis*).[88]

Maple is denser, and thus heavier, than ash. All factors being equal (and in this instance, they are not!), a denser bat will drive the ball a greater distance. The wood properties chapter has more detailed density information.

Players typically want light lumber to quicken their swing, especially with today's fastballers. Since sugar maple wood is slightly heavier than white ash, maple bats tend to have thinner handles than their predecessors. As any player at any level knows, a thin-handled bat is more likely to break when the hitter is jammed by the pitcher. Also, the grain pattern of maple is not always easy to see compared to ash. This led to hairline wood fractures and other unexpected defects creeping into the game. Consequently, broken bats became more common in the professional game, especially in the first decade of the 21st century.[89] The "broken-bat-issue" led to an investigative study by MLB in 2008. The MLB report and conclusions are detailed in Chapter 7.

Pests have wreaked havoc on North American trees in the maple-bat era. The emerald ash borer (EAB) and Asian Longhorned Beetle (ALB) are two invasive insects that have devastated woodlands that supply bat wood to MLB. Although EAB only attacks ash trees, ALB feeds on numerous trees including maple and birch. The good news is that yellow birch has not had the ALB complete a life cycle on it.[90]

Final Thoughts

Baseball, and in particular the baseball bat, has changed over time. As we progress through the 21st century, some fans wonder if aluminum or other materials will replace wood as the choice for major-league bats.[91] Will maple continue its dominance in the game? What is the future of ash? Are insects like the emerald ash borer, the Asian Longhorned Beetle, or other invasive pests a serious threat to the trees that produce MLB bats? Will yellow birch, or another alternative species, require serious discussion in the next 20, 50, or 100 years?

However, what is known, and not debated or challenged, is that the sizes, shapes, and species of wood, bat rules, and player bat preferences change over time.

3

Bat Makers Up
to World War II

I love golf, enjoy its traditions as much as anyone, but if
you don't love **baseball** you have no soul.—David B. Fay,
Executive Director, USGA, 1989–2010[1]

When Lewis and Clark left St. Louis in the fall of 1803 to explore the
530 million-acre Louisiana Purchase, they took with them an array of supplies for their epic wilderness journey.[2] What most Americans don't read-
ily recognize is the number of wooden items needed for their trip. Besides
the obvious articles like bullets, firearms, and food, they were laden down
with items such as wooden buckets, wooden dishes and cups, and wooden
storage containers (mostly for their food). Even their boat, canoes, and
paddles were primarily constructed from wood.

The exploration of the vast Western continent by the party of Lewis
and Clark's Discovery Corps could not have been possible without the
bounty of trees. In the 21st century, over 200 years after the expedition,
the U.S. dependency on wood for various products is still evident (houses
and paper goods are examples).

After the exploration of the Louisiana Purchase, America's fascina-
tion with baseball grew. The expanding interest in baseball included clever
and sharp-minded individuals who tinkered with the game, on and off
the field. Everything imaginable about baseball in the 19th century was
fertile territory for inventors and like-minded people. From box scores
and catcher's mitts to fielder's gloves and even Cracker Jack, all were introduced before 1900. Even the design of the baseball bat was studied
long and hard, and just like the Lewis and Clark supply list, wood was the
obvious choice (and perhaps the only choice) to serve this function. The
first United States patent issued for a bat was to Philip Caminoni in 1864.
While the patent is now buried in obscurity, it took two decades before the
manufacturing of a baseball bat from a tree grew into its own industry.[3]

3. Bat Makers Up to World War II

Another important non-baseball event occurred in the 1800s. Immigrants from around the globe flocked to the new country to seek a better life for themselves and their families. One of these immigrants was German-born J. Frederich Hillerich.

J. F. Hillerich's family emigrated to the United States in 1842 and settled in Louisville, Kentucky. In 1859, the 26-year-old J. F. opened a job turning business to make items like bed posts, hand rails, bowling pins, and butter churns. A few years later, John Andrew "Bud" Hillerich was born.

Bud enjoyed baseball as a young boy and teenager. However, Bud's father had a different opinion of the game. J. F. viewed the sport as foolish and a waste of time, akin to drinking and gambling. Some Americans saw baseball as the working-class man's excuse for skipping an afternoon of labor. It was in this context that Bud went to the ball park to see the Louisville Eclipse professional baseball team in 1884.[4] He was supposed to be at his father's wood shop, carving bedposts and bowling pins. Bud Hillerich got his business start playing hooky when the 17-year-old Kentuckian was cheering on his hometown Louisville Eclipse baseball team.

Bud's favorite player for the hometown Eclipse was playing that afternoon (they were in the American Association). Bud's hero, Pete Browning, was the team's star outfielder who posted a .343 career batting average. Browning had played for the Eclipse since 1877, starting as a teenager when he was 16.[5]

Unfortunately for Browning, he broke his favorite bat in the game. The 17-year-old Bud noticed that the star of the team seemed distraught and discouraged with his fate. Young Bud approached Browning at the end of the game and offered to make him a new bat. Browning took Bud up on his proposition and accompanied him to the Hillerich shop.[6]

As legend has it, Bud selected a piece of ash and began turning the wood on his Dad's lathe. Every now and then Bud stopped working, took the bat off the lathe, and handed it to his hero. Browning took a couple practice swings, made some suggestions to Bud, and handed the bat back to his young woodworker. Bud followed the recommendations, made the necessary corrections, removed the bat from the lathe again, and handed it back to Browning for more practice swings. This process continued for some time (some modern writers claim "through the night") until Browning was satisfied with the bat's length, weight, and handle (feel).[7]

The next day, Pete Browning stepped into the batter's box with his new lumber. He collected three hits with the Hillerich-made bat. Soon afterward, other players (Browning's teammates *and* opponents) wanted Bud to make them their own custom-designed bats.[8]

According to legend, Pete Browning had his first Hillerich & Bradsby bat crafted by 17-year-old Bud Hillerich (Library of Congress).

Bud realized that maybe, just maybe, there was an untapped market in making baseball bats. However, first he had to do a hard-sell on his father, who didn't like the idea of making a product, as J. F. stated, "for a mere game." Eventually J. F. relented, and Bud began making and marketing baseball bats.[9]

Bud Hillerich's bats were initially called Falls City Sluggers. Within a few years, the bats were called Louisville Sluggers, with the name surviving to the present. In 1894—Pete Browning's last season—Bud decided to patent his invention.[10]

The J. F. Hillerich turning business thrived in the 1880s and 1890s. More and more of the products were not the ones J. F. dreamed about making and selling, but rather baseball bats. J. F. realized that maybe his son was on to something bigger than bedposts and butter churns. With the popularity of the bat business, J. F. could no longer ignore its progress and potential. Consequently, Bud was made a partner in 1897; the company name was changed to J. F. Hillerich & Son.[11]

During the late 19th and early 20th century, Bud focused on the baseball side of the business, and J. F. took the lead on the woodworking end. However, Bud never fully gained the trust of his father, who was wary of turning over the entire business to him. Eleven years after making partner in the firm, an unexpected catastrophe slammed the business, and Bud was removed as partner of J. F. Hillerich & Son.[12]

Between 1897 and 1910, J. F. Hillerich & Son had deals with many companies, including Chicago Sporting Goods, Goldsmiths, Rawlings, and Montgomery Ward. However, the bat makers' most successful retail partner was Simmons Hardware. A young Simmons Hardware employee, Frank Bradsby, helped the firm grow into a national power. J. F. took a liking to Bradsby, often discussing business with him. This relationship was a rounding success for both men in the near-term. In 1910, fire burned to the ground (destroyed) the J. F. Hillerich & Son plant. Insurance money from the fire was scant, and J. F. was nearing retirement and without the necessary finances to rebuild. He approached 33-year-old Frank Bradsby about buying controlling interest in the business. Bradsby had the finances, eagerness and vision, so in 1911 he took the plunge and bought the bat-making company.[13]

Immediately, Bradsby realized that Bud Hillerich was the backbone of the bat business. One of Frank Bradsby's first moves was to hire Bud back into the firm as company president. Bradsby also sold part of the business back to Bud Hillerich. By 1916, the company name was finalized to Hillerich & Bradsby[14]—a name still synonymous with baseball at every level of the game.

Bud Hillerich and Frank Bradsby were a dynamic duo. Hillerich focused on his passion—baseball. He maintained his close relationships with players, making sure key professionals had bats built to their personal specifications. As a complement to Hillerich, Bradsby was a sharp business person. He concentrated on sales, marketing, and overall strategy for the firm. Together, Bud Hillerich and Frank Bradsby made the dream team of baseball bat producers.[15]

From their humble beginnings in the 1800s, baseball bats were not the only product that rolled off assembly lines at Hillerich & Bradsby. In 1916, only five years after Frank Bradsby joined the firm, golf equipment was added to the company's lineup. Bradsby loved golf and believed the sport would grow quickly in America. His prediction was correct, enabling Hillerich & Bradsby to increase its reach beyond baseball and diversify its business.[16] Nearly two decades after launching the golf business, Hillerich & Bradsby expanded, and their clubs were renamed PowerBilt. Babe Ruth was one player who used PowerBilt clubs in the off-season.[17]

Prior to renaming the golf clubs, Hillerich & Bradsby had signed World Series champion Babe Ruth of the Boston Red Sox to a bat contract in 1918 for the princely sum of $100.[18] The firm began manufacturing the Ruth model R43 shortly thereafter.[19] The following year, Hillerich & Bradsby sold 276,000 Louisville Sluggers and started a marketing effort aimed at young boys. By 1923, the company sold almost 1.7 million bats, the number one bat seller in the world.[20]

In 1937, the Ohio River flooded and did significant damage to the nearby Hillerich & Bradsby plant. According to the Louisville Slugger Museum, Frank Bradsby worked almost nonstop for weeks to repair the factory. The round-the-clock labor wore down Bradsby, and he died later that year. Bradsby had no heirs, but the Hillerich family kept his name on the business as a tribute to his contributions to the growth of the company.[21]

Hillerich finally took the helm of the firm he had launched. He was thrilled by the game, especially in 1941, when Louisville bats came through for Boston's Ted Williams and his .406 average and Joe DiMaggio and his 56-game hitting streak.

During World War II, Hillerich & Bradsby made M1 carbine gunstocks for American GIs. It's amazing to think the U.S. army was carrying rifles that in part were produced at a bat factory.[22] The war effort didn't end with gunstocks, however. Tank pins, Billy clubs, and other gadgets were made for the military.[23]

Shortly after the war, en route to Los Angeles for baseball meetings,

Bud Hillerich suffered a heart attack and died at age 80. The company has been led by a member of the family ever since.

Hillerich & Bradsby and Other Bat-Makers

The list of big leaguers who swung a Hillerich & Bradsby Louisville Slugger prior to, and during, World War II is endless: Cobb, Ruth, DiMaggio, Williams, and "Stan the Man" Musial are just the most recognizable names. In fact, one year before the U.S. entry into World War II, Hillerich & Bradsby sold two million bats. The stature of the Louisville Slugger baseball bat had risen dramatically in prestige and sales. This same year—1940—90 percent of big leaguers swung a Louisville Slugger, plus many Negro Leaguers, minor leaguers, and Little Leaguers as well. Clearly, Hillerich & Bradsby's Louisville Slugger dominated the baseball bat market.[24]

In the early years of Hillerich & Bradsby, there were other companies that made baseball bats. As the 1800s moved into the 1900s, there were three additional firms—all sporting goods companies—that seemed to stand out from the crowd—Spalding, Wright & Ditson, and A. J. Reach. None of them, however, had the lasting power in the baseball bat business of the firm from Louisville. (The Spalding firm still remains in business but the focus is not on bats.)

Spalding

Albert Goodwill (A. G.) Spalding was a star pitcher before his sporting goods company produced baseball bats. Spalding pitched only seven seasons but won over 200 games. In 1875, hurling for the Boston Red Stockings in the National Association, he was victorious 54 times while only losing five games.[25] In 1876, Spalding moved to the Chicago White Stockings (now the Cubs), where he was named player-manager and part-owner of the club. Spalding was a key figure in organizing the NL that same year in addition to winning 47 games. Also in 1876, he and his brother opened the A. G. Spalding & Bros. Company.[26] In the early 20th century, Spalding led the fight to establish baseball as being invented in the USA, eventually leading to the Doubleday Myth and the Cooperstown location of the Baseball Hall of Fame.[27]

During his initial year in Chicago, Spalding's firm produced the first major league baseball for the NL, which they did from 1876 to 1976. He also produced baseballs for the AL for nearly a century. In 1877 he sold a new-fangled invention called a baseball glove. The following year, Spalding published the first "Official Rules Guide for Baseball." A Spalding football for American play hit the market in 1887, followed by a basketball in 1894. While the Spalding enterprise was making these various sporting good products, his firm was also cranking out baseball bats. By 1900, according to the Spalding website, he was the largest manufacturer of bats in the U.S., producing over one million per year.[28]

Albert Spalding built a sporting goods empire and was a leading bat manufacturer for many years (National Baseball Hall of Fame and Museum, Cooperstown, N.Y.).

Unfortunately for Spalding, Frank Bradsby was a baseball bat marketing genius. Bradsby took the Louisville Slugger brand and helped propel Hillerich & Bradsby past the Spalding firm in the 1920s.

One of Spalding's strategies, beginning in the late 1800s, was to buy out other bat-making firms. He didn't purchase Hillerich & Bradsby, but he acquired the Wright & Ditson and, later, A. J. Reach companies.[29] These firms became part of the Spalding empire, which produced over 50 percent of athletic equipment sold in the U.S. In a shrewd business move, the purchased companies kept their doors open, independently selling their wares despite being owned by Spalding. This ploy created the public perception of choice for the consumer, enabling Albert Spalding to maximize his profits.[30]

Bat-makers were always looking for a new way to differentiate their product from the competition. A. G. Spalding and Brothers were no different. They devised the unique Mushroom bat, which featured a round knob and a promise of even weight distribution.[31] The Spalding firm also marketed the Wagon Tongue brand bat, made with or without a knob.[32]

Many MLB players used a Spalding bat, including Harold "Pie" Traynor, Miller Huggins, Frankie Frisch, and Pete Reiser.[33]

Wright & Ditson

The surname "Wright" was easily connected to both cricket and baseball in America in the mid-and second half of the 19th century. Sam Wright emigrated with his family to New York in 1837. Sam, who was born in Sheffield, England, played cricket for the St. George Club in New York City. In 1844, he represented the USA in the first-ever international cricket match. Sam's son, Harry, also enjoyed the game. Harry developed into an outstanding cricket player. He also took up the new sport that was sweeping across the country—baseball. In the late 1850s, Harry joined the Knickerbocker Base Ball Club. His simultaneous competition in cricket and baseball is just one indicator of the blurred boundaries between the two sports. After the Civil War, Harry left New York for western Ohio. While playing professionally for the Union Cricket Club in Cincinnati, Harry joined a local baseball team and soon rose to captaincy. By the late 1860s, Harry was managing a baseball team considered the best in the game. In 1869, Harry's leadership propelled the Cincinnati Red Stockings (the first professional baseball team) to an undefeated season. One of Harry's star players during the 1869 season was his younger brother, George.[34]

George Wright was one of baseball's superstars after the Civil War. At the young age of 22, his $1400 per year salary led all other players. In his first season with the Cincinnati Red Stockings, he hit .629 and blasted 49 home runs in only 57 games (yes, these numbers are correct!).[35] Since Wright's hitting feats occurred prior to the formation of the NL (1876) and AL (1901), baseball-reference.com does not provide data on Wright's Cincinnati accomplishments.[36] George and his brother Harry moved to the Boston Red Stockings in 1871 after Cincinnati disbanded as a professional team. (Along with the Wright brothers came a 21-year-old pitcher by the name of A. G. Spalding.) George retired after the 1882 season to focus on his sporting good business, Boston-based Wright & Ditson.[37]

George Wright and Boston businessman Henry Ditson opened a business in 1871 that catered to the sports of baseball, golf and tennis. By the early 1880s, Wright & Ditson offered a complete line of uniforms and equipment for baseball (including bats!), polo, lawn tennis, cricket, lacrosse, football, bicycling, camping, and fishing.[38] However, Spalding bought the firm in 1892 after 35-year-old Ditson died suddenly of a heart attack. Although Wright remained a stakeholder in the new firm, his role was more of *figurehead* than anything else.[39]

Despite being owned by the A. G. Spalding & Bros. business, the line of Wright & Ditson baseball bats continued to exist. The line got a boost in 1903 when Cleveland/Philadelphia star Nap Lajoie (HOF 1937) signed an endorsement deal (Lajoie led the AL with a .344 batting average in 1903). Wright & Ditson manufactured a bat with *two* knobs—one at the end and a second (called the shoulder) a few inches up the handle. The idea was that a batter could hold one hand on each knob. The innovation made sense since many hitters of the era, like Ty Cobb and Honus Wagner, hit with their hands apart. Unfortunately for Wright & Ditson, the unique design of the two-knob bat didn't catch on with many players. Production and sales ended after a decade.[40]

A. J. Reach

The A. J. Reach firm is often mentioned as an early manufacturer of baseball bats. However, limited information (in baseball books) has been published about the company as an early pioneer in the bat-making business. The short article about the firm at baseball-reference.com mentions only baseballs, footballs, boxing gloves, batting helmets, and the popular baseball guide.[41] However, a baseball bat article by former MLB player Bernie Mussill in *Oldtyme Baseball News* does note that Reach was a prominent manufacturer at the turn of the 20th century.[42]

A. J. (Alfred James) Reach was one of the top players in the early years of baseball in the National Association. During the Civil War, Reach played for the Eckford Club in Brooklyn before moving to the nearby Philadelphia Athletics (A's) in 1865. He helped the A's win the first professional baseball pennant in 1871.[43] When Reach retired in 1875, he turned his attention full-time to his sporting goods business.[44]

According to *Sweet Spot*, the A. J. Reach Co. sold thousands of baseballs and bats while the firm was in existence.[45] In addition to bats and balls, Reach produced his first *Base Ball Guide* in 1883, the greatest rival to the Spalding guide. The two guides were published simultaneously, and "independently," until the guides were merged in 1939. The *Spalding-Reach Official Base Ball Guide* was sold in 1940 and 1941 and then replaced by the *Sporting News Baseball Guide*.[46]

Reach also was a founder of the Philadelphia Phillies franchise and served as team president from 1883 to 1899.[47] In addition, he served (with

George Wright) on the 1905 Mills Commission, set up by A. G. Spalding, to investigate the origin of the game.[48]

The Reach Company sold all its properties, including baseball bat production, to the Spalding firm in 1934, and its name disappeared from use.[49] The Reach name, however, lives on, especially among collectors of items from the earlier days of baseball. An Internet search in late 2017 showed a number of Reach items available for sale, including baseballs, baseball guides, fielding gloves, and baseball bats.[50] Another Internet example featured a Bing Miller bat. Miller, an outfielder who played in three World Series (twice winning championships) with the Philadelphia Athletics, posted a .311 lifetime batting average over 16 seasons between 1921 and 1936. A photograph of the bat with a prominent "AJ Reach Co." trademark was auctioned in 2014.[51]

Other Baseball Bat Manufacturers

Hillerich & Bradsby, Spalding, Wright & Ditson, and A. J. Reach were not the only firms in the early years of the game vying for market share. Manufacturing baseball bats was a competitive endeavor and not for the faint of heart.

In the late 1890s, Zimmerman Manufacturing Co. in Michigan made a variety of wood products, including axe handles, dumbbells, Indian clubs, Billy clubs, and baseball bats. The Zimmerman bat logo or trademark was sometimes a baseball with crossed bats. The Zimmerman Lifter bat was a popular model. For a time, players on the Detroit Tigers were some of the firm's top MLB customers. Hillerich & Bradsby bought the Zimmerman Company in the 1920s.[52]

Peck & Snyder Sporting Goods Company was founded in 1866. Based in New York City, the firm is considered by many to be the first enterprise to mass manufacture baseball cards. One of their initial offerings was an 1869 team photo card of the famous Cincinnati Red Stockings. However, the company also sold baseball bats in addition to retailing other sporting good items like baseball caps, tennis rackets, and roller-skates.[53] An 1873 ad depicted Peck & Snyder offering ash and willow bats for a dollar with a promise that a broken bat could be returned. Before the turn of the 20th century, it was not uncommon for bat makers to offer a guarantee similar to the one offered by Peck & Snyder.[54] In the mid–1890s, A. G. Spalding purchased Peck & Snyder Sporting Goods, adding to the ever-growing Spalding conglomerate.[55]

Pontiac Turning Company of Pontiac, Michigan, was founded in 1893 as a horse-drawn carriage company. The plant also made baseball bats. In the early 1900s, the firm established an independent corporation in Oakland County, Michigan, to focus on motorcars. The Oakland plant became a General Motors division in the 1930s. The Pontiac plant continued to make baseball bats until 1915.[56]

Pontiac Turning Company might be best known today for their trademark logo of an Indian chief in full headdress. The Ottawa Indian logo is in honor of Chief Pontiac, whom the city was named after. The Pontiac factory was acquired in 1912 by J. F. Hillerich & Sons (famous for the Louisville Slugger and later to become Hillerich & Bradsby). For a few years after the purchase, the Pontiac bat brand continued to be used.[57]

Frank Chance, Napoleon Lajoie, and Hughie Jennings were three Baseball Hall of Fame players who swung a Pontiac bat for a portion of their MLB careers.[58] In fact, a Pontiac model was the bat of choice for Frank Chance in his 17 years in the major leagues (15 with the Chicago Cubs).[59]

Another firm that made a mark in the bat-making business was the Hanna Manufacturing Company. Founded in the second decade of the 1900s in Athens, Georgia, the company was known for making handles for shovels as well as hand and farm tools. In 1926, Hanna started making baseball bats from regional ash. However, the inconsistent Southern growing season caused problems with the wood grain. To solve the problem, Hanna purchased land and built factories in Pennsylvania and New York. The dowels (billets) were shipped to Athens for sorting, inspection, drying, and turning. Once a bat was made, it was branded either Batrite or WTA (both brands were top grade), or Hanna (next grade).[60]

Hanna Manufacturing originally produced toy bats for department stores. The company advanced from small, souvenir-like bats to full-size "game bats." These bats were sold to sporting good firms, colleges, and the major leagues.[61]

Lou Gehrig, a Hall of Fame first baseman during the 1920s and 1930s, needs no introduction to baseball fans. Suffice it to say, Gehrig's achievements included leading the American League three times in home runs, five times in runs batted in, and four times in runs scored, and winning the MVP (Most Valuable Player) Award twice. These are remarkable accomplishments, especially in light of batting *behind* his New York teammate, Babe Ruth, for much of his career. However, Gehrig is best remembered for his 2,130-game playing streak, which unfortunately ended due to ALS.

Gehrig died in 1941, a few weeks shy of his 38th birthday. The illness which cut short his life is today known as "Lou Gehrig's Disease."[62]

Lou Gehrig periodically used a Hanna, Batrite model bat during the late 1920s and early 1930s.[63] In 2015, a Batrite bat was authenticated as the same bat the Yankee great was holding in a 1930 Comiskey Park photograph. The old black-and-white picture, featuring Gehrig posing with Babe Ruth and Bob Shawkey, was published in the defunct *Chicago Daily News*. For 85 years, the Gehrig bat's origin was a mystery and had unknown value to the non-baseball family that owned it. (The bat was given to the family by a relative of a former Yankee Stadium groundskeeper.) The owner used the bat for over a quarter-century as a protective weapon and kept it stored behind their family's front door. When the owner had the bat researched by an auction house, a decision was made to put it on the market. The bat generated great interest among serious collectors, with bidding beginning at $20,000. The final selling price for the Gehrig Batrite bat was over $400,000.[64]

Hall of Fame second baseman Eddie Collins was only 19 years old when he debuted with the Philadelphia Athletics in 1906. Collins had a career batting average of .333, was a member of the elite 3,000-hit club, and appeared in six World Series. He led the American League four times in stolen bases, three times in runs scored and once in pinch-hits. For his final season in 1930, Collins used a 36-inch Batrite model. His bat was stamped "Hanna Mfg. Co., Athens, GA" and featured the company's prominent flying bat logo.[65]

One of the innovations pioneered by Hanna was the cupped bat. Hanna made a bat, starting in the late 1930s, with a scoop of wood removed from the barrel-end. Unfortunately for Hanna, cupped bats were not allowed at this time for major league play. The Hanna Manufacturing Company went out of business in 1976, only a year after the cupped bat was legalized in MLB.[66]

There were other firms that made and/or sold bats under their own brand (logo) in the late 1800s and early 1900s. Names such as Goldsmith, Pennant, and Stoutenburgh & Van Cott Brothers might be recognizable by a few folks, especially collectors. However, none of these or other firms prior to World War II had the name recognition, production numbers, or MLB player approval of Hillerich & Bradsby and their Louisville Slugger.

4

Bat Makers from World War II to Boutique

We started in a garage in 2004 ... and built our name on consistency and craftsmanship.—Jack Marucci, Marucci Sports

At the conclusion of World War II, America was eager to see the 500+ MLB players who served their country return to the diamond.[1] The bat business was going well for Hillerich & Bradsby. The company was anxious to again make Sluggers for the boys coming home after their victorious mission in foreign lands. Hillerich & Bradsby led all other firms in baseball bat sales throughout the country.

When Harry Truman's presidency ended in 1953, Hillerich & Bradsby still remained the kingpin of bat-makers. In 1956, sales of Louisville Sluggers reached three million per year. Near the end of Dwight Eisenhower's second term as President (1959), the 100 millionth Louisville Slugger rolled off Hillerich & Bradsby's production line. By 1972, Louisville Slugger topped six million bats per year, and shortly later sales peaked at about seven million per year.

In the early 1970s, the familiar Hillerich & Bradsby name was dropped from the bat, focusing solely on the Louisville Slugger brand. The thinking behind this decision was that the Louisville Slugger trademark was the brand to lead the company into its second century as a family-owned business. Since sales exceeded $100 million, the prospects for the company looked bright.[2]

Slugger Harmon Killebrew (13-time All-Star and 12th on the all-time home run list in 2019 with 573) proclaimed (as quoted in *Sweet Spot*), "Every home run that I hit in the major leagues was with a Louisville Slugger."[3] George Brett, who collected 3,154 hits during his 21-year career, added in *Sweet Spot*, "Never, never once did I use any other bat but Louisville Slugger."[4] And Derek Jeter of the New York Yankees used the same

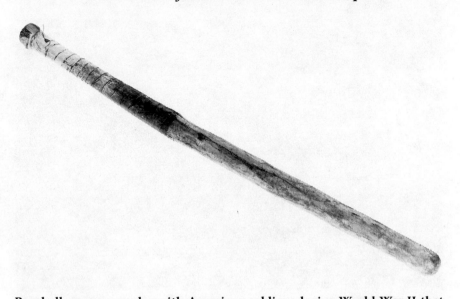

Baseball was so popular with American soldiers during World War II that they made their own bats when none were available (National Baseball Hall of Fame and Museum, Cooperstown, N.Y.).

Louisville Slugger model (P72 but later renamed DJ2) for all of his 12,500+ plate appearances in 20 MLB seasons.[5]

However, three major trends/changes in baseball bats started in the 1970s and continued through the early years of the 21st century. In hindsight, Hillerich & Bradsby was rather slow to react to all three, diminishing their bat sales. First, aluminum/metal bats became popular at all levels except for professional leagues, where a solid wood bat was still required. Second, there was a shift away from ash bats to maple. And third, but certainly not least, there was unprecedented growth of new competitors in the bat-making business. These businesses (usually small with few initial employees) were called "boutique" firms.

In 2009, at the 125th anniversary of the first Louisville Slugger, John A. Hillerich IV, the President and CEO of Hillerich & Bradsby, and the fifth generation of the family to lead the company, remarked in *Sweet Spot*, "He [Bud] would probably be amazed at how much remains the same. Everything we do relates to how it all started. Baseball is about tradition, and so is bat-making. We have never wanted to let go of that string that runs through time, tying it all together."[6]

Bud Hillerich would have been pleased to hear John's comments in 2009. Yes, much tradition was maintained by Hillerich & Bradsby. But

In the early 1960s, Hillerich & Bradsby Company made bats by the millions every year (courtesy eFootage LLC).

Bud could not have imagined the changes in bats from the 1800s, particularly the ones that impacted the town on the Ohio River in Kentucky.

John A. Hillerich IV's tune changed a bit in 2015 when he announced the sale of the Louisville brand to Wilson Sporting Goods. Hillerich said, "[he and the company] firmly believes that a new business model is necessary to realize the enormous potential of this brand in the future. We recognized from our first conversation with Wilson that they would be a great partner and steward of the brand our family created and so many have nurtured for 131 years." The agreement did not include the sale of all divisions of Hillerich & Bradsby. For example, the PowerBilt golf brand, one year shy of its 100th anniversary, was retained by the company.[7]

Soon after World War II, another firm, Adirondack, entered the fray and tried to win the hearts and minds of MLB players. The new firm never achieved the status (or sales) of Hillerich & Bradsby, but the bat-maker did produce lumber that was swung by some famous major leaguers.

Adirondack

When most people think of New York state, they immediately envision the bright lights, hustle and bustle, and huge population of New York

City. However, there is a vast region of the northern portion of the state that encompasses the cities of Albany, Syracuse, Rochester, and Buffalo, to name just a few. Smaller communities and millions of trees dominate the countryside. Cooperstown, headquarters of the National Baseball Hall of Fame, is one of these small towns. The tree-covered areas in New York state are best known for two large parks, the Adirondacks and the Catskills.

The northern area of New York State is referred to as "upstate New York" and boasts quite a lineup of innovations and new products. According to newyorkupstate.com, the list of pioneering inventions (often uncredited to the area) in the 1800s and early 1900s included Pepto-Bismol, the air conditioner, Pyrex bakeware, potato chips, Jell-O, fish hatcheries, and the American Express Company. Since World War II, upstate New York has introduced a host of other inventions, including chicken nuggets and the NBA shot clock.[8] Additional inventions credited to the area include the photocopier, Corning Ware, and the digital camera.

In the 1890s, German immigrant Joseph Kren started turning bats on his lathe for youngsters in Syracuse. Soon Kren went into business, manufacturing only baseball bats (youth and adult) and police Billy clubs. His most popular brand with MLB players was the Kren Special. Kren's business flourished as many major leaguers toured his small factory when players stopped in town once the Hall of Fame was established (it is only a 90-minute drive from Syracuse to Cooperstown).[9]

Kren's son, Joe Jr., who worked in his dad's factory told Syracuse's *Post-Standard* newspaper that in the early 20th century, he remembered visits by Honus Wagner, Lou Gehrig, and the Sultan of Swat, Babe Ruth. Gehrig testified under oath in a baseball bat competition lawsuit that many major leaguers preferred a Kren bat. The younger Kren also recalled a busload of Negro Leagues players who visited the factory and bought dozens of bats.[10]

When Joseph Kren, Sr., died in 1953, the business essentially died as well. None of Kren's boys ever learned how to turn a bat, so a year after Joseph's passing, the enterprise was sold and Joseph's tools donated to the Hall of Fame.[11] In this bat-making tradition, entrepreneurial spirit, and regional setting, Adirondack Company emerged.

In the 1940s, a small sawmill and woodworking shop began operations in a 2,500-resident community, about 75 minutes by automobile east of Syracuse. The mill originally produced boards for the woodworking industry and billets (round dowels about three feet in length) for producers of baseball bats. The small mill and shop owners decided after a couple years to make their own bats. Consequently, in 1946 the Adirondack Company was founded in Dolgeville, New York, roughly 200 miles north of New York City.[12]

One of the entrepreneurs who started Adirondack was a Dolgeville woodworker and sawmiller named Edwin McLaughlin. His partner was Charles Millard, who joined with McLaughlin during the last year of World War II.[13] One advantage the McLaughlin and Millard partnership had was the abundance of white ash in the surrounding area (then the wood preferred by MLB players). With their business' raw material growing nearby, McLaughlin and Millard began making bats. A smart move Adirondack immediately made was the hiring of good friend and ex–New York Giants pitcher Hal Schumacher. It was Schumacher's job to show the bats to former teammates in hopes that the players would use an Adirondack in major league action.[14]

Schumacher won 158 games with 121 defeats for the New York Giants and pitched in three World Series. He had a 13-year career in MLB, with an ERA of 3.36. Over three consecutive years, his regular season won-lost records were 19–12, 23–10, and 19–9. Schumacher broke in with the Giants in 1931 and ended his career in 1946. Schumacher's last year for the Giants was the first for a promising rookie named Bobby Thomson.[15]

Although Adirondack bats had been swung in the major leagues prior to the 1950s, the firm's big break came thanks to Bobby Thomson. In 1951, the Giants outfielder/third baseman hit a fastball from Dodgers pitcher Ralph Branca for a home run to win the winner-take-all game of the National League playoff. The victory sent the New York squad to the World Series rather than the Brooklyn Dodgers.[16]

Thomson's blast came on October 3, 1951, at the Polo Grounds in New York, and is known to baseball fans as the *Shot Heard 'Round the World*. The white ash bat Thomson wielded for his historic blow was a 34-ounce, 35-inch, model number 302, manufactured by the Adirondack Company. Thomson bought the bat from his former teammate, Hal Schumacher.[17]

Another Giant who hit a historic home run with an Adirondack bat was Willie Mays. Mays, elected to the Baseball Hall of Fame in 1979, slugged his 600th career home run on September 22, 1969, in San Diego. At the time, only Babe Ruth had hit more home runs than Mays.[18]

Willie Mays, nicknamed the "Say Hey Kid," finished his 22nd season MLB career with 660 home runs, four times leading the National League. Mays was voted Rookie of the Year in 1951, earned two MVP Awards, was a batting champion in 1954, and won 12 Gold Glove Awards.[19]

Of all the home runs Mays hit, his 600th round-tripper, of course, was quite memorable for Mays. It was also memorable for the workers at the Adirondack factory in Dolgeville, New York. A few years later, another memorable occasion occurred with an Adirondack bat. This time the event took place in the factory's home state.

In Game 6 of the 1977 World Series, Reggie Jackson, wearing the pinstripes of the New York Yankees, hit three home runs—with an Adirondack bat—off three Los Angeles Dodgers pitchers to clinch the championship for the Yankees.[20] The three home runs propelled out of Yankee Stadium on October 18, 1977, by "Mr. October" was Jackson's crowning achievement in a long and storied career. With 21 seasons in MLB, 563 home runs, 14 All-Star Games, the 1973 AL MVP Award, five World Series Championships, and two World Series MVP Awards, Jackson was a first-ballot member of the 1993 class of the Baseball Hall of Fame.

Controversy seemed to follow Jackson wherever he played, and the three World Series home runs in 1977 were no exception. Soon after Jackson's heroic feat, Hillerich & Bradsby took out an ad congratulating him on the achievement. The ad included a photograph of Jackson's Louisville Slugger bat. Rawlings, the owner since 1975 of Adirondack and its Big Stick, struck back a few weeks later with an ad of their own. According to Stuart Miller's *Good Wood* book, the Rawlings ad declared, "H&B... How do you sleep at night? Doesn't it bother you just a little to capitalize on Reggie's glory, when he set all those World Series slugging records with an Adirondack bat? It bothers us."[21]

Along with the text of the ad, Rawlings showed a picture of Jackson in Game 6 using a bat with the distinctive Adirondack Pro Ring. Jackson did have a contract with Hillerich & Bradsby, but he used an Adirondack Big Stick on numerous occasions. To make matters even murkier, Jackson was said to have painted the Adirondack ring on some of his Louisville Slugger bats. Regardless, the Adirondack Big Stick still receives the credit and recognition as the lumber used to launch Jackson's three World Series home runs.[22]

Jackson's bat controversy was not unique. Mike Schmidt, Philadelphia's slugging third baseman, is a member of the 500-home run club like Jackson. Once Schmidt proudly stated that he was probably the only player to achieve this home run milestone using an Adirondack bat exclusively throughout his career. Schmidt confessed in the same statement that if he ever used a different bat, he'd be sure to tape a ring on it so it looked like an Adirondack.[23]

There was no bat controversy in 1998 when Mark McGwire of the St.

The Baseball Bat

Louis Cardinals stepped to the plate. The single-season home run record was being assaulted, and baseball fans were captivated.

During late summer and early fall, McGwire, who hit with an Adirondack (by now owned by Rawlings) Big Stick, was locked in a home run race with Sammy Sosa of the Chicago Cubs. As both men chased the ghosts of Roger Maris and Babe Ruth, the on-field action turned into a once-in-a-lifetime event for the citizens of Dolgeville and the workers at the Adirondack factory where McGwire's Big Stick was made.[24]

Everyone in Dolgeville and the Adirondack factory became a fan of the St. Louis Cardinals slugger, rooting for McGwire to beat Sosa in their epic battle. Even folks who weren't baseball fans got caught up in the day-to-day drama of the home run chase. The *New York Times* reported that one long-time Adirondack factory worker stated, "I never paid much attention to baseball, really." The worker then admitted, "But you just couldn't help getting excited about it. I mean, these are our bats."[25]

At season's end, both McGwire and Sosa eclipsed Ruth's 60 homers in 1927, and Maris's 61 home runs in 1961. McGwire finished 1998 with 70 round-trippers and Sosa had 66.[26]

In 2003, another change—at least from an ownership perspective—occurred with the Dolgeville bat-maker. Adirondack's parent firm, Rawlings, was bought by K2, a Los Angeles–based company. K2 Inc., best known for skis and other sporting goods, wanted to break into the team-sports equipment business, and Rawlings offered them the opportunity. While Adirondack's parent company changed hands a couple times over the next 15 years (Kohlberg & Company bought the firm in 2017), the bat factory in tree-covered upstate New York continues its tradition of supplying lumber for MLB.[27]

Twenty-first century players continue the tradition of swinging an Adirondack. Joe Mauer, retired from the Minnesota Twins in 2018, is an example.

The St. Paul, Minnesota native Mauer exemplified the small-ball game of baseball popular in by-gone days. While winning three AL batting titles (.347 batting average in 2006, .328 in 2008, and .365 in 2009) and one MVP Award (2009), Mauer had 548 hits and 282 walks during these three years, but only 50 home runs. Mauer's preferred lumber was an Adirondack.[28]

The 2017 World Series featured the Houston Astros and Los Angeles Dodgers. The Astros had never won a World Series title since their MLB franchise beginning (as the Colt 45s) in 1962. The Dodgers had not won the championship since 1988, a span of 29 years. The Series went seven games with the Astros prevailing. Carlos Beltran of Houston and Justin Turner of Los Angeles both used Adirondack bats during the fiercely fought games (additional players may have used an Adirondack during the series, but the Beltran and Turner bats were clearly identifiable on the television broadcast).[29]

Aluminum.... But Not in MLB

The first patent for an aluminum bat was made in the early 1920s by an archery company founded by James Easton. Initial aluminum bats were too heavy for baseball and, consequently, never caught on the way the inventors had hoped. Through the years, however, technology improved until aluminum bats came of age in the 1970s.[30]

In 1970 in a tannery in Tennessee, a firm by the name of Worth made a baseball bat, not from wood, but aluminum. The thinking by the son of the owner was that the only way to successfully enter the industry dominated by the Louisville Slugger brand was to make a bat from an entirely new material. By 1971, Little League Baseball approved the aluminum bat. In 1974, the NCAA also gave its blessing to aluminum bats. Following closely on the heels of Worth, the California-based Easton Company introduced an aluminum bat in the mid–70s that reduced weight and increased distance and power over wooden bats. While the aluminum bat craze swept across the country, some bat manufacturers, most notably Hillerich & Bradsby, sat on the sidelines regarding technological improvements to the aluminum bat.[31]

Hillerich & Bradsby's wooden bat sales dropped almost overnight from seven million to one million per year. The MLB market, requiring a wood bat, could not sustain Hillerich & Bradsby. With an undeniable trend in non-wood bats at the amateur level, Hillerich & Bradsby entered the aluminum business in 1978 by buying a plant in California.[32] Even though Hillerich & Bradsby began making their own aluminum bat, profits plunged until the company perfected the technique. One estimate of Hillerich & Bradsby profits from 1980 to 1985 pegs their sharp decline at 90 percent.[33]

The Spalding Company was not as direly impacted by the move to the non-professional level aluminum bat as Hillerich & Bradsby. While the Spalding name is well-known in the 21st century, the baseball bat manufacturing era is forgotten by most people. As of late 2017, Spalding was the world's largest basketball equipment supplier, including the official backboard of the NBA and the NCAA. Spalding also makes a range of other products for volleyball, American football, soccer, softball, and baseball. The Spalding business component that specializes in the "national pastime" of the U.S. is currently focused on the object a pitcher throws (ball) rather than the lumber a batter uses (bat).[34]

Boutique Firms

Thirty-two different firms were licensed to supply MLB with bats for the 2017 season, whereas in 1993 there were just 10 companies.[35] Some of the "old guard" companies, and their branded bats, like the Louisville Slugger from Hillerich & Bradsby and the Adirondack-made Rawlings bats, were included on the 2017 list. However, the vast majority were small firms with a knack for either woodworking, sports, marketing, public relations, or a specialty not directly related to the crafting of a baseball bat. These enterprises were relatively obscure, and were David-Compared-To-Goliath companies like Hillerich & Bradsby and Spalding. The 21st century trend of wooden baseball bat producers threw a curveball to large corporations with a long history of providing professional players with their lumber. The new wave of wooden bat-makers are often referred to as boutique firms.

Boutique bat-makers flourished in the 1990s thanks to many firms, including Glomar (headquartered in California), Kissimmee (Florida), Hoosier Bats (Indiana), and Carolina Clubs (Florida). The most famous, perhaps, of the 1990s boutique bat-makers was a carpenter, woodcarver, and longtime stagehand for Canada's National Arts Centre. The individual's name is Sam Holman, and *Sports Illustrated* credits him with unleashing the boutique bat business.[36]

As the story goes, Holman was relaxing at The Mayflower bar in his hometown of Ottawa, Canada, when he spotted a familiar face. The acquaintance was a Colorado Rockies scout and recent returnee from baseball's spring training. The scout complained to Holman about the large number of bats that players had broken that spring. Holman was not a huge baseball fan, but he could talk for hours about wood. The scout knew Holman's background and issued a challenge: Could Holman design a better wooden bat?[37]

Holman took the scout's challenge seriously. He read everything he could find on bats and bat making. Holman even reviewed the 200-plus bat patents and found that the patents dealt with ash. He realized he

Paul Lancisi, owner of Dove Tail Bats, is one of the recent "boutique bat" makers (courtesy Mary Stevens).

probably couldn't improve on the ash patents, so he looked for an alternative wood. Since Holman lives in Ottawa, which is surrounded by hard maple, and since he knew a lot about maple, he shifted his search in that direction.[38]

After purchasing a used Italian lathe and converting his garage/basement into a workshop, Holman crafted his first bat from a left-over maple bannister from a home renovation. In 1997, he formally launched his Sam Bats company. A few years later, Holman got the big break he was looking for.[39]

According to *Sports Illustrated*, at spring training in 1999 in Scottsdale, Arizona, Barry Bonds was introduced to the gray-haired, 53-year-old, Canadian carpenter. Holman convinced Bonds to take a few swings in the batting cage with his north-of-the-border-made sugar (hard) maple bat. Bonds was a bit skeptical about the new wood since he and the majority of his MLB colleagues had swung white ash bats throughout their big league careers. However, after his session in the cage, Bonds changed his tune. The San Francisco slugger thought the maple bat felt harder than his ash bats, and the ball jumped off the bat with more zip.[40]

After Holman followed Bonds' design suggestions for improvement, the Giants' left fielder began swinging Holman's maple bats full-time in the second half of the 1999 season. Then in 2001, using a Holman-crafted bat, Bonds bashed 73 home runs with an .863 slugging percentage. The rise of the boutique bat-maker (and maple bats) had begun.[41]

In 2017, there were dozens of boutique bat-makers scattered across the land. MaxBats in Minnesota, D–Bats (Texas), Axe Bat (Washington), Victus, BWP, and Chandler (Pennsylvania), Old Hickory (Tennessee), Zinger (Arizona), Trinity (California), Dove Tail (Maine), and B45 (Quebec) are just a few. And Sam Bats, while the company was sold by Sam Holman in 2008 to investors, continues its tradition of producing bats in the Canadian province of Quebec. However, the biggest name in the boutique bat-making business is Marucci Sports (founded as Marucci Bat Co.), based in Baton Rouge, Louisiana.[42]

Jack Marucci started an obscure, tiny company in the early 21st century that made wood bats. According to *Sports Illustrated*, the growth of his small business within the game "has been an underground social explosion, far from the eyes of all but the most scrutinizing fan."[43] For example, the Marucci bat brand (or bat companies owned by Marucci Sports) dominated the starting line-ups in the 2017 World Series. For the decisive Game 7 of the Series between the Dodgers and Astros, 14 bats used in the starting lineup were identifiable, nine of which (64 percent) can be attributed to Marucci Sports. The famous Louisville Slugger and Rawlings-brand bats had only one each. In an interview in late 2017, Jack Marucci estimated that more than one-half of MLB players used his bats in the 2017 regular season.[44]

Marucci's unlikely story started in 2002. When his eight-year-old son, Gino, wanted a wooden bat to use in his Little League games, the elder Marucci took notice. Gino loved the bats of big leaguers, so he asked his dad for a bat like the ones he saw MLB players swing on television. Jack Marucci did what many dads would do for their child—he tried to find a wooden bat that an eight-year-old could swing. He called several bat companies, but none of them made a small bat. So Marucci took matters into his own hands—and this is where his actions differed from many fathers posed with a similar problem.[45]

Marucci bought a cheap wood lathe and used tools inherited from his dad. He tried to remember what he learned in ninth grade wood shop, and he moved the lathe and memories of his junior high training into a 54-square-foot tool shed in his backyard. After a few failed attempts on the wood lathe, Marucci crafted a bat suitable for his son. Gino liked the bat, and so did his teammates and opponents. Soon, many Little Leaguers wanted their own wooden bat and asked Marucci to make them one. As demand grew for Jack Marucci's bats, his hobby was quickly becoming a full-time job.[46]

When Marucci started crafting youth bats, he had an advantage over most others. First, he called a contact in his native Pennsylvania and ordered high-quality wood billets for his bat-carving experiment. Second, since Marucci is the head athletic trainer for the Tigers of Louisiana State University (LSU), he had ready access to LSU athletes. A retired professional baseball player, Joe Lawrence, who was playing football for the Tigers (still 20-something in age), gave Marucci valuable bat-making tips. Third, Marucci was entering the boutique bat business when other small companies (like Sam Bats) with superior craftsmanship were rocking the establishment. As popularity of Marucci bats skyrocketed beyond the youth market, he had an in-place distribution network with former LSU alumni who were playing professional baseball. All the stars were seemingly lining up, and Marucci took advantage of each one.[47]

Success in business often hinges on good decisions at the beginning, and Jack Marucci can point to his. Marucci said, "I had an idea ... an inspiration ... but I needed help to move beyond my own backyard. I partnered with Joe [Lawrence] and hired Kurt [Ainsworth] and they helped my little bat company go to the next level. In 2006, sales really took off."[48]

After tearing his ACL, Lawrence became a regular in the university training room run by Marucci. Marucci and Lawrence developed a close relationship and felt they could work together. Lawrence encouraged Marucci to expand the brand. Marucci gives Lawrence a lot of credit in growing the brand and providing confidence to move forward in the Marucci bat journey.

Another smart decision was made in 2003, when Marucci reached out to Eduardo Perez of the St. Louis Cardinals. Perez, the son of Hall of Famer Tony Perez, played college ball in the early 1990s at Florida State, where Marucci was a trainer before his move to LSU. The friendship between Marucci and Perez was formed in Tallahassee, FL, and deepened when they met in St. Louis. Marucci convinced his friend to try a couple of his Louisiana-made bats, and Perez was thrilled with them. Perez helped spread the gospel by telling teammates (like Albert Pujols) and ex-teammate (Barry Larkin) about the benefits of Marucci's bats.[49]

Marucci gives Perez most of the credit for the growth of his bats in MLB. Perez, according to Marucci, was the key person, "Who was a game changer for the company."[50]

By 2008 the company was growing to the point where Marucci

The finishing process at a bat firm, boutique or elsewhere, can last four days or more (author's collection).

decided to take the plunge and purchased a wood mill in Pennsylvania. As of 2018, 100 percent of the wood billets used to make bats are sourced from mills owned by Marucci. He said, "The best wood for bats comes from Pennsylvania and southern New York. We ship all of our wood to Louisiana from Pennsylvania."[51]

Consistently crafting a quality product has been the forte of Marucci Bats. For instance, most players, after getting a new shipment of bats, make three piles—game use, batting practice, and scrap. Marucci said, "Bats in a Marucci shipment to a MLB player land in the game use pile only, which contributes to the reputation of consistency and craftsmanship."[52]

One of the reasons the Marucci brand has flourished with big leaguers is the company's player advisory board. Marucci stated in late 2017, "We formed a board of former and current MLB stars to help us design products and give us feedback along the way." Based on Marucci's website (https://maruccisports.com/about/), players on the board, either active or retired, include Andrew McCutchen, Albert Pujols, Jose Bautista, Chase Utley, and David Ortiz.[53]

Marucci is also quick to satisfy a player's immediate needs. A case in point is the experience of Chase Utley (who finished the 2017 season with the Los Angeles Dodgers). Utley placed his first order with Marucci in 2006 and was quickly impressed. Three years later, prior to the 2009 World Series, Utley (then with the Philadelphia Phillies) called Marucci to order a special bat to use against Yankees closer Mariano Rivera. Utley wanted a one-inch shorter bat with a slightly larger barrel than his regular model (in an attempt to neutralize Rivera's cutter). Marucci's company complied and rushed the special-order bat to him. Although Utley's debut in the series against Rivera resulted in a ground ball double-play, it likely had less to do with the bat than with the man on the mound. Later, Utley invested in the company.[54]

In February 2017, Marucci acquired five-year-old bat company Victus, based in King of Prussia (near Philadelphia), Pennsylvania. 2017 World Series Champions Jose Altuve, Carlos Correa, and MVP George Springer swung Victus bats for Houston in the deciding seventh game of the Series. The acquisition made sense from a MLB reach and facility distribution standpoint. The CEO of Marucci Sports, Kurt Ainsworth, told *Baseball America,* "Victus makes a great product [and] they're [run by] great guys. I kind of saw myself and [Jack] Marucci and us eight years ago. What we could basically do is help them [Victus] avoid some of the mistakes we've made along the way…. We know what we can do to help them grow their brand."[55]

As baseball moves into the third decade of the 21st century, the dominant MLB bat-makers have certainly changed since the 1800s, not only in name but in their approach as well. The industry's future, from bat-style and type of wood to location of manufacturing plant and distribution network, is not easy to predict.

5

Wood Properties and Features and Their Relationship to Bats

We may use wood with intelligence only if we understand wood.—Frank Lloyd Wright (1867–1959)

It's important to remember that wood comes from trees. It's also important to recognize that whatever shortcoming a wood object exhibits, such as breaking or shattering into pieces when impacting a speeding baseball, can often be traced back to the tree. Wood evolved as a functional tissue of plants and not to satisfy MLB or the players who swing the objects known as bats.[1]

The nearly century-old quote from architect Frank Lloyd Wright is appropriate when discussing baseball bats.[2] I'm not sure if Wright played baseball or was a fan of the game, but his comment on wood, with an extension in thinking to wooden baseball bats, is right on target.

A good primer on properties and features of *wood* can be found in a 2016 Dr. Gene Wengert article, published by *Sawmill & Woodlot*. Anyone seeking a non-technical overview of wood should read this short piece.[3]

Unfortunately, most people take for granted, or have a vague understanding of, the material called *wood*. However, many properties and features of wood directly impact MLB and the bats professional players rely upon. A few components are discussed below, in hopes of increasing appreciation for, and knowledge of, wood.

Atoms and Molecules

Three atoms make up wood—hydrogen, oxygen, and carbon. These three atoms combine to form a molecule called glucose sugar. Glucose sugar molecules join together into a long chain to form *cellulose* (known as polysaccharides). As an example, cotton is basically cellulose.[4]

A second long-chained molecule that builds the wood substance is called *lignin*. Lignin is the stiffener that gives wood its strength (e.g., to propel a baseball 400 feet or more). Lignin also is the glue that holds the wood together.[5]

Other chemicals, like sap or resin, may also be found in a tree. Regardless, they are made of the same three building-block atoms—hydrogen, oxygen, and carbon.[6]

Cells

Look closely the next time you hold a piece of wood in your hand. You might notice that the material we call *wood* is made up of tiny cells. Cells are formed by the long molecule chains discussed in the previous section. They are hollow, tiny structures that look like miniature soda straws. Cells are so small they might not be visible except with a magnifying glass or microscope.[7] A one-inch cube of wood can have five million cells! The number of cells in a large tree is astronomical.[8]

Almost all cells in a tree run vertically, from the bottom to the top of the tree. Newly formed vertical cells tend to be hollow tubes that are greater in length than in diameter. These cells move water and nutrients from the roots to the very top of the tree. This transport, especially in a tall tree, is quite an engineering feat. The redwoods in California pump water and nutrients 300 feet!

Within the leaves, a process called photosynthesis occurs, which many of us learned about in school. Water combines with carbon dioxide from the air, and with the right mix of sunlight and chlorophyll, sugars are produced.[9] These sugars then move downward via cells through the inner bark of the tree in the form of sap. Some sap continues downward to the roots, assisting root development and providing an energy source for new growth at the beginning of a growing season. Sap is the building block used by the tree to create the unique substance known as wood.[10]

The common name for these water- and nutrient-carrying cells is *sapwood*. As these cells age, they often acquire a darker color. The aging process of sapwood cells can be anywhere from several up to 50 years. Old sapwood cells are called *heartwood*.[11]

Wood Vessels or Pores

Trees in North America that lose their leaves in the autumn are called deciduous trees. *Hardwood* trees are typically deciduous, with examples including hickory, oak, ash, maple, and birch, to name just a few. The term conifer refers to *softwood* trees that are usually evergreen and characterized by needle-like or scale-like foliage. Familiar examples include pines, spruces, firs, hemlocks, and cedars.[12]

Current MLB bats are made from hardwoods like ash, maple, and birch. Also, hardwoods are often used for, but not limited to, cabinets, furniture, flooring, paneling, cutting boards, tool handles, decorative veneer, and fuel wood. Softwoods typically are the species of choice for products like construction lumber (think 2 × 4's) (due to their light weight and high strength), utility poles, stadium scorecard pencils, and newspapers. In some ballparks, bleacher or dugout seats might be made from softwood trees.

There are anatomical differences between hardwoods and softwoods, but the terms simply distinguish the two broad groups of trees. The term is *not* indicative of the hardness or softness of the wood. As an example, cottonwood is light in weight (soft) but is classified as a hardwood (deciduous) since it loses its leaves in autumn. On the other hand, Southern yellow pine is actually harder than cottonwood. However, since Southern yellow pine retains most of its needles year-round, it is classified as a softwood (conifer).[13]

One way in which hardwoods differ from softwoods is that all hardwoods have relatively large diameter cells known as vessels (often called pores).[14] The pores of a hardwood tree, like ash, maple, and birch, can be thought of as pipelines that carry water and nutrients throughout the tree.[15]

Growth Rings and Wood Grain

Tree growth, the result of cell division just under the bark, continues from year to year when the tree is living. In the temperate climate in much of the U.S. and Canada, the typical growth cycle includes a growing season and a dormant season. Nearly all trees follow this same cycle, resulting in growth layers or annual rings. When rings are visible and there is a sharp contrast *within* a single growth ring, the viewer is seeing the contrast between wood grown early in the year (called *earlywood*) and wood grown

Joe Jackson, prior to his banishment from MLB, had little trouble seeing a bat's grain pattern (National Baseball Hall of Fame and Museum, Cooperstown, N.Y.).

later in the season (*latewood*). The transition from earlywood to latewood may be abrupt (called *ring-porous*) or gradual (*diffuse-porous*).[16]

White ash is ring-porous with an eye-catching distinction between early and late wood. When a white ash begins growing in the spring, there are concentrations or bands of large-diameter wood cells. As the growing season moves into late spring and summer, there is a shift to smaller-diameter, latewood cells. Other familiar ring-porous trees are the oaks and hickories.

Consequently, white ash growth rings and grain patterns are relatively easy to see. As opposed to ash, both sugar maple and yellow birch have a somewhat even distribution of smaller-sized wood cells across the growth ring. Both maple and birch are termed diffuse-porous. The grain of diffuse-porous trees is difficult to see with the human eye.

Slope of Grain

Since the majority of wood cells run vertically in a tree, a section of wood from the tree (e.g., a sawn board), reveals what we refer to as the grain. For baseball aficionados, the grain of a bat runs from one end to the other.[17]

Grain can be either straight in a tree or at an angle. Perfectly straight grain results in a piece of wood with maximum strength. Any deviation from straight grain results in strength loss. As an illustration, wood with 10 degrees slope-of-grain (SOG) decreases strength approximately 70 percent. Even slight angles like a mere 2–3 degrees SOG decrease strength by roughly 10 percent. Structural lumber, for example, with a SOG greater than a one to five ratio (20 degrees or more), is considered very weak and is dropped from standard grades.[18]

Due to the difficulty of seeing maple grain, severe grain slope was overlooked during the maple bat inspection process during the early years of the species introduction. The inspection flaw contributed to a huge problem for MLB in the initial years of the 21st century. MLB bats began breaking frequently into multiple pieces and becoming airborne. The erratic maple grain angle (slope-of-grain issues) was blamed for the catastrophic rise in shattered bats through 2008. Since then, new bat requirements have been in place, and MLB bat breakage has significantly dropped. (See the next chapter for a discussion of the new requirements.)

Rings per Inch

There is disagreement among former MLB players who used ash bats about whether wide-grain or narrow-grain is best.[19] Wide-grain indicates a fast-growing tree and produces a bat with a low number of growth rings per inch. Narrow-grain bats come from slow-growing trees and result in a higher ring count per inch.

Rings per inch are easily seen on the bat knob (courtesy Leatherstocking Hand-Split Billet Co.).

Ted Williams, as an example, insisted on a narrow-grain bat.[20] Williams wanted his bats to be 10 grains or fewer per inch, while Willie Mays preferred wider grains.[21] George Brett wanted a precise number of grains in his ideal bat—seven, to be exact.[22] "Stan The Man" Musial used a wide-grain bat and liked to have a knot right on the hitting surface.[23] Though many players consider a pin (small) knot as a defect, some, including Babe Ruth and Carl Yastremzski, preferred the small knots, thinking their bat had tougher wood.[24] Although some of these men—Williams, Mays, Brett, Musial, Ruth and Yaz—had differing views on grain width and knots, all were great hitters. And all are in baseball's Hall of Fame!

According to Miller's *Good Wood* book, scientific studies support Williams' theory that narrow-grain bats are best, but some players simply believe otherwise. A veteran bat-maker at Hillerich & Bradsby, per *Good Wood,* said that even scientific data wouldn't end the debate between narrow- and wide-grain proponents. The bat-maker summed it up by stating, "Players are the most superstitious people you will ever meet. They're all nuts."[25]

Density

Density is the weight of wood per unit of volume. The Forest Products Laboratory (FPL), a division of the United States Forest Service, noted that the standard reference for wood weight (density) is the term specific gravity. Specific gravity is based on wood weight when completely dry and wood volume at a specified level of moisture (often 12 percent). Consequently, sugar maple (specific gravity of 0.63) is indeed heavier and, thus, denser than white ash (specific gravity of 0.60). (For perspective, the specific gravity of mockernut hickory is 0.72, and that of balsa is approximately 0.19.)[26]

Remember the joking question: What weighs more: one pound of feathers or one pound of steel? The answer, of course, is that they weigh the same amount—one pound. The difference is that one pound of steel would fit into your hand, whereas one pound of feathers might fill a basket or large bag. In other words, steel is denser than feathers. The same principle holds true for different species of wood. Thus wood density is a good predictor of *hardness*.[27]

Density of wood can also be thought of as the porosity of the species, i.e., the proportion of void (empty space) volume of the material (think about the steel and feathers example). In addition to hardness, wood density is a good indicator of *strength*.[28] Some experts argue that wood density—when comparing samples of different species that have equal quality—is *the* single-most important indicator of strength.[29]

Another example, this time comparing different species of wood, should drive home the point. Pick up a block of balsa wood[30] (or imagine picking it up) and pick up the same size block of white ash, sugar maple or yellow birch. The balsa block will feel much lighter (and it is!) than either the ash, maple or birch block. In other words, balsa is less dense, and does not have the hardness or strength of ash, maple or birch.

However, maple is slightly denser than ash. As noted above, density is a good measure of *hardness* and the key indicator of *strength* of wood. However, ash has more *flexibility* than maple. Also, ash is *lighter* than maple, leading to thinner-handle maple bats to compensate for swinging a heavier wood. Despite the flexibility and weight issue, many players are convinced that a maple bat gives the ball more pop. According to *Good Wood*, "The pop theory is not scientifically true when comparing maple versus ash bats."[31] Regardless, ballplayers believe what they want to believe.

Prominent wood scientists A. J. Panshin and Carl de Zeeuw stated in their classic *Textbook of Wood Technology*, "It is frequently overlooked [or not known] that variability in the properties of wood of the same species may be of even greater significance than the relatively minor discrepancies in the wood characteristics among different species."[32] One of these over-looked or unknown characteristics is *density*.

Wood density can vary with a number of factors including location in a tree, geographical location where the tree grew, growing conditions such as rainfall and soil type, and the tree's genetic make-up. For example, an-other prominent wood scientist, Dr. Jim Bowyer, remarked that the density of 10 to 25 percent of sugar maple trees is *lower* than the highest-density soft maple tree. In other words, some pieces of hard maple wood can be less dense (less hard or less strong) than some pieces of the closely-related soft maple. Also, density variability with maple is not easy to spot with the naked eye. With ash, lower density wood pieces can generally be seen, in the sawmill or by the bat maker, by looking at the pores in the growth rings.[33]

Interestingly, hickory wood is very dense and was used often in mak-ing bats over a century ago. However, with its unusually high strength-to-weight ratio, ash was deemed special. Consequently, white ash out-competed the denser, but heavier hickory, as MLB players' favorite wood for bat-making in the 20th century.[34]

Dr. Robert Adair of Yale University wrote in his book *The Physics of Baseball*, "A hickory bat with the same dimensions as the 33-ounce ash bat used by Roger Maris to hit 61 home runs [in 1961] would weigh about 42 ounces."[35] Just as ash wood dominated over hickory in the 1900s, maple bats have a sizable lead over ash as the preferred choice for MLB players in the 21st century.

Moisture Content

The amount of water in wood, or an item made from wood like a baseball bat, is called moisture content (MC) by wood scientists. Wood can gain or lose moisture content by picking up or losing water vapor from the surrounding air.[36] Consequently, a baseball bat can gain or lose weight depending on the climate, whether at a stadium or in transport from one city to another. This is one reason Ted Williams was meticulous about not having his bats lie on the ground after he took his turn at the plate.

Even the *New York Times* and a host of others weighed in on the sub-ject of wooden bat moisture by noting what methods some great MLB players used. Ichiro Suzuki, they noted, took great care that his bats did

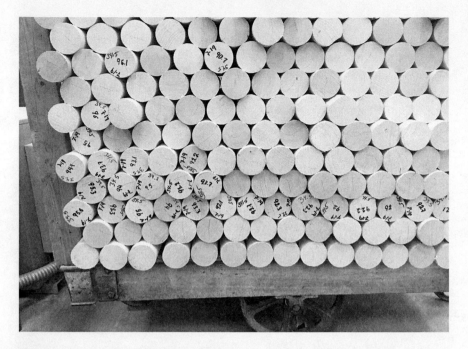

Moisture content is critical and is often marked on the billets prior to bat making (author's collection).

not accumulate moisture and thus gain weight. Suzuki's solution: he stored his bats in humidors, one in the clubhouse and another, a portable one, for the road. Rod Carew fought moisture by storing his bats in a box full of sawdust in the warmest part of his house. "The sawdust acts as a buffer between the bats and the environment," he explained, "absorbing any moisture before it can seep into the wood."[37]

Moisture content of wood can affect its strength. A white ash, sugar maple, or yellow birch baseball bat, for example, will become stronger if the moisture content of the final product is below roughly 25 percent.[38] Reaching this threshold moisture content is typically not a problem with baseball bats at any level.

However, sugar maple and yellow birch trees have a much higher sapwood moisture content (72 percent) than a typical white ash tree (44 percent).[39] Baseball bats are made from a tree's sapwood. Consequently, maple and birch billets (the round dowels from which bats are crafted) originally have more moisture than ash billets. To compensate for this difference, maple and birch billets are sometimes dried for slightly longer time periods, using different drying methods, compared to ash. Consequently, the extra drying time and different drying methods can lead to more brittle wood.[40]

Longitudinal, Radial and Tangential Surfaces[41]

Pick up a wooden bat made from ash, even if you're not ready to hit the diamond. A hickory bat will also serve as an appropriate prop, but not a maple bat (I'll explain later why maple might not be appropriate). The following discussion of *surfaces* of wood will be clearer if you have an ash or hickory bat in your hands.

The *longitudinal*, or end surface, of wood, is the circular surface when looking at either a stump or end of a log (often called the cross-sectional surface). This surface is perpendicular or longitudinal/cross-wise to the direction of tree growth. On a baseball bat, the longitudinal surface can be easily seen by looking at the end of the barrel or knob, where the bat length or player jersey number is sometimes stamped.

The *radial* surface of a piece of wood comes into view when a cut is made *across* the growth rings and *along* the length (axis) of the log. This is the hitting surface or edge of an ash or hickory bat, regardless of whether

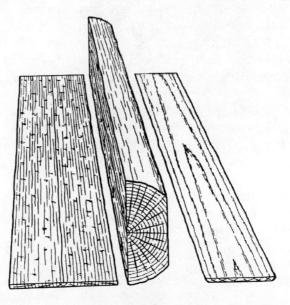

The three surfaces of wood: Radial (left), Longitudinal (center), and Tangential or Flat-Sawn (right) (U.S. Forest Service, Forest Products Laboratory).

the batter swings right- or left-handed. The radial surface shows the long, parallel grain that runs from the knob to the barrel of the bat. Hitting a ball on the radial surface of a bat is similar to making contact with the edge of a deck of cards. Radial or edge-face grain contact transfers the impact of ball hitting bat across the diameter of the bat barrel.

The *tangential* surface of wood is seen when bark is peeled from a log. Like the radial surface, the tangential surface runs *along* the length of the log. However, the tangential surface is, more or less, *parallel* to the growth rings. In a log, the tangential surface is curved, and sawn lumber is often called flat-sawn or plain-sawn. The tangential surface is where the trademark is placed on an ash or hickory bat and other bats made from ring-porous trees. Since 2009, the tangential surface is NOT where the trademark is placed on bats made from diffuse-porous trees like maple and birch!

"Impact bending strength," a term used by engineers and wood scientists, is the wood property most related to baseball bat strength. Surprisingly to many observers, the radial surface (often called the radial "plane") is weaker than the tangential surface of a piece of wood. This phenomena is easily seen in a "tree cookie" (a cross-section of a tree) or piece of firewood. The cookie, or end of firewood if you burn wood for heat, with the passage of time develops a split typically from the tree center (called "pith") to the tree bark (outside edge). The split occurs *along* the *radial* surface (but is *viewed* from the *longitudinal/cross-section* surface). The tangential surface has been demonstrated by scientists as the strongest surface of wood. However, in an ash baseball bat, this is the surface stamped with the trademark (the side opposite the trademark is also a tangential surface). The practice of putting the trademark in its traditional position continued for over a century. However, repeated bat-ball collisions on the tangential surface of a bat manufactured from ash (a ring-porous species) will eventually cause the bat to flake (annual ring separation). Flaking comes from a structural breakdown between earlywood and latewood.

An ash bat with the trademark on the tangential surface warns players which side will deteriorate fastest. Thus, players of all ages are taught to hit with the trademark pointing up. Although this advice with an ash bat results in striking the ball on the radial surface, the trademark up technique slows down bat deterioration. Since flaking does not occur on a maple or birch bat (diffuse-porous species), the tangential surface is recommended for ball-striking.[42]

Some great hitters of the past who swung ash bats hit with the trademark down. For example, Ted Williams hit this way as he wanted nothing at home plate to mess with his mind—pants too baggy, sleeves too tight, hat too small. Williams said, "I even hit with the label of the bat down so I couldn't see it and get distracted."[43] Hank Aaron was another player who didn't want to be distracted by the trademark. Dan Gutman, in *Banana Bats and Ding-Dong Balls*, wrote, "When an opposing catcher helpfully suggested that Aaron hold his bat with the trademark facing up, Hammerin' Hank responded curtly, 'I didn't come up here to read.'"[44]

Sweet Spot

The "sweet spot" on a baseball bat is the position on a bat near, as physicists call it, the "center of percussion." The sweet spot is located between the trademark and the end of the bat barrel. This is the point, regardless of wood species, where maximum force is transferred to the incoming ball but no vibrations are felt in the handle. A bat's sweet spot is where hitters attempt to make contact with the ball.

Like the vibrating string on a guitar when it is strummed, a baseball bat also vibrates when contact is made with a ball. The bat, however, vibrates so fast for a well-hit ball (about $1/1000$ of a second), the movement is not discernible by the human eye. The minimum vibration on the bat occurs when a batter makes contact on the sweet spot. At this point, minimum bat energy is lost due to vibration, and the ball travels the greatest distance.[45]

The bat's sweet spot can also be explained by a familiar child's plaything. Visualize the traditional seesaw often found in playgrounds or backyards. A baseball colliding with a bat is like a rubber ball hitting the fulcrum of a seesaw. The ball bounces the maximum distance. If the rubber ball contacts the seesaw on either side of the fulcrum, the energy is scattered and not concentrated at one point, causing the seesaw to vibrate. This physics principle is why baseballs struck on the bat's sweet spot produce longer hits.[46]

The following sweet spot observation was made by perhaps the greatest hitter in baseball. Ted Williams of the Boston Red Sox played MLB in four decades from 1939 to his retirement in 1960. In his 1971 classic, *The Science of Hitting*, he referred to the sweet spot on the bat as the "joy spot." Since Williams played before maple bats were introduced in the sport, his comments focused solely on ash bats.[47]

Williams contended that an ash bat's "joy spot" was 4½ inches long when "fully exposed." By that Williams meant hitting the ball at 90 degrees

Ted Williams called his sweet spot the "joy spot" (National Baseball Hall of Fame and Museum, Cooperstown, N.Y.).

from the direction of the pitch. A swing too early or too late that produced bat-ball contact at an angle that deviated from 90 to 45 degrees, reduced "the joy spot one-third."[48]

Some modern bat-makers, in discussing the pros and cons of maple and ash bats, acknowledge the sweet spot size difference between the two species. Their websites note that ash bats have a longer sweet spot while maple bats have a smaller one. One manufacturer quantified his comments by saying, "Maple bats have anywhere from a 1–2" smaller sweet spot area [than ash]."[49]

In recent years, maple baseball bats have increased in popularity. Early in the second decade of the 21st century, almost two-thirds of MLB bats were maple.[50] As of the 2019 season, the number of maple bats continues to grow.

Ash Versus Maple Baseball Bats

Wood scientists will tell you that sugar maple (often called hard or rock maple) is approximately 5–10 percent stronger, harder, and tougher than white ash. So why not make all bats out of maple and forget about ash? The brief discussion above points out some wood properties and features that make the decision more complicated than simply a general statement on wood strength, degree of hardness, and toughness.

Also, some current MLB players want the same wood as swung by earlier Hall of Famers like Williams, Aaron, and Derek Jeter (ash in this case). Others want to swing the lumber species that made Aaron Judge, Miguel Cabrera, and Albert Pujols famous in more recent times (maple). And still other players want a bat from the wood they used while growing up—Juan Uribe (ash), or in the minor leagues—Mike Trout (maple).[51]

Regardless of wood species, the perfect bat, like magic, is not easy to define. Scott Podsednik, when he was an outfielder for the Chicago White Sox, summed up the opinions of many players when he told the *New York Times*, "You can't describe it—it's a feel. When you pick it up and take a couple of swings with it, you just know." When this occurs with players as Podsednik described, all information and scientific data about wood properties and features are out the door.[52]

6

Bat Breakage

Think?! How are you supposed to think and hit at the same time?—Yogi Berra

Sometimes a baseball thrown by a major league pitcher breaks a wood bat. Just ask hitters who stepped into the batter's box against flame-throwers like Hall of Famers Bob Feller, Nolan Ryan, and Randy Johnson. Sometimes a break in a wood bat can be expected, as when the hitter makes inside contact with a fastball.

However, sometimes the bat shatters, resulting in what is called multiple-piece-failure, or MPF. When this happens, pieces of flying wood go everywhere. These whirling, spinning shards can injure people—players, umpires, coaches, and spectators.

In the spring and early summer of 2008, media attention was again widespread on the frequency of bats breaking and shattering in Major League games. Numerous horrifying incidents occurred throughout the league: Pirates hitting Coach Don Long had his left cheek slashed (April 15); a fan's jaw was broken in two places when the barrel of Rockies player Todd Helton's bat hit her in the face (April 15); and umpire Brian O'Nora's forehead was cut when Kansas City catcher Miguel Olivo's bat shattered (June 24). These and other heart-stopping breakage events provided MLB with justification to act.

In July, MLB (through its Safety and Health Advisory Committee) assembled an interdisciplinary team of external experts to study the causes and propose a solution for reducing the frequency of broken bats. MLB was particularly interested in multiple-piece failures of bats—in other words, the shattering of bats into many pieces.[1]

The experts and their staff represented the fields of wood science, wood products certification, bat testing, bat manufacturing, and statistics. A research engineer specializing in wood-related issues at the U.S. Department of Agriculture's (USDA) Forest Products Laboratory, a division of the U.S. Forest Service, led the study team: David Kretschmann of Madison, Wisconsin. Other team members included: Dr. Carl Norris, Professor of Statistics at Harvard; Dr. James Sherwood, Professor of Mechanical Engineering, University of Massachusetts at Lowell; and Scott Drake, Vice-President of Operations, Timberco (TECO) Inc., Cottage Grove, Wisconsin.[2]

In what many would call a Herculean effort, MLB gathered every broken bat (over 2,200) from MLB games from mid-season through the late summer of 2008.[3] The goal was to characterize and analyze the failures of the cracked or shattered bats. In addition, a database was compiled with details about each incident, including player, type of bat, bat manufacturer, how the bat broke, the number of pieces and where they landed, and video of the incident.[4] The study also included testing of wood billets/dowels, manufacturing plant visits, and the engineering concepts of dynamic durability testing of bats (bat density and its relationship to bat durability) and finite element modeling of the bat-ball collision (e.g., slope-of-wood grain and pitch speed versus the relationship to broken bats).[5]

From Boston to Seattle and San Diego to Miami, with all MLB cities in between, broken bats were collected and shipped for testing and inspection. The recipient of the failed bats was TECO in Sun Prairie, Wisconsin (TECO has since merged with the PFS Corporation). When the extensive data on broken bats was gathered and analyzed for the period between July and September 2008, the study team put together a report.

Study Findings[6]

One conclusion was that maple bats broke more often and in more dangerous ways than ash bats; this was already known by many players and observers of the game. The report specifically noted that in the 2008 season, maple bats were "three times more likely than ash bats to break into two or more pieces [multiple-piece failure]."[7] The question that needed an answer was "Why?"

The main cause of broken bats—whether maple or ash—according to the final report, was what wood scientists call slope-of-grain, the straightness of the wood grain along the length of the bat. Straighter grain, from the bat handle to the end of the barrel, means less likelihood for breakage, regardless of the wood species. Slope-of-grain can be thought of as the angle, relative to the grain direction in the log, at which a piece of wood is cut. However, maple grain is more difficult for the naked eye to see than ash grain. This fact of nature resulted in a higher percentage of lower grade maple bats showing up in MLB games. Consequently, there were four times more shattering, or multi-piece failures, in maple bats compared to ash.[8]

Another finding from the study related to density of the wood. Low-density maple bats were found to not only crack but shatter into multiple pieces more often than ash bats and higher-density maple bats. The study team demonstrated a significant relationship between density and bat durability.[9]

Recommendations[10]

The study team made nine recommendations, all adopted by MLB with approval of the Major League Baseball Players Association. In the 2009 season, all suppliers of MLB bats needed to comply with those requirements.

First, all bats are required to conform to the slope-of-grain (SOG) wood-grading standards. Billets for bat-making have to meet a five degrees maximum deviation from perfectly straight grain, along the ⅔ length of the bat from the handle through the taper region. The five degrees maximum deviation translates to a SOG ratio of one to 20 (1:20). The ratio applied to the traditional hitting (radial) and traditional trademark (tangential) surfaces of the bat. MLB reasoned that requiring manufacturers to produce bats with a maximum SOG of 1:20 would significantly reduce broken bats flying into the air.

Second, manufacturers must place an ink dot (12 inches from the knob) on the traditional trademark side (tangential surface) of the bat handle of sugar maple and yellow birch before applying a finish. This requirement was adopted since it was often difficult to see the grain on maple and birch. When a drop of ink soaks into the wood, the ink "bleeds" (follows) along the grain. Consequently, the ink dot makes it easier for MLB inspectors, manufacturers, players, etc., to determine slope-of-grain issues on the bat handle.

Third, the logo or trademark on maple and birch bats must be placed such that ball-bat contact is made on the flat-grain (tangential) surface of the bat. Of course, the batter ultimately decides how the bat is held. The new maple and birch (diffuse-porous woods) trademark placement is opposite from ring-porous ash bats that many MLB players swung during most of the 20th century.

As briefly described in an earlier chapter, an ash bat will flake from

The handle dot is now required on diffuse-porous species like maple and birch (author's collection).

repeated ball-bat collisions on the tangential or trademark surface of the bat; maple and birch will not. The "impact bending strength" (a technical engineering and wood science term) of radial or edge-grain wood is less than the tangential or flat-sawn surface. Consequently, since maple and birch are diffuse-porous woods, a bat's trademark stamp could be changed for these species. The new trademark, rotated 90 degrees, takes advantage of the extra impact bending strength (without flaking) of the tangential surface.

Fourth, handles of sugar maple and yellow birch bats must be natural or treated with a clear finish (only implemented through the 2009 season). This requirement made it easier for MLB, or their inspectors, to check for slope-of-grain issues.

As noted above, the recommendations from the study team included guidelines on the manufacturing of bats for MLB. However, the study findings pointed out additional information for MLB beyond the specific techniques of bat-making. Recommendations (requirements following approval) five through nine dealt with bat tracking, MLB random

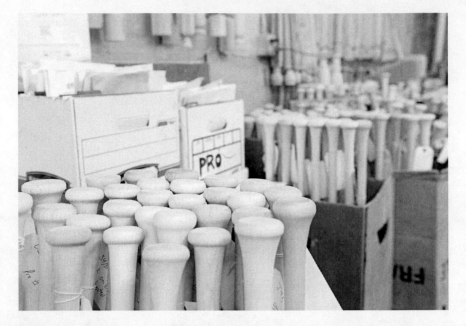

Bat manufacturers must mark all MLB bats for trackability before the lumber is shipped (courtesy Mary Stevens).

visits to manufacturers, audits, workshop attendance, and third-party bat certification.

Specifically, the fifth requirement states that bat manufacturers must have a way of identifying their bats once the bat leaves their shop and travels to a major league stadium. Serial numbers stamped on the bat is one way to do this. A manufacturer must be able to track the bat from its production records to MLB play, and back.

Sixth, representatives of each authorized firm that supplies bats to MLB is required to participate in a MLB-sponsored workshop. The workshop addresses wood science topics as well as engineering properties and grading practices of wood. The goal is to help MLB-approved bat makers better understand the manufacture of solid-wood baseball bats.

Seventh, MLB, or its designated representative, can regularly visit bat manufacturers. The primary purpose of the visits is to audit each firm's manufacturing processes and record-keeping with respect to bat traceability.

Eighth, random audits will be conducted at ballparks in MLB cities to make sure that the new bat requirements are being followed. MLB or its designee can conduct these audits.

Ninth, and last, MLB established a formal third-party certification and quality control program. The program certifies new suppliers, approves new species of wood, provides education and training to bat manufacturers, and addresses issues of non-compliance.

In addition to the nine study-team recommendations, a two-part requirement was implemented by the MLB Office of the Commissioner. All firms supplying bats for use in MLB games were required to increase their annual administrative fee from $5,000 to $10,000. Also, MLB bat suppliers needed to raise their Umbrella Liability Insurance coverage from $5 million to $10 million. The justification by the Commissioner's Office for the rate hikes was "to defray the substantial costs that the Committee [study team] has incurred to conduct its investigation of bat durability."[11]

Reactions

Even before the study team's recommendations were adopted by MLB and the MLBPA, theories swirled like a fast-moving tornado on bat breakage. Stories abounded in clubhouses and beyond about MLB bats breaking/cracking or even "exploding" into numerous pieces. For example, *USA Today* reported in 2005 that Jay Gibbons of the Baltimore Orioles broke 20 bats *before* May 25, less than two months into the season. The same article noted that the Orioles' clubhouse manager claimed the number of bats ordered per player had doubled over two decades. At this point in time, many players were pointing the finger at maple bats.[12]

Players such as Craig Biggio of the Astros and Paul Lo Duca of the Marlins had opinions in 2005 that were reported in major newspapers. Biggio was quoted in *USA Today*, "Bats used to be tapered and have a gradual thinning from barrel to handle. Now you see bats with ultra-thin handles and big barrels…. Players want … bat whip with the thin handle." Lo Duca said that an ash bat would flex at the handle but maple would not. He contended that this was the reason maple broke cleanly.[13]

In July of 2008, when the MLB study team was conducting its tests and before their final recommendations, a Washington State University mechanical and materials engineer weighed in on the maple controversy. Lloyd Smith, as quoted in a *Live Science* article, prophetically proclaimed, "If you have a bat that's not cut straight to the grain, you have a weaker bat." Smith also said the grain of ash is easier to see and straighter than the grain of maple.[14] Both of Smith's theories were ultimately in the study team's report.

Shortly after adoption of the study team's recommendations and new MLB guidelines (increase in supplier fees and insurance), bat manufacturers weighed in on the maple bat controversy. Some didn't trust the science or the safety of some recommendations. Other maple-bat manufacturers worried that the new guidelines would hurt their bottom line and drive some smaller producers out of business.

One point of contention pointed out by some manufacturers was the trademark change for maple and other like species. With the new trademark placement for the 2009 season, players were told to hit using the face grain. An anonymous manufacturer, as quoted by *Yahoo Sports* in January 2009, said, "The players are going to hold the bat how they want to hold it, hit it how they want to hit it. Just because MLB wants them to use the face grain doesn't mean they will."[15]

Another maple-bat maker was disgruntled with the handle dot requirement for maple and other diffuse-porous species. He argued that the dot to check grain slope could be beaten by rubbing the handle with 250-grit sandpaper, thus closing the pores on the wood.[16]

Next Steps ... 2009 Season

Although the new requirements, according to MLB, resulted in all species of bats cracking about one-third less often in 2009, maple bats were more prone than ash bats to break into multiple pieces and dangerously fly through the air. Since 2009, other modifications have been made by MLB in hopes of substantially slowing down the occurrence of broken bats.[17]

2010 Season

In the 2010 season, all bat barrels, regardless of species, were reduced from 2.75 inches to 2.61 inches. The MLB rulebook can be seen at http://mlb.mlb.com/mlb/downloads/y2010/official_rules/2010_OfficialBaseball Rules.pdf. The minimum size of bat handles increased by $\frac{1}{50}$ of an inch to $\frac{86}{100}$th of an inch.[18]

Also, in the minor leagues, restrictions were placed on the density of sugar maple. Since density translates to strength, sugar maple was classified as either high- or low-density.[19] Additionally, silver and red maple bats were banned from minor league play; only sugar maple could be used.

6. Bat Breakage

Bat barrel and handle size were not the problem for George Brett on July 24, 1983, but rather pine tar. Brett's bat is now at the Baseball Hall of Fame (National Baseball Hall of Fame and Museum, Cooperstown, N.Y.).

Both minor league restrictions applied only to non–40 man roster players, thus the MLBPA didn't have to approve the changes.[20]

The 2010 regulations also impacted players who had a history of broken bats in 2009. Any Major Leaguer whose bat broke in two pieces more than 10 times the previous year had to meet with members of the MLB study team and the MLBPA to determine if there were further problems.[21]

One of MLB's requirements from the 2009 season was lifted for 2010 play. No longer did bat makers supplying MLB have to contend with no paint or stain on bat handles of maple, birch, or other diffuse-porous species (see page 75). Colored handles on diffuse-porous species were allowed with one caveat. The ink dot location still needed to be properly placed *and* protected, *prior* to coloring the handle. The protection requirement was accomplished with a small circle or triangular emblem that could be removed after the handle was colored. This "window of no-color" enabled inspectors to check for illegal (and dangerous) wood grain slope.[22]

Despite the well-intentioned efforts to control breaking/shattering bats, dangerous events still occurred. Attention was heightened by a terrifying (and much-publicized) incident in Miami on September 19, 2010. Tyler Colvin of the Chicago Cubs was on third base when Welington Castillo stepped to the plate. Castillo, using a maple bat, ripped a double down the left field line, but the bat exploded on impact. Colvin, running home literally with the crack of the bat, was impaled—a few inches from his heart—with a flying shard from his teammate's bat. Though Colvin scored, he was hospitalized for several days, thus ending his season.[23]

Notwithstanding the horrific Colvin event, an article in *The Chronicle of Higher Education* reported that rule changes in 2009 and 2010 actually *reduced* MLB bat-breaking incidents by more than 40 percent. The same article also noted that like many businesses needing expert advice, MLB sought help from specialists. Donald Halem, MLB's senior vice-president for labor relations (currently Deputy Commissioner and Chief Legal Officer) was quoted as saying, "Bringing science to this issue helped us enormously in understanding it."[24]

2011 Season

In 2011, the rate of MLB broken bats continued to decline. Study team leader David Kretschmann of the Forest Products Lab and his colleagues believed the simple ink dot test on bat handles of less well-defined grain species (like maple) was key in reducing bat breakage. Kretschmann was quoted in *On Wisconsin* magazine, saying, "It took a while [for manufacturers] to get used to doing this efficiently, but we saw an immediate drop [in the number of shattered bats]."[25]

If seeing the numbers translates to believing, the data in the *On Wisconsin* article was compelling. From an average of one shattered bat per game during the last three months in 2008, the number dropped to .65 by the end of 2009 season. The decline continued in 2010 to .55 and was .45 by mid-season 2011 (data for the *On Wisconsin* article only went through mid-season, with the end-of-season rate at .50). Kretschmann noted, "This is not to say we've solved the problem. It's tricky to get everyone to accept our [study team] recommendations. But the numbers are down.... From my point of view, that's something."[26]

2012 Season

For the 2012 season, MLB and its consultants (select members of the study team) continued their pursuit of further lowering the broken bat rate in the big leagues. Since common knowledge dictates that reducing MLB bat breakage to zero is unrealistic, the ultimate goal was to reduce catastrophic failures and make the game safer for everyone.

Study team members note there are two basic principles that must be understood, especially by players: straight grain and density. In a 2012 MLB.com article, Scott Drake, a consultant for MLB and vice president of business operations for Timber Engineering Company (now known as PFS–TECO), said, "Once players and the equipment managers understand the basics, it is like a light bulb going off. We are finally starting to see the impact of all this hard work."[27]

Also, the 2012 season limited the choices of lumber species that major leaguers could carry to home plate. MLB and the players' union jointly approved six types of wood that could be used to craft bats. The bat-tree species were the traditional white ash and the well-known sugar (hard) maple, plus hickory, yellow birch, red oak, and Japanese ash. Other species, most notably soft maples like red and silver, were not allowed.[28]

Bat "drop" was another issue that MLB had been discussing for years due to the widespread adoption of big barrels and thin-handle bats. "Drop" is a term most fans of the game are not acquainted with; simply, drop is bat weight (ounces) minus bat length (inches). Therefore, a 34 oz. bat with a length of 33 inches has a drop of positive 1 (34−33 = 1).[29] The greater the drop, the greater the bat speed. Consequently, increased bat speed with a decrease in handle thickness leads, as one would expect, to an increase in broken bats.

For the 2012 season, the MLB bat drop could be no more than a positive 3.5.[30] This means a heavy bat (say 37 ounces) with a short length (say 32 inches) would have a drop of 5 and be ruled illegal. Jim Anderson, founder of MaxBats, argued in 2011 in *Good Wood* that players shouldn't swing anything with a weight to length difference less than minus 2 (e.g., a 31-ounce bat should be no more than 33 inches).[31]

The other change for the 2012 season related to the density of maple bats per a new Collective Bargaining Agreement between MLB players and team owners. The minor league restrictions regarding low- and high-density maple (see 2010 above) were carried over to MLB, with one significant exception. The new change applied only to players who had never had a Major League at-bat. Any player who had at least one at-bat in MLB was grandfathered in and could use a low-density maple bat for their entire career.[32]

Within a few days of the new density requirement, ESPN.com announced that the president of the Ottawa-based Original Maple Bat Corporation (maker of the Sam Bat) didn't have a problem with the mandate. "It's something that we welcome," Arlene Anderson said. "We don't want [bat] breakage on the field, it's not good for anyone." Anderson said her company already had been regularly reporting wood density data to MLB.[33]

As a recap of past years, the *New York Times* reported that from 2008 through the 2012 season, shattered bats (multi-piece failures) in MLB went from approximately 2,500 to just over 1,200.[34] Clearly, the odds of flying pieces of exploding bats were heading in the right direction.

However, the cries about the new regulations, especially with an eye to maple bats, continued to raise doubts. Jason Rosenberg, the founder and director of the New York Yankees blog, was a vocal critic on the subject. According to a 2012 *SBNation* article, Rosenberg opined:

> Regardless of the remedies now or in the future, as long as the players want the thin handle, heavy barrel bats that create a whip-like action, bats will continue to shatter. According to MLB regulations, the difference between the bat length and weight can be no greater than 3.5. In other words, a 35 inch bat cannot be lighter than 31.5 ounces. Bigger barrels, narrower handles and bats that push the limits of this rule (or exceed them due to player modification [such as sanding the handles for weight narrowness]) all greatly contribute to this problem.[35]

2013 Season

Through roughly the All-Star break of the 2013 season, the MLB study team reported that shattered bats, or the multi-piece failure rate, dropped to 0.47 per game. The rate was down from about 1.0 in 2008. Chuck Schupp, director of professional baseball sales and promotions for Hillerich & Bradsby Co., credited the new rules for the reduction of flying bat shards in MLB. Schupp told the *New York Times* in 2013, "Maple's been around for 13 years. The rules helped make it less a question of safety."[36]

The new bat rules also prompted comments from Don Fine, founder of the boutique firm, Viper Bats, in Washington State. In 2013, he acknowledged that the new rules influenced the way he cut the cylindrical billets before crafting a bat. After the rules were in place, Fine's new goal was to follow the grain, mimicking the action of splitting a fence rail.[37] Fine also was quoted by the *New York Times* with an observation that is rarely reported. He said, "It's created a longer business cycle for wood bats. A guy might have bought six of them every summer until last year. Now he's buying three."[38]

2014–2018 Seasons

There were no bat changes in the MLB rulebook for the five seasons from the start of 2014 to the end of 2018. This fact didn't stop bat breakage from occurring or curtail discussions and opinions on the subject.

6. Bat Breakage

One horrific incident occurred in Fenway Park in Boston in late spring 2015. There were others in the near past, but the one in the land of Paul Revere will suffice to demonstrate that the problem of shattering bats has not been completely eliminated.

Regarding the flying lumber at Fenway, the *Boston Globe* reported, "a [multi-piece bat break] seriously injured [a woman] who sustained life-threatening injuries when the barrel of a broken maple bat went flying into the stands, striking her violently in the face. The gruesome incident, which was witnessed by her 8-year-old son and brought a hush to the ballpark, has renewed calls for tougher restrictions on maple bats, or outright bans."[39]

The Fenway Park incident aroused even current and retired players to speak out on the issue. Mark Grace, a former slick-fielding first baseman with 16 MLB seasons under his belt, ranted about the dangers of flying bat shards during his tenure as an Arizona Diamondbacks broadcaster. Grace commented in 2015, per the *Boston Globe*, "I've been saying all along that we've got to find a way to outlaw maple bats. They're too dangerous. Just use ash bats. Everybody use the same kind of bat and it will be fair."[40]

Banning maple bats and making all bats from ash has been discussed by MLB. However, there are two reasons why professional baseball leagues have not gone down this slippery path. Both reasons are rooted in opinions of the 2008 study team. If maple bats were completely banned and the switch was made to ash, then a continuous supply of quality ash wood to make bats for MLB would be precarious. At least one expert of the MLB study team believes this is true.

A Ken Rosenthal *Fox Sports* article said some firms could produce enough bats to go 100 percent ash short-term. However, Scott Drake, a study team member, noted in the same article, "Each wood species has a sweet-spot for what constitutes professional-grade quality. It's not just how many bats you can produce, its how many professional-grade bats you can produce, and for how long."[41]

Also, the study team stressed in their final report that slope-of-grain, regardless of wood species, was the main culprit in causing a bat to shatter. This finding was the driving force behind the ink dot requirement for maple, since straight grain of this species is more difficult to see than the traditional ash. A participant in the 2008 study team said, "If the bat has straight grain, it should stay in one piece. There are a lot of people screaming about maple, but it's not about the species, it's about the properties of the wood."[42]

2019 Season and Beyond

For the 2019 MLB season, most of the bat changes enacted from 2009 and onward were still in effect after 10 seasons. The handle dot on maple and birch bats (non-plain handles) and trademark placement on these species did not change. For all species, the bat drop or length-to-weight ratio (3.5) and maximum diameters of handle (0.86 inches) and barrel (2.61 inches), are still in place. In addition, maple bats were not banned by professional baseball.

Final Thoughts

Wooden baseball bats will always break due to poor wood quality, prolonged bat use, incorrect contact with the ball, pitch speed, and other reasons too numerous to name. However, the goal of MLB, players, fans, coaches, spectators, researchers, and others is to *reduce* bat breakage to a level acceptable to all.

As the 21st century marches on, MLB continues its drumbeat with bat makers via education, training, workshops, and plant visits to ensure that proper manufacturing processes and record-keeping protocols are followed. In addition, the random audits that started in 2009 continue at major league ballparks to ensure that bats conform with MLB requirements.

Also started in 2009, the bat certification and quality control programs remain in place. The certification and quality control process evaluates, and approves, new species of wood for making major league bats. Members of this group also are responsible for investigating issues related to non-compliance with MLB rules and requirements.

7

U.S. Forests

Unless we practice conservation, those who come after us will have to pay the price of misery, degradation, and failure for the progress and prosperity of our day.—Gifford Pinchot, Chief, U.S. Forest Service (1905–1910)

On a hot and humid fall day in upstate New York over a century ago, a frequently unemployed, 28-year-old man from Cleveland waited for the president of the U.S. Just the day before, the same man, in a crowd of 50,000 onlookers, listened to a speech delivered by the popular president. This day, however, the man was coming face-to-face with the most powerful man in the country. Consequently, he endured the uncomfortable weather, along with an excited crowd of people, in the long presidential receiving line at the Temple of Music in Buffalo, New York.[1]

The occasion for the large gathering was the Pan-American Exposition that had been in the planning stages for years. The Exposition considered it a coup to host the current U.S. president at the event.[2]

Finally, after two hours of standing in line, it was Leon Czolgosz's turn to meet the president. Since Czolgosz's right hand was wrapped in a white handkerchief, the chief executive reached to shake Czolgosz's left hand, assuming the right hand of the man was injured. At this very moment, on September 6, 1901, Czolgosz fired two shots from a revolver hidden beneath the handkerchief. Both bullets struck William McKinley in the chest. McKinley lingered for eight days but died in the early morning of September 14. That afternoon, Theodore Roosevelt, a self-proclaimed conservationist, was sworn in as the 26th president.[3]

What's the connection here? What do the McKinley assassination, the sudden ascent of *environmentally leaning* Theodore Roosevelt to the presidency, and Major League Baseball have in common? The common thread, overlooked by most, is the bat, made from wood, which is the miracle product manufactured from trees.

19th Century and Earlier

Douglas MacCleery eloquently stated near the turn of the 21st century, "Forests are a key element in the broad sweep of United States history. Informed choices about the future of our forest and wildlife should be based in part on knowledge of how they came to be what they are today."[4]

During the three centuries prior to 1900, forests in the United States were viewed as inexhaustible. In 1600, estimated tree acreage covered nearly two thirds of land now known as the U.S. Today, about one third of the U.S. is blanketed with forests.[5]

Throughout the long history of the swath of land known today as the U.S., people depended on the bounty of the forest both personally and commercially. Native Americans, pioneers, and early Americans used trees for nearly everything. Examples include fuel, tools, building products, and eventually transportation.

Wood was virtually the only fuel used until the decade before baseball's first professional team. By then, wood supplied more than 90 percent of the nation's heat energy needs. In fact, fuel wood was the main product supplied by trees until the 1880s, when the amount was finally exceeded by lumber.[6]

Trees, in fuelwood form, not only warmed the body but cooked food as well. Food originally came from the forest in the form of wild turkey, deer, bear, and more. Eventually, the wild game diet was augmented by food grown on the land (agriculture use). Regardless of where the food was from, fuelwood was used as a critical step in its preparation.

Trees were indispensable in fashioning everyday implements. Eating utensils, water buckets, tools, and other necessities such as brooms, hitching rails, pitchforks, scythes, game-hunting weapons, etc. were made from trees.

People used lumber, timbers, and other structural forest products for a host of activities: constructing houses and barns, building factories and stores, assembling bridges, erecting fences, and even controlling water flow in dams and locks. To cite one example, farm fences accounted for enough wood to go around the earth 120 times.

As a young nation grew, the demand on the bounty of forests continued as well. Wood was key in producing iron, driving locomotives, propelling steamboats, and powering stationary engines. Incidentally, after 1850, railroads began expanding rapidly, and by 1900 just the demand for RR ties required up to 20 million acres of forestland.

Railroad ties exemplify the use of wood in the 1800s (courtesy Forest History Society).

Based on our nation's reliance on wood, it's not surprising that during the 1800s, forests in the U.S. were cut at an alarming rate. The emerging game of baseball can't be blamed for the big decline of U.S. forestland, but other statistics are staggering. The amount of wood used in 1850 was nearly six times the amount used just 50 years earlier.

Trees were viewed as both a blessing and a curse to a young nation. A blessing in that they provided the early settlers much of what they needed to survive in a harsh environment. A curse because trees did not provide a steady supply of food. From 1850 to 1910, 190 million acres of forests were cleared for agriculture, some of these acres on highly erodible lands. This immense forest removal was justified by the need to feed a growing population and provide sustenance for draft animals which were required for food production. In other cases, where food planting and gathering was not the primary objective, trees were simply cut for timber products and the residual abandoned, leaving wildfire to take its toll.[7] Cut-over lands dotted the landscape, the amount of timber cut greatly exceeded growth, and sawmills and logging operations were inefficient. Tree-planting provisions were nonexistent. By 1900, people viewed natural resources as not inexhaustible, as they had in earlier centuries. To put this forest-loss time period into a baseball perspective, the 60-year span ran from shortly after the Knickerbockers drafted the rules of baseball to when Ty Cobb was in the middle of leading the American League in hitting for nine straight years. New approaches were needed, but the specifics of how these approaches would be accomplished were not clear.[8]

The alarming rate of forest removal before 1900 caught the attention of numerous groups of people. Organizations that expressed concern for the forested environment included the American Forestry Association (formed in 1875) and the Sierra Club (1892). There were also numerous individuals in the late 1800s who pushed for protection of U.S. forests. Chief among these movers and shakers of forest conservation were Henry David Thoreau, Ralph Waldo Emerson, and George Perkins Marsh. At the beginning of the 20th century, the stars were aligned for a change.

Then came the unexpected McKinley assassination in 1901. Theodore Roosevelt suddenly occupied what he called the "bully pulpit" and set in motion an aggressive natural resources agenda.

The 20th Century

During Roosevelt's 7½-year tenure as chief executive of the U.S. (1901–1909), he established himself as the Conservation President. Roosevelt had a tremendous impact on forestland in the U.S. During his time in office, he established the U.S. Forest Service, signed into law the creation of five national parks, and proclaimed 18 new U.S. national monuments. Roosevelt also designated 150 million acres of National Forest and established 51 bird preserves and four game reserves.[9]

Roosevelt's policies and his dynamic advocacy, implemented by his friend, mentor, and chief forester Gifford Pinchot, sought to demonstrate that trees could be grown on a renewable cycle. Both Roosevelt and Pinchot were influenced strongly by progressive era thinking, which put great faith in science and a rational approach to problem-solving.[10]

Although Roosevelt primarily set his goals on the West, which was still mostly unpopulated and not yet fully explored at the turn of the 20th century, his battle cry from the bully pulpit was a call-to-arms for the conservation movement. No chief executive, according to historian Char Miller, writing in 2016, has been more sympathetic to, or forceful in, his advocacy of the need to protect America's natural resources and its spectacular landscapes.[11] The Roosevelt presidency set the stage for policies impacting forests throughout the country for over a century.

During the years when Babe Ruth was in his heyday as a pitcher in Boston and slugger, forestland in the U.S. was at an all-time low. Fortunately, when Aaron Judge of the Yankees first stepped to the plate in the 21st century, U.S. forests had stopped their steady decline since the first settlers stepped ashore in the 1600s. In fact, the acreage of U.S. forests is the same since the time of Ruth, even though U.S. population has tripled during this same time period. (The expansion of U.S. forests would be greater if the 20–30 million acres of tree-covered land in urban areas were included.)

One of the reasons for the stabilization of forestland in the United States after the turn of the century, in addition to progressive era politics, was simply that the nation did not need for everything to be made out of wood. For example, fossil fuels replaced wood fuels as the primary energy source for home heating, transportation, and the like. With coal and oil replacing U.S. energy needs, fuelwood demand dropped from 90 percent in 1850 to about 10 percent in 1920.

Wood substitutes, such as steel and concrete, replaced wood in structural applications. Even major league franchises got in the act. Prior to 1900, all baseball stadiums were made from wood. One of the first to be constructed primarily of concrete and steel was Forbes Field in Pittsburgh.[12] Opened in 1909, the new ballpark was christened by Honus Wagner and his Pirates teammates in a World Series win over the Ty Cobb–led Detroit Tigers.[13]

Also, stabilization of farmland was a boon for the forest. Prior to the Babe Ruth era, land devoted to agriculture, including crops, pasture, and hay, was enormous. Before tractors, farmers also used draft animals which had a large appetite and needed to be fed. All these enterprises—farming, ranching, and the like—removed millions of acres of forestland. The clearing of forests was an essential and vast task in feeding the U.S. When the 20th century neared the 21st, U.S. farmland produced five times more food per acre than in 1920, enabling less land to be devoted to growing food.[14]

By the 1930s, the decade when Dizzy Dean won 30 games (1934) and Hank Greenburg hit 58 home runs (1938) to challenge the single-season record, scientific forest management and conservation in general were making inroads in the U.S. The old style of "cut and get out" logging, exemplified by the large pine trees in New England and the Lake States that were felled in the late 1800s and early 1900s with little regard to future generations of trees and people, was fading.[15]

The Baseball Bat

From the 1940s to the end of the century, the conservation movement regarding U.S. forests was in full swing. For example, forest acreage expanded throughout the country, including land that supplies lumber for baseball bats. College and university graduates with forest science degrees increased 60 percent along with expanded forest research. Annual forest loss due to wildfires dropped from 30 million to roughly 7 million acres. Tree planting accelerated, and eastern national forests grew in number and size.[16]

The 21st Century

The amount of goods or products that can be made from our trees, like baseball bats, kitchen cabinets, and 2×4s has more than doubled since 1953 (two years after New York Giants' Bobby Thomson broke the hearts of Dodgers fans with his pennant-clinching home run). Today in the 21st century, the growth of trees far exceeds the harvest or cut of these trees. In other words, current U.S forests provide our nation more products while at the same time growing faster than removals.[17]

Interesting, and surprising to many, is the ownership breakdown of U.S. forests. The overwhelming majority of forestlands in the 50 states is privately owned, including land that supplies the lion's share of wood for MLB bats. The vast majority of these private forests are non-corporate; private ownership is made up of individual, joint, family, trust, estate, business (non forest-related), association, and nonprofit owners. Think of most tree-covered land you might own, and you'll likely get the picture. Private non-corporate owners also dwarf any other category of ownership, including federal and state government.[18]

The proportion of forestland that provides a variety of commercial products, including baseball bats, is called timberland. Nearly one-half of the timberland area is owned by *private non-corporate entities* (242 million acres). The other one-half is divided between government ownership and corporations.[19]

The trees growing on timberland are referred to as timber growing stock. This fancy term is used by foresters simply to refer to volume or amount of timber. Since 1953, timber growing stock has substantially increased in the U.S. The northern, southern, and Rocky Mountain regions of the country had a healthy growing stock increase of 52 percent as defined by the U.S. Forest Service, the volume in the 20 states of the northern region nearly tripled.[20]

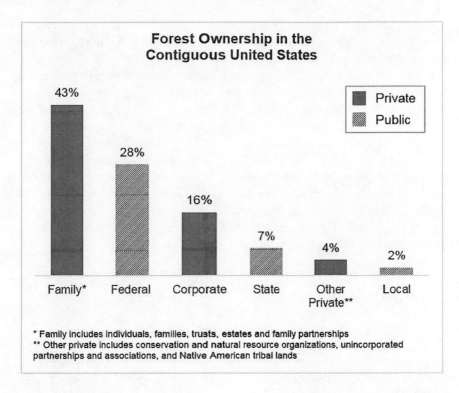

Forest Ownership in the Contiguous United States

* Family includes individuals, families, trusts, estates and family partnerships
** Other private includes conservation and natural resource organizations, unincorporated partnerships and associations, and Native American tribal lands

Family forest owners and their acreage considerably outnumber all other ownership groups (Forest Service, United States Department of Agriculture).

The modern success story of U.S. tree growth exceeding tree harvest was put in place by the actions of Theodore Roosevelt and his adviser, Gifford Pinchot. Most people, including baseball fans, believe, as a country, that we are running out of trees. However, the notion of a tree shortage is simply not true. Yes, there are regions of the country where forestland is declining compared to earlier times. And yes, there are U.S. tree species that are in peril due to fire, drought, pests, and other calamities. However, the "running out of trees" comment often used today in a broad, paint brush-like fashion, is not accurate for the nation, and certainly not accurate in the primary baseball-bat-producing area of the country, Pennsylvania, New York and other northeast states. Ironically, both Roosevelt and Pinchot predicted a timber famine that never occurred, as did a number of land managers of their era.[21]

However, the status of U.S. forests at the end of the second decade of the 21st century is paradoxical. When viewed from a national perspective, the number of acres of forestland is stable, tree growth vastly exceeds harvest, and timber growing stock is up substantially. At the same time, specific regions have experienced declines in forest area. Because forest loss is personally experienced at the local level and viewed from a local perspective, national statistics often offer little comfort to people and communities that experience declines in their local forests. A baseball analogy is that batting averages in MLB might have been **down** for five consecutive years, but batting averages of the World Series-winning teams might be **up** over this same time period. However, the trees crafted into MLB bats are primarily found—growing naturally and *not* planted by a human—in the northeast U.S. Fortunately, this region of the country has spreading forestland, increasing tree growth, and expanding timber growing stock. This is good news for everyone—baseball and non-baseball fans alike.

MLB Bats

There are two main species and one "up and comer" used for MLB bats in the early 21st century. These species will be discussed in light of the above comments.

White Ash

One of the tree species that benefited from Roosevelt's actions was the white ash. For more than a century, white ash was the primary tree used to fashion baseball bats.

I swung white ash during my Little League through American Legion baseball years in the 1960s. Most players, young and old, did the same for decades before, and after, my brief youth career.

The list of famous major league players who used a white ash bat is endless: Joe DiMaggio, Ted Williams, Stan Musial, Jackie Robinson, Willie Mays, Mickey Mantle, Roberto Clemente, Harmon Killebrew, Hank Aaron, George Brett, and Cal Ripken, to name just a few. Yes, these and other players all tinkered with their batting stance, bat coverage of home plate, where they stood in the batter's box, the bats' weight and length, and other hitting factors in order to survive or excel in MLB. But despite their differences, they had one common denominator: a white ash bat.

Through trial and error, and with the input of baseball players, bat manufacturers made an important discovery. It was determined that the

White ash painted/marked by a forester and ready for harvest (courtesy Collin Miller).

best place to find an ash tree that made a top-quality bat was the region of the country between northern Pennsylvania and upstate New York (fittingly, Gifford Pinchot was governor of, and made his retirement home, in Pennsylvania, and Theodore Roosevelt was born in New York). Many companies that manufactured baseball bats during the 20th century bought land in this prime white ash-growing habitat. The Hillerich & Bradsby firm was one.

A white ash tree growing in the southern U.S. has a longer growing season and produces annual rings which are too far apart for many players, with fewer growth rings per inch. Conversely, white ash trees too far north of the Pennsylvania–New York border region have a short growing season. These two scenarios can result in annual rings which are either too close together, or too far apart. As a result, trees growing in the deep South of the U.S. or too far north in the continent did not (20th century and earlier), and still do not (21st century) produce a "choice bat."

White ash is one of dozens of tree species in the ash genus or group. A genus is a taxonomic term for a collection of closely related species. In the U.S., white ash is more plentiful and commercially important than any other American ash.[22]

In addition to white ash which grows in the eastern U.S. and limited parts of southern Canada, other notable ash species are green, black, blue, and Oregon ash.[23] Of these, the green ash (*Fraxinus pennsylvanica*) is the most widespread, growing naturally in the eastern U.S., the Great Plains, and southern Canada. Green ash has also been planted extensively in urban areas throughout the U.S. and Canada due to its tolerance of climatic extremes and soil types.[24]

White ash typically grows to 70–80 feet in height and may reach 6–9 feet in circumference and 2–3 feet in diameter. A 2016 study in the northern U.S. reported that all ash species (living trees about the width of two baseballs and not still-standing dead trees) make up only two percent of the trees in a 10-state study region which included Pennsylvania and New York.[25]

In a separate 2016 Pennsylvania inventory, both white ash removals and mortality were greater than tree growth for the first time in five years. Another way to state this finding is that the Keystone State had net tree growth (volume/amount) of white ash *less* than the amount either cut or dead.[26] Clearly, the Pennsylvania finding is not a welcoming thought for MLB and their batsmen swinging ash lumber. However, the good news is that New York nearly doubled its growth of white ash compared to tree removals for all products (furniture, flooring, etc., including baseball bats). White ash mortality in New York also significantly lagged behind net growth.[27]

In a prime specimen, the white ash trunk is long, straight, and clear, ideal for baseball bats. White ash is often found in deep, moist, and fertile soils growing beside northern U.S. trees such as black cherry, basswood, oaks, hickories, and other hardwood species. In the South, white ash can be found with sweetgum, willow, and loblolly pine in addition to various hickories and southern oaks.[28]

The best white ash baseball-bat trees grow on the north- or east-facing side of a hill. The soil's depth and its quality, including moisture-holding ability, are excellent in this type of location compared to slopes that face either south or west.[29]

White ash reproduces through seeds which are produced every year, although the tree really flourishes with seed production at three- to five-year intervals. Since white ash reproduces naturally, there is no need to plant new trees, a boon to foresters, landowners, and Major League Baseball.

Maple[30]

Worldwide, there are over 100 different species of maple trees and shrubs. However, there is only one that grows in North America that is made into baseball bats used by major league players—the sugar maple, often called "hard" maple. In the U.S., sugar maple (*Acer sacharrum*) can be found growing naturally in New England and the South, extending as far west as Kansas. Canadian sugar maple trees grow primarily in Nova Scotia, New Brunswick, Prince Edward Island, southern Quebec, and southern Ontario. The cities of Montreal and Toronto are located in these latter provinces.

Sugar maple is similar to white ash as far as maximum height (upwards of 80 feet) and diameter (two feet). Sugar maple, again like white ash, when grown in close proximity to neighboring trees, develops a clear, straight trunk. Unlike white ash, which needs direct sunlight early in life, sugar maple seedlings can survive in a dense shade. Sugar maple's *tolerance* of shade and other growing conditions is important, including soil, climate, root competition of neighboring trees, etc. Young trees of many species die if their leaves receive little or no direct sunlight, or have their growth hampered by nearby larger trees. Fortunately, this is not the situation for MLB's foremost current choice for the wood that hitters carry to the plate.

In Pennsylvania, a state historically known for trees that supply baseball players of all ages with bats, the net growth of sugar maple in 2016 was almost twice the amount of removals due to tree cutting.[31] New York's sugar maple growth and removal rate is positive and similar to Pennsylvania.

The Baseball Bat

5494830

In fact, sugar maple has more "large" trees (as measured by amount of wood) in the Empire State than any other species.[32]

Sugar maple, before the baseball bat craze of the 21st century, was best-known, perhaps, as the tree that provide the syrup that breakfast-hungry folks pour over their pancakes and waffles. Sugar maple also provides the brilliant yellow, orange, and tangerine colors during the MLB playoffs in the fall. It thrives in forested landscapes advantageous to many kinds of trees, including the white ash—deep, fertile, and well-drained soils. Sugar maple can also be found in unfertile and barren locations, but those are never in the batter's box.[33]

In upstate New York, primarily in mature, previously uncut forests, MLB-quality sugar maple trees often grow in close proximity to yellow birch. Yellow birch is the baseball bat tree that is the new kid on the block. Additional information on yellow birch is provided in the next section.[34]

South of New York's Adirondack region, sugar maple often grows with a group of trees known by foresters as central hardwoods, including hickory, oak, and white ash. Consequently, the three trees that make up the bulk of bats in MLB (white ash, sugar maple, and yellow birch) can be found growing in relatively close proximity.[35]

Sugar maple can produce millions of seeds in the fall, "winged fruit" known by some folks as "helicopters."[36] Like white ash, mother nature does the tree planting, a process called natural reproduction/regeneration. If the prolific seed crop of sugar maple somehow fails (it usually doesn't!), harvested trees can still regenerate a forest by sprouting from the stump. Many hardwood tree species like the oaks, hickories, ashes, and birches also perform this stump sprout trick.

Birch

Birch trees are in the *Betula* genus, with 15 species growing in the wild in the cooler regions of North America.[37] Common types of birch trees are paper birch (sometimes called white), river or red, black, gray, and yellow. Yellow birch poses the most interest to MLB and players, bat manufacturers, baseball researchers, and fans.

Yellow birch (*Betula alleghaniensis*) has cracked the starting lineup as one of the top three tree species selected for bat-wood by MLB players.

Opposite: **Sugar maple is the primary tree now made into baseball bats (T. Davis Sydnor, The Ohio State University, c/o bugwood.com).**

Although yellow birch trails sugar maple by a whopping margin in MLB use, its popularity in minor league baseball is not as far behind maple in the major leagues. In MLB, yellow birch is within striking distance of second-place white ash.

Yellow birch can be found on tracts of wooded land from southern Canada through the eastern U.S., extending as far south as Georgia and west to Minnesota. The geographical distribution of yellow birch is similar, although smaller, than both white ash and sugar maple. Yellow birch prefers moist, cool locations such as north-facing slopes. In mountainous areas, yellow birch often grows near, or with, sugar maple. Like sugar maple, yellow birch produces some seed every year and an enormous quantity at irregular intervals.[38]

The growth rate of yellow birch is generally not as rapid as white ash or sugar maple. However, when growing in a forest as opposed to a relatively open pasture or similar setting, the tree trunk (the prime location for a baseball bat) is usually straight, without branches.

New York's yellow birch trees, suitable for baseball bat manufacturing and growing on land eligible for harvest, increased two percent (as measured in amount of wood) from 2012 to the most recently published inventory in 2017.[39] Pennsylvania, another key state in MLB bat making, has only a fraction of the number of New York's yellow birch trees.

In addition to providing wood for baseball bats, yellow birch trees also produce wintergreen oil. Methyl salicylate, an active pain-killing ingredient in Bengay liniment, is in wintergreen oil. Consequently, in addition to the batter's box, MLB players may be unwittingly using yellow birch in the clubhouse as well.[40]

Climate Change

Regardless of opinion on what is driving climate change, whether it be primarily human-induced, long-term climatic cycle-induced, or a combination of the two, one fact is clear. Temperature trends are on the rise both in North America and the world.[41] A U.S. Forest Service research scientist said,

> Although people's worries about global climate change most often focus on things like summer heat, drought, flooding, rising sea levels, and polar bears, there's another big worry that isn't so well publicized—the effects of all these changes on plants, particularly trees. People and animals can walk, run, swim, or fly to a more suitable habitat, but trees can't escape the heat.[42]

Reasons differ as to why tree populations move in one direction or another, and the speed of their migration. A tree's geographical location can be due to temperature, rainfall, seed dissemination (animal or wind), elevation, latitude, pest populations, calamities like wildfires and severe storms, land use, and a host of other factors, some of which are yet undiscovered. However, a changing climate (i.e., long-term temperature and precipitation) has been found to impact a species' location, especially in the eastern U.S.[43]

Based on tree inventory data, white ash, sugar maple, and yellow birch have moved northward since late in the 19th century.[44] Theoretically, climate change could push these species farther north, resulting in fewer trees for baseball bats in the U.S., but more suitable trees for MLB in Canada. However, luckily for the northeastern U.S., the northward shift of these species will be measured over decades, not individual baseball seasons.

Bottom Line

Forests and the trees that grow in them have always been connected to baseball via the bat. Over 100 years ago, many influential individuals such as a U.S. President, presidential advisor, environmental leaders, and concerned citizens believed the U.S. would run out of trees if drastic measures were not taken. Fortunately, policies and programs, including applying scientific principles to the care of forests, were adopted.

Instead of cutting trees without concern for the future, methods were used that insured U.S. citizens would have trees, and by extension, baseball, beyond the 21st century. Specific trees favored by MLB batsmen continue to change, but the abundance of wood in the U.S. and its northern neighbor, Canada, remains strong.

Challenges, such as climate change, still remain and are on the minds of many, including MLB, players, and fans. However, the game of baseball is strong, and the supply of wood for big league bats is increasing. The future for trees and MLB looks good.

8

Killer Pests

It's like the children's book, "The Very Hungry Caterpillar," but with a bad ending because of a beetle.—*Environment Newsletter*, Fairfax County, Virginia

Imagine this scene: In 1992, a dock worker at the Port of Detroit unloaded a shipment of automotive power-steering equipment from China. This was not the first time the dock worker legally moved a crate from an ocean-going vessel to the shores of the U.S., where it then moved into the metropolitan suburbs of Detroit. However, this time was different. Unknown to anyone at the time was that the untreated wooden shipping crates that protected the imported goods harbored the hungry worm-like larvae of the Emerald Ash Borer (EAB). While the used crates were stacked in a pile and awaited pick-up from a recycler, the hidden EAB larvae evolved, then emerged, as half-inch-long, bullet-shaped, metallic-green beetles, smaller than the penny's portrait of Lincoln. The beetles, which only live about three weeks, flew to nearby ash trees that were common in southern Michigan. Each female EAB beetle, after escaping from the crate, then deposited up to 100 eggs on or in a crevice of a healthy ash tree's bark. Without fanfare, those eggs also hatched and grew into beetles that traveled further, accidentally spreading through movement of small nursery trees, firewood, logs or lumber with some bark on its edges.[1]

In reality, no one knows precisely when or where the first EAB larvae came into southeastern Michigan, but all signs point to a scenario like ours that started with the dockworker. Within the next decade, citizens, tree workers, foresters, and others all realized something was wrong with many of the ash trees in the Detroit area. Southeastern Michigan's ash trees were showing aggressive dieback—when the branches of an infested tree die first near the top and eventually work downward to the base of the tree. Also seen was more prevalent woodpecker damage, which is consistent with insect pest infestations, and profuse branching, especially along the trunk. S-shaped galleries (tunnel-like paths) under the bark from larval feeding, and D-shaped emergence holes, created when well-fed adult beetles burrow out of the tree to mate and reproduce, were also observed. The symptoms weren't quite consistent with any known diseases or causes of decline. Both rural and urban ash trees were impacted, with the trees often dying within just 3–4 years of showing symptoms.

In late summer 2001 (when Cal Ripken, Jr., was playing his final games at Camden Yards), a Michigan State University (MSU) horticulture specialist collected larvae from infested ash trees. The larvae were raised in a laboratory under the proper conditions to produce adult beetles, a process that took months. The following year, the beetles were sent to a MSU entomologist in an effort to determine the identity of the mysterious insects. These specimens were circulated to additional experts at Michigan State University, the Michigan Departments of Natural Resources and Agriculture, universities across the country, the U.S. Department of Agriculture, and the Smithsonian Museum of Natural History. Unfortunately, no positive identification could be made. However, the experts agreed that the beetles were likely from another country. Finally, in early summer of 2002, Eduard Jendek of the Institute of Zoology, Slovak Academy of Sciences, Slovak Republic, was contacted for assistance. Jendek, a noted authority on Eurasian metallic wood-boring beetles, identified the troublesome insect as *Agrilus planipennis,* the Emerald Ash Borer. This was the first confirmation of EAB in North America.[2]

EAB larvae—which do the damage that kills trees— are cambium-feeders. The cambium is the living layer of the tree. It lies just underneath the bark. The cambium layer moves the tree's uptake of water and nutrients from the roots, similar to how a drinking straw moves water from your glass into your mouth. When EAB larvae break up the structure of the cambium's microscopic cells, they effectively put holes into the straws, therefore starving the tree to death.

As of late 2016, EAB was

Size of Emerald Ash Borer (EAB) compared to a penny (bugwood.com).

EAB devastation to ash trees in forests (bugwood.com).

confirmed in 30 states and in two Canadian provinces.[3] The "Green Menace," as some experts call it, has already killed untold millions of ash trees in the U.S., primarily from New England through the upper Midwest. In Michigan, the epicenter of the EAB invasion, at least 25 million ash trees have been destroyed in two decades due to the pest. Jessica Simons, a forester in southeastern Michigan who has been active in the fight to stop the pest and develop new markets for urban ash trees noted, "Since the arrival of EAB, it has attacked any ash tree it has found—healthy or struggling, large or small. Whether along Detroit's streets or within the acreage of National Forests, no ash tree in Michigan is safe."[4]

The state of New York alone has an estimated 857 million ash trees growing within its boundaries, according to Melissa Fierke of the College of Environmental Science and Forestry at the State University of New York in Syracuse. In acknowledging the continuing EAB onslaught across North America, Fierke stated that the invasive species "causes 99.9 [percent] ash mortality" in the areas it infests.[5]

The EAB is a native pest of China, where it causes only minor damage. In Far-Eastern countries, EAB has co-existed for centuries with Asian ash trees. Ash trees from Asia have evolved defenses against EAB attack, whereas North American ash trees seem to have no defenses against EAB. For this primary reason, EAB in Asia only kills ash trees that are already under stress or damaged. Tree death caused by the EAB in Asia is minimal compared to the devastation it inflicts in the U.S. and Canada due to the lack of tree resistance. It is unfortunate for everybody, including home-owners, foresters, and baseball fans, that EAB attacks all North American species of ash (the *Fraxinus* species). The white ash, the preferred tree for baseball bat production for nearly a century, is at risk.[6]

The Spread of the Emerald Ash Borer

Emerald Ash Borers in the adult beetle stage are relatively weak fly-ers. Most EAB fly only about a half-mile, but a few can take wing for up to three miles. Using a baseball (and geographical) analogy, one-half mile is roughly the distance from Fenway Park in Boston to the nearby Massachusetts Institute of Technology (MIT). Consequently, the rapid spread of this invasive pest is likely due to what experts call artificial movement or human-assisted spread. People move small trees from a nursery or land-scape business, as well as untreated wood products like logs and lumber, and, of course, firewood.

Although quarantines are in place in all of the infested states and provinces to prevent movement of potentially infested ash wood, experts point to firewood as the primary means of artificial movement of EAB. Agencies have been promoting firewood safety messages in areas where the EAB has been either detected or anticipated, urging those using fire-wood for home heating, warming cottages and cabins, and enjoying the ambience of outdoor fire pits to source their wood as close as possible to where they use it. Luckily for fans of America's Pastime, this message does not apply to the purchase or use of ash baseball bats!

In Pennsylvania, where EAB has been found in all counties and ash tree growth is ideal for baseball bat manufacturing, firewood movement messages are evident around the state. According to Stuart Miller in his 2011 book, *Good Wood*, the EAB was enough of a threat to the bat-making industry that Louisville Slugger teamed with The Nature Conservancy on a firewood movement campaign.[7] Miller also noted that not only are well-known bat manufacturers concerned about EAB, but smaller firms as well. Miller quotes Kevin Lane, co-owner of Carolina Clubs, a Florida-based bat maker with manufacturing facilities in New York, as saying, "There is a sense of panic [regarding EAB]."[8]

Michigan was the first state to launch a "Do Not Move Firewood" educational effort with billboards, bumper stickers, and posters to promote the message. Other states and Canadian provinces have followed suit in getting the word out about the dangers of moving firewood and spreading the EAB.

Currently, there are no long-term solutions for eradicating EAB in North America. Unfortunately, it is likely that the vast majority of native ash will be lost. However, there are a couple of options for managing EAB. First, some insecticides work very well, but they are expensive. Also, they need to be reapplied every few years, so are best used on high-value landscape trees such as in a yard, along a street, or growing in a park. Second, small parasitic wasps have been introduced from Asia to kill EAB larvae and eggs. The wasps help keep EAB populations at lower levels and could slow the spread of both EAB infestation and tree mortality. Third, heat treatment of ash products like firewood is an option for processors to create safer products, but is an added step that increases costs and time. Hopefully, resistant or tolerant ash trees will be found that can be used to start developing new varieties of ash trees that have defenses against EAB attack. The American mountain ash, *Sorbus americana Marsh*, popular as an urban tree, is technically not an ash and is not susceptible.

Another Pest That Threatens MLB Bats[9]

The Emerald Ash Borer is not the only threat to major league players who step into the batter's box. Although not as widespread, fast-moving and devastating as the ash borer, the Asian Longhorned Beetle (*Anoplophora glabripennis*), referred to as ALB, is another invasive pest that threatens our national pastime. Unlike most other beetles which are limited to one species, the ALB feeds on numerous trees, including elm, birch, willow, poplar, and black locust. However, one of its favorite trees to dine on is maple. Since maple has surpassed ash as the preferred choice of big league batsmen, the ALB also poses a threat to Major League Baseball. According to Kelli Hoover, an entomologist at Pennsylvania State University, when tree-covered land populated with maple is infested with ALB, the only course of action is to remove all the host trees. As of 2016, ALB was a serious problem with maples in Massachusetts, Ohio, and New York. The U.S. Department of Agriculture warns that nearly 30 percent of wooded land in the U.S. (71 billion trees) is at risk of death by ALB since the beetle feeds on so many kinds of trees.[10] High-value and

ALB-desirable trees growing in villages, towns and cities add to the potential mortality.

ALB was discovered in New York City in 1996. Like the Emerald Ash Borer, the suspected culprit in bringing ALB into the U.S. was wooden shipping crates and pallets from China. Later, ALB was found in other major shipping centers such as Chicago, Jersey City, and Toronto, as well as in European countries. Fortunately, ALB has been eradicated in Chicago. However, a continuing effort still exists to completely eliminate the pest from the U.S.

The damage inflicted by ALB is similar to the Emerald Ash Borer in that both pests cut off the flow of nutrients in the tree. However, several weeks after the ALB larvae burrow into the living layers of the tree just under the bark, larvae of ALB move deeper into the woody part of the tree (unlike EAB). Deep within the wood is where the worm-like ALB larvae continue to feed and develop over the winter. As the ALB larvae feed, they make tunnels or galleries in the tree stem and/or limbs. Sawdust-like material, called frass, from the insect's burrowing can be found at the bottom of the trunk and branch bases of infested trees.

Over the course of a year, ALB larvae grow into adults and chew their way out of the tree. One report noted that even cold New England winters didn't stop this process.[11] Adult ALBs can reach one inch or more in length with antennae that stretch twice as long as their bodies. Adult beetles are black with small white spots, and adult antennae are banded in black and white. The adult beetles leave round, three-eighths-inch exit holes that are big enough to insert a pencil. After emerging from the tree, adult beetles feed on bark or leaves for up to two weeks. The fully grown ALB then mates, lays eggs, and the entire process begins again.[12]

ALB tunnels are actually not as damaging to the tree's life as the EAB tunnels that wind around just under the bark. Trees attacked by ALB can be riddled with tunnels deep in the wood and branches, yet remain alive. But over time, branches begin to break from wind, ice and snow; eventually, the tree dies. The wood inside ALB-infested trees is of no value for baseball bats since the tunnels extend into the bat-making area of the trunk.[13]

Control of ALB is similar in some ways to EAB.[14] When many trees are infested in rural areas with ALB, complete tree removal is the only option. In urban areas, chemical control over a three-year period is an option, although it can be expensive. Biological control of ALB is questionable. Natural predators like wasps have not been successfully used to control ALB in China, so therefore may not be effective in the U.S. either.[15]

The U.S. Department of Agriculture (USDA) says, "the Asian Long-horned Beetle could be worse than Dutch elm disease, chestnut blight, and gypsy moths."[16] This is not good news for industries like the maple syrup business that depend on healthy maple trees for their livelihood. The USDA warning, although not specific to MLB, also puts baseball bats manufactured from maple in peril.

Invasive Tree Pests in America

The Emerald Ash Borer and the Asian Longhorned Beetle are not the only threats to trees in our front or backyard, neighborhood, town, wood lot, or forest. According to a 2016 article in *Sawmill and Woodlot* magazine,[17] over 400 invasive species have hitchhiked to the U.S. Once here, they move throughout the country by natural means, or artificial movement such as firewood transport.

One of the tree species devastated in the past by an invasive pest was the American chestnut. Although the wood of the chestnut was not used for big-league bats, the demise of this tree is a case history of the damage that can be inflicted by a non-native pest. Over a century ago, the disease known as blight arrived from overseas in a shipment of seedlings destined for a tree nursery. In the absence of natural enemies, and with millions of U.S. chestnut trees with no natural defenses, the blight spread quickly. Within four decades, over four billion chestnut trees covering 200 million acres in the Appalachian area were killed. Today in the 21st century, only a few American chestnut trees remain.[18]

Another example of the destruction wrought by an invasive pest is the demise of the American elm. In 1930, imported elm lumber was infected with a disease that was unknown by the importer. The disease, a fungus, spread from one elm tree to another, killing the trees. The true devastation didn't begin, however, until the arrival of the European elm bark beetle, a bark-burrowing beetle which carried the disease efficiently from tree to tree. The American elm that once dominated rural and urban areas was essentially wiped out by the combination of these non-native pests. Fortunately, isolated American elm trees are still surviving to maturity, and some show resistance to Dutch elm disease.[19]

Until the last few decades, the impact of invasive pests on Major League Baseball was minuscule. From before the days of the New York Knickerbockers in the 1840s through the 20th century, scant mention was made of foreign insects and diseases affecting baseball in North America.

Everything changed, however, when EAB and ALB invaded the U.S. These two killer pests threaten a key ingredient—bats—of our national pastime. Steve Rushin, sportswriter and author of *The 34-Ton Bat*, in reference to EAB and its impact on ash bats, said "an Asian monster [is] laying waste to the landscape in the manner of Mothra, Godzilla's nemesis."

What to Do?

As America continues on a path to be part of a global society, there will be increasing opportunities for exotic pests to reach our shores. The U.S. is working with other countries to prevent other likely catastrophes from occurring. Strategies being used include inspections at ports of entry, quarantines, and treatment of materials that may harbor pests. State and local governments, forestry professionals, concerned citizens, and impacted industries, to name a few, are working on action plans to limit the destruction caused by hitch-hiking exotic pests. Hopefully, these efforts will reduce the threat of new invasive species from getting a foothold in the U.S., leading to much easier control.[20] Although MLB is not the primary focus in keeping nasty exotic invaders from coming ashore, the actions being taken will benefit baseball and its traditional icon—the wood bat.

Looking Ahead and MLB

The traditional wood species for bats in the 20th century—white ash—is threatened with extinction by the Emerald Ash Borer. In addition to the EAB issue, ash has already lost its MLB lead role to maple in the eyes of players. However, the Asian Longhorned Beetle is a threat to the future of maple as a MLB bat. Of course, both ash and maple may be spared the fate of American chestnut or American elm. Future research may discover a cost-effective cure for EAB infesting ash trees and ALB devastating maple, both species destined for use in a MLB batter's box. If a cure is not found, then one option is to look for other tree species suitable for bat use in MLB. Fortunately, a species has already been found that might be a replacement for ash and maple.

Yellow birch (*Betula alleghaniensis*) is making inroads into MLB bat manufacturing and use. In fact, Mark Trumbo, playing for the Los Angeles Angels of Anaheim, hit two of the seven longest home runs of the

2013 season with a Trinity birch bat.[21] According to Trinity, "birch has the perfect combination of flexibility and hardness [and] is considered a 'hybrid' wood type between ash and maple."[22] Scott Drake, a wood scientist in Wisconsin, notes that birch has an additional advantage. Drake, part of the team used by MLB in its 2008 study of bat breakage in the big leagues, points to the fact that birch has a higher impact strength than maple and can better withstand the shock of contact with a baseball traveling at high speed.[23]

Many consider the B45 Company as the first to use yellow birch. B45 was founded in 2004 in Quebec City, Canada. The B is for birch, bat, and baseball; the wood comes from the 45th parallel. The B45 firm, like the Trinity Bat Company, from Fullerton, California, believes yellow birch is the best of both worlds when comparing it to ash and maple. In 2015, former MLB pitcher Éric Gagné led a new ownership group of B45. The firm is still based in Quebec City and makes yellow birch bats from youth to the professional level.

Another bat-maker that uses only yellow birch is the Birch Bat Company. Founded in 2006, the firm notes that birch has several great properties for use as a baseball bat. Chief among them is the shear rate, the point at which the wood grain splits, which is higher than ash and just under maple.[24]

MaxBats is a Minnesota-based company started in the early 21st century. Currently a division of Glacial Wood Products in Brooten, Minnesota, MaxBats founder Jim Anderson sees the growth potential of big leaguers stepping into the batter's box with a birch bat in their hands. The biggest difference he sees between a birch and a maple bat is the flex or whipping action. Anderson claims, "Birch definitely has more flex than maple, but it doesn't compare to the flex of ash."[25]

Unfortunately, some birch trees, like grey, river and European white, are also attacked by the Asian Longhorned Beetle. Yellow birch has been infested although the ALB has not completed a life cycle on this species.[26] Luckily, the devastation to birch trees is not comparable to ALB's onslaught on maple. However, if maple disappears from the tree-covered land of North America, birch could be the next tree species that the hungry ALB dines upon. This scenario is purely conjecture, but the potential threat to yellow birch is sobering to all of us, including MLB.

9

Tree to Billet

I think that I shall never see
A poem as lovely as a tree
—Joyce Kilmer

I didn't think about baseball bats coming from trees when I was young and playing in Little League, Pony League, and American Legion. And I didn't think much about it during college, where I studied Forestry. In fact, during my entire career as a forester, I didn't give the subject much thought. Today's top players, such as Mike Trout and Kris Bryant, do not typically make the connection between trees and bats. These players, and other MLB hitters, are too focused—as they should be during games—on pitchers, pitch selection, game situation, and the like. Maybe MLB players think about their bats and trees during the off-season or in the clubhouse, but the tree-to-bat thought is likely fleeting. What a player's mind concentrates on during the season is hitting the ball squarely, upping their batting average, mastering the intricacies of hitting, helping the team win games, and so forth.

However, the fact is that at the MLB level, bats come from trees. But first the tree has to be cut and converted into a billet. A billet is a round, dowel-like piece of wood from which bats are crafted. Bat makers in the past usually produced their own billets. However, most today either buy billets or deliver them to their bat-making factory from company-owned operations. Typical billet size is slightly over three feet in length with no taper, and less than three inches in diameter.

The manufacturing process to make a billet can vary with company, but one example discussed in this chapter will be illustrated.

Trees are felled and cut into *logs*. The logs are cut again at the mill, usually with a chainsaw, into 40-inch-long round *bolts* (similar to making firewood). Bolts are then cleaved into triangular chunks of wood called a *split*, as with firewood. The splits are then converted into rectangular lumber often called a *square* (the lumber is square on the ends, often four inches by four inches, with a length of 40 inches or less). The squares are dried and manufactured into round *billets* akin to a shortened baker's rolling pin without the handles. Some firms saw or core·billets directly from bolts, and the process just outlined is slightly different.

The billet is eventually processed into a bat. Although the bat-making process has improved since the 1800s, the typical journey begins on tree-covered land with either a forester or logger, or both.[1]

A forester's main duty is planning for the desired future condition of the land while taking into account the multiple goals of the landowner such as outdoor recreation, wildlife conservation, and aesthetics. A forester applies scientific principles to evaluate and manage trees for what products the land is suitable for growing in the future. Consequently, timber harvesting is a method a forester may use while working together with a logger to achieve the owner's long-term goals for the land.[2]

Some folks refer to a logger by the terms woodcutter, woodsman, faller, cruiser, or lumberjack. Whatever the label, loggers are the men and women who work outdoors daily with trees and wood products. One of their main jobs, is to convert an upright tree into a log (i.e., cut trees). Other primary duties may be conducted like buying trees or logs from an owner. Loggers can also build temporary trails or roads to move logs from the woods to a central location called a "landing," and load logs on a truck for the journey to a sawmill.

Leatherstocking Hand-Split Billet Company

Leatherstocking Hand-Split Billet Company is one firm that specializes in making billets, selling the billets to a bat-maker. Leatherstocking exemplifies the billet-making process and is used throughout this chapter as an example.

Background

Matt Kent grew up around his Dad's machine shop. Kent gained valuable experience from his early exposure to the business world. With an appetite for tinkering and entrepreneurship, Kent decided to pursue a career in the trees surrounding his childhood home.

Kent spent over 20 years in the log and lumber business, with the last 15 as a full-time log broker. As a broker, Kent purchased logs from independent loggers and landowners and resold them to manufacturers that made a variety of products including paper, lumber, and veneer.

During this time period, Kent devised a strategy to add more value to high-quality logs. In 2009, he founded, and currently is president, of Leatherstocking Timber Products, Inc. DBA Leatherstocking Hand-Split Billet Co. Kent's billet plant is located in Oneonta, New York, a small city of approximately 14,000 residents about 175 miles northwest of New York City.[3]

Leatherstocking Hand-Split Billet Co. is located in upstate New York. The specific locale of the billet company is called the Leatherstocking Region, perhaps best known for the author James Fenimore Cooper, the son of the founding father of Cooperstown, New York. James Fenimore Cooper penned *The Leatherstocking Tales* which included the novel *The Last of the Mohicans*. The main character in the *Tales* was known by many names, one of these being Leatherstocking. Hence, the name's origin of the billet plant run by Kent.[4]

Matt Kent's billet company was launched after the recession in 2008. At the time, log markets were depressed and he had an excessive number of high-quality, hard maple logs. Also, 2008 coincided with MLB's study on broken bats, which included slope-of-grain issues with maple. Kent's knowledge of tree growth, tree harvesting, and wood structure plus his love of baseball were the pillars of his venture into the business of wood baseball bats. His firm produces the white ash, hard maple, and yellow birch lumber that will one day be swung by major leaguers and other players as well. Kent—through his parent company, Leatherstocking Timber Products—also sells various wood products outside of the billets destined to be crafted into baseball bats, like wood chips and unprocessed logs. Billets not meeting baseball bat standards are sold by the billet company as turning blanks for furniture manufacturers and specialty shops, who make a host of products like baseball bat beer mugs and pepper mills.[5]

The Leatherstocking billet firm has grown over the past decade. As of 2018, it had a payroll of over 40 full-time workers and dozens of customers.[6]

Trees—The Beginning of a Billet

An area up to 300 miles in all directions from the Oneonta mill is heavily scoured by Leatherstocking timber buyers to find trees and logs which meet Kent's company specifications. Kent said, "We search for good

Trees that will become MLB bats (courtesy Leatherstocking Hand-Split Billet Co.).

logs as far east as Vermont, south to central Pennsylvania, north to the Adirondack Mountains, and as far west as the Finger Lakes region of New York. During our busy time, one of our buyers might travel as much as 1,800 miles per week."[7]

The Leatherstocking region is ideal not just for Kent's billet firm but for others as well. Numerous sawmills and manufacturers of hard maple, white ash, and yellow birch billets and baseball bats are found scattered throughout the region. This wooded, rolling terrain is mostly remote and outside of the glitz and glamour of major cities like New York, Philadelphia, and Boston. The Leatherstocking region has the right amount of sunshine, the proper rainfall, and the correct mix of glacial till (unsorted glacial sediment) to grow supreme trees for bat-making.[8]

Kent added, "There is no doubt about it—we are in the sweet spot for growing bat wood. It's no wonder why the big bat makers set up shop in this region several decades ago."[9]

One of those big bat makers referred to by Kent is the former Rawlings plant started as Adirondack. This bat-making facility is just over an hour's drive from the Leatherstocking plant.

Another firm that recognized the quality of the region's trees is

Hillerich & Bradsby (now owned by Wilson Sporting Goods) in Louisville, Kentucky. John Hillerich IV, named CEO and president of the company in 2001, was quoted in *Sweet Spot* as saying, "It is all about the wood." Hillerich went on to say, "We have people ... who know what [wood] to look for. It made a difference for Ted Williams, and it makes a difference ... today." His remarks were a testament to the New York and Pennsylvania timberlands and sawmills first purchased in the 1950s by this pioneer bat-maker.[10]

Of course, not all trees, even the ones that happen to be hard maple, white ash, or yellow birch, are destined to be in the batter's box with major league players like Bryce Harper or Aaron Judge. According to Leatherstocking's experience, for every straight and forkless tree growing in the wild, another dozen or more grow awkwardly with crooks and bends that disqualify them from being turned into a MLB-quality bat. A similar analogy can be found with a red spruce sounding board on a violin. The right species doesn't automatically mean the violin will play like a Stradivarius.[11] Another estimate, found in *Sweet Spot*, is that only one tree out of 20 growing in the wild will be good enough to produce a MLB bat.[12] The vast majority of maple, ash, and birch trees are rejected due to numerous reasons including size, straightness, growth rate, knots, and scars from fire or over-grazing.

Even straight trees are often cut into logs that don't meet the standards for a bat. Kent remarked, "Of the logs we procure, a small amount will be turned into bats. Of this portion, a much smaller amount will make the quality for a MLB bat."[13] Stuart Miller wrote in *Good Wood* that a 10-foot log could theoretically make two dozen bats if the wood is acceptable, but only one out of 10 logs is good enough to produce bats, whether or not they reach MLB, Little League, or anything in between.[14] Louisiana bat-maker Jack Marucci, who sources his wood from New York and Pennsylvania, put the estimate at potentially 12–24 bats per tree, with the caveat "the actual number is quite variable."[15] Another approximation early in the current century for ash—not maple or other species—was that for 10–12 million board feet of lumber, the proportion turned into bats—by volume—was less than two percent.[16]

Kent noted that high quality "bat trees" (as he called them) are often found growing on cooler, north-facing slopes. He said, "Bat trees like a calcium-rich, well-drained, upland soil. Our soil and climate tends to give us tighter growth rings as compared to trees farther south. Our region produces ideal wood for high-quality bat-making."[17]

A typical bat tree is often 80+ years old and 16 inches in diameter or larger.[18] (Foresters measure tree diameter or width at 4½ feet above the ground, on the tree's uphill side. This measurement is called DBH—diameter at breast height.) Many of Kent's higher-quality trees meet this age category and size range, growing in the conditions he described. Unfortunately, maple trees tapped for syrup are eliminated as potential bat trees due to tap holes and the resulting discoloration of the wood.

Any firm around the world, regardless of specific billet or bat-maker, follows roughly the same procedure in converting trees (vertical orientation) to logs (horizontal orientation). A tree is usually felled in the direction it is leaning, as most trees are heavier on one side. First, an area called the landing zone is cleared of debris. The landing zone is where the tree should fall once it is correctly felled. A notch in the shape of an open bird's mouth is cut into the tree with a chainsaw, placed in the direction of the landing zone. Next, a "back-cut" is sawn into the tree from the opposite side of the notched tree. The back-cut stops when it reaches close to the notch to have enough un-cut wood to hold the tree and guide it as it falls. Once on the ground, lopping is done by severing the top and limbs to make one straight log. Depending on tree type, age and growth rate, logs can be upwards of 40 feet long. The log is then hitched by the chain of a tractor-like machine named a cable "skidder," or grabbed with metal tongs by a grapple skidder. Lastly, the skidder moves the log along a trail to a landing area (not to be confused with landing zone) where the log can be picked up by a truck.

Billet companies either (1) own their own land and thus their own trees, (2) purchase trees before converting them to logs, or (3) directly buy logs. Any combination of these three wood-procuring methods is also a viable option. The Leatherstocking firm uses all three methods to get the required wood for their operation.

Leatherstocking's tree purchases primarily come from privately-owned family forests. These forests in the East are often called woods and include, but are not limited to, tree-covered land on farms, ranches, hunting camps, and residences (either primary or second homes). Leatherstocking's forester is the point person for *tree* purchases (often called "standing timber").

Kent noted that butt logs—the portion of the tree immediately above the ground—is his "go-to log" for high-quality bat wood. However, he said, "Upper logs can be used if the tree grew straight and is free of branches, bumps, and defects."[19]

The majority of Kent's *logs* are bought from either loggers not employed by the Leatherstocking Company or independent sawmills/log yards. Leatherstocking employs log buyers to handle these transactions. Logs are lined up on the ground and the Leatherstocking log buyer does an inspection and selects logs (based on species, size, defects, amount of sapwood, etc.) that are needed by the mill. Logs are then end-marked with paint, a price is negotiated, and they are loaded onto a Leatherstocking truck. The truck is self-loading in the sense that the driver sits atop the truck and runs a crane with a claw at the end for picking up logs and placing them on the truck.[20]

Regardless of the raw material—trees or logs—the majority originate on small tracts of timbered land, not owned by corporations or government.[21] These small tracts of timberland are the source of bat wood for most bat manufacturers in the U.S.

As more and more MLB players switch to maple for their lumber, the bat industry is following the lead. For example, maple (both hard, i.e., sugar [80 percent], and soft, i.e., silver and red [5 percent]), account for the majority of wood species that find their way to the Leatherstocking plant. This makes sense from a supply viewpoint since these species of maple are predominant in New York State; the soft maple makes an excellent wood for souvenir, fungo, and youth bats. White ash (5 percent) and yellow birch (10 percent) account for the remainder of bat wood manufactured by Leatherstocking. Kent said, "Most of our ash logs are exported to China. They use ash over there as an alternative to red oak."[22]

The pest threat to trees in the U.S. impacts not only owners of home and land, but also the baseball bat industry. Kent said, "There is a lot of ash being cut now due to the potential damage from the Emerald Ash Borer. Most EAB-killed trees are still nearly 100 percent usable if cut within a couple years after death. The Chinese are very interested in ash. They are paying more for ash logs than we can make from value-added products like bat-billets."[23]

Kent also said, "Veneer logs are the most valuable logs. Since veneer is often thinly sliced or 'peeled' similar to peeling an apple, the material goes much further than most wood products. However, a good veneer log does not always make a great bat-log, and vice versa."[24]

From Logs into Bolts

The logs are 10 to 14 feet in length and over 16 inches in diameter when they arrive at the Leatherstocking mill. Logs are unloaded from log trucks by an attached crane and claw (called a "picker"), and are laid on

Unloading logs at the billet manufacturer (courtesy Leatherstocking Hand-Split Billet Co.).

the ground for a second visual screening. Logs destined for bats are separated from the others.

Each truck can carry enough logs to make about 1,000 bats. However, since most logs are not up to MLB-quality, each truck, on average, can only provide enough good wood for one

Cutting logs into 40-inch bolts (courtesy Leatherstocking Hand-Split Billet Co.).

major league player's bats for a single season (50–100 bats). Leatherstocking anticipated this reality and has other markets for non-bat logs such as timber beams (often pine), pulpwood (for paper-making), and wood chips (for heating educational and other facilities).[25]

Dave Rama, Leatherstocking sales manager, said, "After one of our employees gives a visual inspection to a log, we cut the bat-logs by chainsaw into lengths of 40 inches, long enough to give us a 37-inch billet. These 40-inch chunks of wood are what we call bolts."[26]

From Bolts to Splits

There are two primary methods—splitting and sawing—used to convert bolts into billets. The splitting method cleaves pieces of wood from the bolt by hand or machine, similar to the backyard method of making firewood. The other technique is to saw the bolt into a rectangular section, slightly larger than a bat, before shaping it into a round billet. Sometimes sawing is accomplished with a tube saw that bores a round billet from the bolt, like a cook using a cookie-cutter on flattened dough.

The 40-inch Leatherstocking bolts are transported from the log yard to the wood splitter via a tractor-like machine with front-end grapples. The firm's wood splitter was designed in-house for the task of splitting the hardwood bolts. A Leatherstocking employee stands the bolts upright— small end pointing to the sky. Next, the surface facing up of each bolt is marked on the sapwood near the bark with a series of hash marks that are spaced evenly using a circular "jig" (template). The jig is about the diameter of the barrel end of a bat or the size of a hockey puck. The first mark is drawn on a natural crack in the wood which indicates where the wood wants to split. Using the jig as a spacer, hash marks are drawn around the rest of the bolt to approximate the location and number of splits to make.[27]

Most firms, Leatherstocking included, only use the sapwood found in the portion of the bolt near the bark. Heartwood (the interior of the tree/ log/bolt) is avoided as the outer growth provides the best wood. Consequently, about 50 percent of the bolt is used in the bat-making process. At Leatherstocking, the other half is fed into a wood chipper and either sold or used internally as fuel to heat the mill.[28]

After the hashes are drawn, the split technician lines up the bolt with the splitting machine, which is similar to, but larger than, the hydraulic machine sometimes used to split firewood. Each split is made on a hash mark and follows the direction of the grain. This ensures that the resulting billets—and thus, eventual bats—will be straight-grained.[29] Depending on the size of the bolt, approximately 4–8 splits will be cleaved from one bolt.[30]

A Short Primer on Splitting Versus Sawing

For over a century, ash was the most commonly used species for bats in professional baseball. Splitting, in the old days, was a common process. Splitting an ash log followed the grain of the wood.

Splitting a log by hand was a labor-intensive process. However, splitting produced triangular pieces of straight-grain wood called splits or staves. After the splits

Splitting bolts along the grain (courtesy Leatherstocking Hand-Split Billet Co.).

were dried, they were placed on a lathe and turned into round billets. Ash wood was used not just for baseball bats, but other products such as handles for tools like hammers, axes, and shovels.

Dave Rama explained, "One hundred years ago or so it was an ash and hickory dominated business. Logs would be cut into four-foot bolts and split in the woods with a froe, sometimes called a shake axe. The froe, which is the basis for the Leatherstocking logo, is a tool designed to cleave wood. Each split followed the log grain thereby retaining the strength that nature intended. The splits were then air-dried and taken to a lathe where they were turned into bats and other products."[31]

Today in the 21st century, with higher-production equipment and increased demands for yields and efficiency, a much faster option is available: directly sawing billets. The sawing process can increase the risk of baseball bats with a higher grain angle. Although many MLB-approved bat-makers use the splitting technique, the issue is complicated due to whether or not the grain is visible to the human eye. Ash trees produce baseball bats with a wood grain that is easily seen. This is not true for today's primary bat-making wood species, maple (and birch as well).

Matt Kent believes, "Regardless of tree species, wood *splitting* results in a superior bat when compared to the sawing method of bat production." He noted that the benefits of splitting maple and birch are often even more significant than with ash, due to various factors. Kent said, "White ash trees often grow straighter than sugar maple and yellow birch. Additionally, due to the greater flexibility of ash, they are less prone to breaking into multiple pieces. However, straight grain is perhaps the most important quality aspect in every bat used. Consequently, I use the splitting method 100 percent of the time."[32]

Kent added, "Bolts made into billets with a tube saw (boring billets from a split)—a common milling process used by major companies—perhaps increases the number of billets per log, but quality suffers because the integrity of the grain—the way mother nature intended it to grow—is not preserved. In a sense, we like to think we are going back to the future. Leatherstocking is doing what worked in the past but with more knowledge and safer, more efficient manufacturing practices."[33]

Splits to Squares

The splits at the Leatherstocking mill are shaped into 3-inch-thick rectangles called squares (12/4 lumber for wood aficionados) before being loaded into the drying kiln. For this conversion of splits to squares, Leatherstocking uses a proprietary technique.[34]

Some bat-makers use a "roughing" lathe on the triangular splits instead of producing a square. A roughing lathe can have dozens of sharp knives that transform the split into the rough shape of a billet. When the billet is completed (trimmed to size, etc.), then drying occurs.[35]

Squares to Billets

Wood is hygroscopic. This simply means wood absorbs water from the air because of changes in humidity. This property is one of the most distinctive characteristics of wood.

Final product from the billets manufacturer (author's collection).

A baseball bat, regardless of whether it is maple, ash, or birch, will give or take moisture from the air until it reaches a steady-state with the environment (ball field, dugout, clubhouse, etc.). Wood scientists call this the equilibrium moisture content, or EMC, for short. Since a bat's dimensions, like any wood item or product, will change with a drop or rise in humidity, kiln drying becomes important relative to the bat's efficient use. Besides removing excess water, kiln drying makes the bat lighter, stronger, and more resistant to pests like insects and disease.[36]

Dave Rama notes that kiln drying is necessary for proper machining like billet-making. Bat makers require a consistent EMC to determine which billets are to be used to produce their various models.[37]

Interestingly, according to Peter Morris in *A Game of Inches*, over 100 years ago, kiln drying was viewed as an inferior method of bat-making. Morris noted that a 1909 *Washington Post* article stated, "The timber that is to be made into a first-class bat must be seasoned outdoors at least four years, and seven is better."[38] Fortunately, lumber kilns have greatly improved since the early 20th century. Current lumber drying technology has given billet and bat manufacturers a level of sophistication that was unimagined in the playing days of deadball stars like Ty Cobb.

9. Tree to Billet

The most commonly used kilns in the lumber drying industry are conventional (the use of steam) and dehumidification. Solar and vacuum kilns are used for special applications and conditions; vacuum kilns are used for the majority of MLB billets.[39]

Since many billet and baseball bat companies use a vacuum kiln to dry their wood, the question asked by many is, what is a vacuum kiln? A follow-up question is often: Why are vacuum dry kilns popular in the bat industry?

The answer to the first question is relatively simple. A vacuum kiln is basically a chamber containing only lumber where all the air is pumped out of the chamber, creating a vacuum. The vacuum lowers the boiling point of water to below 212 degrees Fahrenheit, thus drying the lumber at a reduced temperature compared to most traditional lumber kilns.[40]

In the Leatherstocking vacuum kiln, courses (rows of squares) are separated by plates which carry hot water to heat the wood. The vacuum removes the water and air that accumulates in the kiln.

One reason to use a vacuum kiln is speed. What used to take 6–8 weeks or more in a conventional kiln is now performed in about a week. A quick turn-around time can be a plus if speed is important. However, rapid drying can lead to cracks and checks in the wood, so experience and following the manufacturer's recommendations are critical.[41]

Leatherstocking's lumber (called squares) is usually dried to the pre-determined moisture level in a week or less. For hard maple, an eight percent water amount is the target for removal from the kiln. Ash moisture content is slightly higher than maple when exiting the kiln. Kent noted, "Another benefit for us is that vacuum kiln drying disallows oxidation. Oxidation is a process between air and lumber that results in the discoloration of wood. Much like an apple with a bite taken out of it, wood will turn quickly to a brown color when exposed to the air. In a vacuum, where air is removed, wood can dry while maintaining its bright color."[42]

Leatherstocking uses a number of vacuum kilns with varying capacities to dry their baseball bat blanks. Kiln sizes range from a capacity of 400 to over 4,000 squares (each square can produce one bat). Even though a vacuum kiln is pricey compared to a high-end traditional kiln, Kent and Rama both believe vacuum-dried wood is cleaner, brighter, and makes a better bat.[43]

The vacuum kilns plus the mill, office, and inventory storage at Leatherstocking are heated by wood-chips. The chips are scraps and sawdust by-products from the entire manufacturing process. Therefore, from an energy perspective, Leatherstocking's entire drying process plus other buildings are self-sufficient.[44] This energy self-sufficiency is true for many other wood processing mills, whether or not they are connected to the baseball bat industry.

When the squares come out of a Leatherstocking kiln, they are loaded on a pallet and moved to the moulder machine, which shapes the maple, ash or birch squares into round dowels called billets. The billets are inspected and end-marked either prime (the best), select, choice, or economy. Short billets (down to 31 inches and often soft maple) are sold as mini-bats for advertisers and public relation events. This assortment of billets is what Leatherstocking sells to bat-makers.[45]

Before shipping, however, all billets are graded again for quality, trimmed to 37 inches in length, and weighed. The average billet weight is 5.5 pounds (88 ounces).

Rama said, "At Leatherstocking a final inspection of the billets looks for cracks, checks, knots, color, and other imperfections in the wood. The billets are then horizontally stacked on a pallet and loaded onto a covered truck."[46]

To the Bat-Maker

Leatherstocking ships billets to a number of baseball bat manufacturers throughout the U.S. Many of these manufacturers supply bats to MLB players, while others focus on youth, high school, and collegiate teams.[47]

Since individual trees are unique, billets of the same species and exact same dimensions can vary hugely in weight. Kent said, "We have four weight classifications for our billets varying from less than 82 ounces to 99 ounces and up. MLB hitters prefer a billet range of between 87 and 93 ounces for their bats."[48]

The number of billets sold at one time to a bat-maker varies by the billet manufacturer. At Leatherstocking, billets are sold as a full pallet (333 billets) or a short pallet (250 billets).[49]

Final Thought

It's a long journey from a seedling in the woods to a grown tree and then to a billet which will be transformed into a baseball bat. The complete journey usually requires more than 80 years, if the tree's age is considered. A combination of hand labor and modern-day technology is involved.

Matt Kent's Leatherstocking Hand-Split Billet Company is one example. Kent said, "Simply stated, a quality billet makes a quality bat."

10

Billet to Bat

> They give you a round bat, and they throw you a round
> ball, and then they tell you to hit it square—Willie Stargell
> (also attributed to Ted Williams, Pete Rose, and others)

Josh Hamilton, five-time MLB All-Star, remarked to his hitting coach, Johnny Narron, in 2009, "This is the best bat I've ever hit with." Johnny Narron, former professional player, is the brother of Jerry Narron, who should be familiar to long-time New York baseball fans. When Thurman Munson's plane crashed in 1979, Jerry Narron had the daunting task of becoming the regular Yankees catcher.

The bat used by Hamilton was crafted by David Chandler. Chandler, a native of Detroit, was living in Durham, North Carolina at the time. Chandler made a couple of experimental bats for his nine-year-old son, Noah, who was having a difficult time finding a suitable wood bat. Noah's hitting coach happened to be the same hitting coach working with Josh Hamilton during his rehabilitation period in 2009.

The coach, Johnny Narron, gave one of Chandler's bats to Josh Hamilton to try, and within a year a new MLB bat company emerged. Chandler said, "An endorsement from someone like Josh Hamilton got me thinking, 'I can do this.'"

Chandler Bats, founded in 2010, is now located outside of Philadelphia. The firm is considered by many as a "new breed representative" of one of the dozens of smaller boutique bat-makers in North America. David Chandler found his niche in high-end bats and is pleased with his position in the pecking order of bat-makers. Chandler Bats is not the biggest manufacturer nor the smallest in the baseball bat industry. Chandler said, "I don't want to be *everything to everybody*. You need to figure out who you are and decide the most effective manner to have an impact on something. This thinking is especially important when you're new or just starting out in a business. This is what we're striving for at Chandler Bats."

David Chandler's prior profession was in the design field, with a successful career as a high-end furniture-maker before the switch to crafting baseball bats. Once Chandler transitioned from building tables and chairs to building an integral part of our National Pastime, he hasn't looked back.[1]

In the Beginning

The art and craft of making a wooden baseball bat hasn't changed in principle for nearly two centuries. When Daniel "Doc" Adams was supervising bat-making for the New York Knickerbockers prior to the Civil War, the same basic techniques used in the 1840s remain the same in the 21st century. Good trees, straight-grained billets, lathes, knives, and sandpaper were all used long ago as well as today. What has changed over the years, however, is specialization and the use of scientific principles.

For example, it is not uncommon for current, state-of-the-art, bat-making firms to buy billets from a company that specializes in making billets. This was not the case in bygone days. Today, there are dozens of billet producers scattered throughout the country that sell their product to bat-makers. Many of these billet producers are located in, or near, the northeastern U.S. since this is the growing area of prime maple, birch, and ash.

Also, when the New York Knickerbockers were in their glory, or when Bud Hillerich supposedly turned a bat for Pete Browning in 1884, the science of baseball bats was in its infancy. Ball-bat collisions, bat-swing velocities, ball spin and the Magnus force, coefficients of restitution, and altitude and humidity effects, among others, were principles either unknown or not properly understood by early bat-makers.

At many bat-making factories, billets arrive at the standard industry quantity of 333 per pallet. Billet length and diameter is typically 37 inches by 2⅞ or 3 inches. Most billets-makers are located in upstate New York and Pennsylvania. The majority of billets are hard maple with the remainder being northern white ash and yellow birch.

Billets can be used by the bat-maker the day of arrival at the manufacturing plant. However, they often rest for a couple days in the mill's storage room. The storage period gives the billets a chance to acclimate to the humidity they'll experience on the shop floor, where they are transformed into bats.

Once the billets are unloaded at the bat-maker, a visual inspection is conducted. Any billets that have knots, structural defects noticeable

Bat-making is more complicated in the 21st century, as exemplified by the Chandler Bats conference room (courtesy Chandler Bats).

by the naked eye, or other blemishes, are either discarded or selected for other baseball products (mini-bats for stadium sales, souvenir or commemorative bats, training bats, etc.).

Often, the next step is a check on the weight of each billet. Each billet is placed on a scale and typically marked on one end with the weight, species, date, or other information that is deemed appropriate. This slender stick of wood will soon become the tool of America's National Pastime.

The heft of a billet is a good indicator of moisture and density. The weight of each billet can be quite variable. The weight depends on many factors including tree species, time of year the tree was felled, drying time, length of time the billet sat on the delivery truck, the billet cover on the truck (i.e., tarp), outside weather conditions, etc.[2]

Billets are often separated into weight classes upon arrival at the mill. Categories can vary every ½ ounce such as 88 to 88½ ounces, 88½ to 89, and so forth, up to 105 ounces or whatever is the heaviest billet. This categorization makes locating the correct billet much simpler among the many hundreds in storage. Every firm will have its own system for choosing the correct billet for an order.

Billets at bat manufacturer with the moisture content on ends (courtesy Chandler Bats).

Players typically want a specific bat-weight to carry to the plate. Giancarlo Stanton, for example, prefers a 32-ounce maple bat to use against MLB pitchers. Bat-makers know that a weight of 32 ounces, along with Stanton's typical bat length of 34 inches, requires a maple billet of a certain weight class.[3]

A billet might have 60 ounces of wood or more removed in the bat-making process. Sixty ounces is nearly four pounds of wood, about the weight of a bag of sugar. Consequently, for the Stanton example above, an appropriate billet (weight class is important!) is selected and the bat manufacturing process begins.

The Shop Floor

The bat-making shop floor is where most of the action takes place. The roar of lathes, sanders, and saws means billets are becoming baseball bats.

When a bat manufacturer receives an order from a major league player, great care is taken to get the correct dimensions. Various scenar-

Sample bats hanging on the wall are used to check dimensions for new bats (courtesy Chandler Bats).

ios are likely, including the following, or a combination of these possibilities. Some firms use a metal template or a lathe with pre-set knives if the bat order comes from a return customer. These templates are entered into the memory of a computerized lathe, and the worker can watch the bat-turning rather than doing it by hand.

Another firm might use a player's discarded bat (broken, for example) from the company "bat library" to check all the specific dimensions. A sample of the player's previous bat, regardless of manufacturer, might be selected from the bat library and used as a prototype to craft the new bat.

Other firms first make a prototype with a master bat that is thicker, longer, and heavier than the bat's final dimensions. The duplicate master is then used to craft the real McCoy.[4]

Hand-Turning vs. Automatic-Lathe

A simple definition of a wood lathe used to make baseball bats is a tool, sewing machine-size or larger, that turns or rotates a billet along a horizontal axis against a fixed, chisel-like tool. This process of turning a bat from a billet is also called shaping.

Not every bat company follows the exact same steps in turning a bat, but the basics are relatively similar. Before the electric age, all bats were hand-turned on a human-powered lathe. This labor-intensive hand-turning was first done with assistance from a hand crank or foot pedal. In the late 1800s, a steam-driven implement provided the power. Hand-turning a bat took roughly 15–30 minutes, about the length of time today to enter a MLB stadium and locate your seat. Today, bat-turning by hand is essentially obsolete, especially for high-volume bat producers. However, these same large bat-makers still occasionally tweak a bat by hand before it is deemed game-ready.[5]

In the 21st century, an automatic-lathe, referred to as a computer-ized- or CNC-lathe, does the lion's-share of the bat-shaping work. Some of these CNC-lathes (computerized numeric control-lathes) can shape a billet into a bat in under 45 seconds. Most bats destined for the major leagues, regardless of bat-making firm, are turned on a CNC-lathe.[6]

CNC-lathe that transforms billets into baseball bats (courtesy Chandler Bats).

Some CNC-lathes can weigh eight tons or more, about the size of a small car, and often are imported from around the world. To get the maximum precision that MLB and other players require, lathes can be mounted on the floor to reduce vibrations and produce a perfect bat.

Even though a pricey, exceptionally accurate lathe might be used, the exact bat size can't be taken for granted. The prototype is sometimes the official and final arbitrator on bat dimensions.

Cupping

The barrel end of the bat was solid with no scoop of wood removed in the days of Hank Aaron, Jackie Robinson, Stan Musial, Ted Williams, Joe DiMaggio, Babe Ruth, Ty Cobb, and most other players before the 21st century. However, bat cupping is in favor in the 21st century. Game 7 of the 2017 World Series is a good illustration. The starting lineups for the Astros and Dodgers had 12 of 18 players with a small cup—tea cup size— at the end of their bat.

Many players, especially at the MLB level, seek a bat-maker that can satisfy a host of requirements for their lumber. Bat *length,* bat *weight,* and *species* of wood are conditions that must be met by the bat-maker. Another requirement more common today with players is the request that their bat be cupped on the barrel end. Player reasoning is that the cup increases bat speed and enables them to whip the bat through the hitting zone.

The allowable indentation on a big league bat is limited to a maximum of one and one-quarter inches in depth and two inches in diameter. The minimum diameter of the cup is set by MLB at one inch. The cup or indentation must be curved with no foreign substance added such as cork.[7] These requirements must be adhered to by manufacturers producing MLB bats.

Cupping is accomplished primarily by placing the bat in a fixed, horizontal position and boring the end with a fast-moving drill bit (wood router). Also, cupping can be done starting with a billet on a CNC-lathe. The actual process varies by individual bat-maker.

Jose Cardenal, playing for St. Louis in the early 1970s, was one of the first big leaguers to use a cupped bat. Cardenal was given a cupped bat by George Altman, a former player who took his talents to Japan, where bat cupping was commonplace. Cardenal liked the cupping on the Altman bat and ordered a dozen from a Japanese company. The Far East firm also explained their opinion on the benefits of cupping. Cardenal used the bats in games against the protests of opposing players. To alleviate any confusion on this innovation, Commissioner Kuhn stepped in and declared the cupped bats legal in 1975.[8]

Dan Gutman, author of *Banana Bats and Ding-Dong Balls,* a book on unique baseball inventions, weighed in on the subject. Gutman stated in 1995, "Cupped bats have a slightly altered center of gravity, but it has not been proven that they drive a ball harder or further than conventional bats."[9] Barney Mussill, a former major leaguer with the Phillies, wrote in the late 1990s for *Oldtyme Baseball News,* "[Cupping] removes extra end weight and moves the center of balance toward the Trademark, giving the batter better whip-like control."[10]

In 1987, Robert Adair, Ph.D., and Yale University physics professor, was dubbed by Bart Giamatti, then President of the National League and future MLB Commissioner, as "Physicist to the National League." Consequently, Adair wrote a fact-based report on baseball for Giamatti that the latter suggested expanding to a book, *The Physics of Baseball* (2002, 3rd edition, but originally published in 1990, prior to the Gutman and Mussill comments).[11]

Adair's book analyzed baseball with discussions and research results on bat weight, barrel size, and indentations, but not end-cupping per se. Written before the cupping craze of today, Chapter 6—Properties of Bats— is required reading for youth baseball players as well as professionals.

Adair wrote, "It is not possible to conclude categorically that a specific physical change in a bat is good or bad.... It seems possible that for [the *weight of the batter,* i.e., 180 vs. 250 pounds], a slightly lighter—or slightly heavier—bat may lead to a better (-timed) swing and a larger energy transfer to the bat.... And this could well override any ... derivation of an ideal *bat* weight."[12]

Shortly after Adair published his ground-breaking book, Robert Watts and Terry Bahill wrote *Keep Your Eye on the Ball.*[13] In research they conducted, Watts and Bahill found that (not surprising!) a lighter bat produced a faster swing. And again, as expected, there was a bat weight where the ball leaving the bat—called exit velocity—would decrease. However, and this is one of the study conclusions rarely discussed or seen in print, there possibly could be an *optimum* bat weight and an *ideal* bat weight. Whereas an optimum weight would enable a hitter to maximize his batted-ball speed (exit velocity of the ball) an ideal bat weight (lighter) would give the hitter better bat control and allow more time before swinging.[14]

Increasing bat speed via a reduction in bat weight supports the views of many baseball researchers and ballplayers, including Ted Williams. While end-cupping a bat *can* accomplish improved bat speed and *can* reduce bat weight, there is more to hitting a baseball than the bat cup. Robert Adair wrote, "[T]o survive in professional baseball, one must hit the ball *often* as well as *hard*"(emphasis added). According to Adair, a light bat decreases distance only slightly but gives the batter extra quickness, leading to good contact more often. Adair noted that the complexity of the bat swing is often ignored on bat weight issues, and he did not specifically mention cupping. He opined that great batters often have a "beautiful" swing, thus supplying maximum energy to the bat as it hits the ball—most players do not.[15]

Player preference, requests for bat styles of current MLB stars, and MLB explicit approval are just three of the many reasons bats are now often cupped. Only time (probably decades) and additional research will determine whether bat-cupping as practiced in the 21st century will remain part of our National Pastime.

Trimming and Sanding

Once the bats have been turned, either manually or automatically, the next step is removing the end-wood (nubs) that held the billet on the lathe. A band saw is often used to trim the excess wood from the bat knob and barrel-end. This wood, along with the shavings and other scraps, are often used for building heat or sold to farmers for animal bedding.[16]

After the trimming, the entire bat is sanded either by hand or with a belt-sander. Lower to higher grit (coarser to finer) sandpaper is the tool of choice. Sanding smooths the cut marks left by the lathe and rounds the ends.[17]

Boning the Bat

Ted Williams said, "I always worked with my bats, boning them down ... forcing the fibers together. Not just the handle, the whole bat."[18] According to *Good Wood*, Chuck Schupp of Hillerich & Bradsby agreed with Williams by noting, "Boning helps close the pores and harden the bat's surface, making it more durable and providing more power."[19] Some manufacturers contend that proper bat boning is an art that can separate them from the competition.

10. Billet to Bat

Boning or bone-rubbing a bat to strengthen the wood has been practiced for decades.[20] Players have endlessly rubbed hard objects over their bats—primarily the barrel—including rolling pins and glass bottles, being careful the bottle does not break. However, rubbing the bat with an animal bone was the most popular. During the first decade of Ted Williams' playing days with Boston, the National League Philadelphia Phillies attached a hambone to a table in their clubhouse. Other MLB teams followed suit by attaching animal bones to benches, desks, and tables. This step was taken to help players gain an edge by preparing their lumber.[21]

Mark Grace, longtime Chicago Cubs first baseman, preferred a cow femur to harden his bats. Hall of Fame catcher Gary Carter favored a porcelain sink over an animal bone.[22]

In the distant past, Hillerich & Bradsby's Louisville Slugger bats carried the words "Bone Rubbed" just above the trademark. According to *Good Wood*, one of the selling points in the firm's marketing strategy was to capitalize on the players' old trick of hardening the wood by rubbing a bone or other hard object on the bat. After many decades, Hillerich & Bradsby switched to the word *Powerized* along with a bolt of lightning. With this change, the "Bone Rubbed" phrase disappeared completely from the Louisville Slugger; the marketing ploy was successful.[23]

Since players have always been protective of their bats, various alternatives to boning were practiced to make their lumber stronger. For example, Pirates star Honus Wagner was one of MLB's greatest hitters of the early 20th century. Wagner reportedly boiled his bats in creosote, the ingredient used in preserving the life of utility poles, railroad ties and other outdoor wood products. Creosote, an oily and sticky substance, comes from the distillation of wood tar or coal tar.[24]

Some players tried other remedies to harden and extend the life of their bats. According to legend, Frankie Frisch, while with the Giants and Cardinals, toughened his bats by burying them in a dung-hill. The New York Mets' Howard Johnson covered his bats with dirt, followed by a coating of pine tar, and then repeatedly slammed a batting doughnut on his weapon until the dirt and pine tar filled in the grain. Jim Frey, a MLB manager and two-time minor league batting champ, soaked his bats in motor oil.[25] Pete Rose also used motor oil to soak his bats in a tub in his basement, followed by hanging them up to dry.[26]

Players in modern times remain protective of their bats and continue testing different methods to harden them. However, 21st century bat boning is a fading art that some players simply ignore. Today, younger players are not accustomed to fixing or modifying a product right out of the box.

A refrain one might hear when a player receives a shipment of bats that have not been boned, "What do you mean, I have to do something to the bat? I just want to play baseball."[27]

Another factor in the decline of boning is science. Robert Adair said in 2002 in reference to boning ash bats, "The benefit from any effort by players to harden their bats ... must be considered largely psychological."[28] Writing in *Good Wood*, Stuart Miller states, "Maple bats already have a compressed grain ... so boning them is unnecessary; also, any bat with a lacquer finish can't be bone-rubbed because it would destroy the finish."[29]

Regardless of the different methods used in the past, boning or bone-rubbed remains popular with most MLB players and their bats. Since the technique was used by superstars of the past like Williams and DiMaggio, and since some modern players expect their bats to arrive ready to use, many bat-makers offer the boning process.

Bat-makers who subscribe to the theory of bat boning have their own methods. However, the boning process is straightforward in many regards. Before applying the finish, a hard object, like a steel rod, is rubbed against all sides of the bat. This can be accomplished with the bat spinning on a small lathe. The rod, as an example, functions like a lathe-knife as it moves over the rotating bat. In some situations, the bat barrel is previously made slightly larger than final size, and boning reduces the size to the correct dimension. In the eyes of many manufacturers, bat-boning is a testament to the hardness of their bats.

Looking for Defects

With any bat-maker, constant attention goes into identifying blemishes on both billets and bats. Visual inspections are done throughout the manufacturing process. All workers are on the lookout for defects that might compromise the final bat. However, even though a turned bat might look perfect, there still might be an internal problem not visible.

Chandler Bats, as an example, uses a flex test before finishing, engraving, and trademark application to locate hidden problems that often go undetected, like embedded bark or an internal knot. All bats are positioned in a vice-like device, with the handle secured and the tangential side of the barrel facing up. The barrel is then flexed (bent) three to four inches. Bat handles that do not break from the pressure applied to the barrel pass the test.[30] The flex test is akin to the bending of a door stop spring.

David Chandler also noted that the test is important for the wood species he uses for the majority of his bats. "One of the characteristics of maple is internal bark in the tree. For maple bats in particular, any minor injury to the handle will cause it to break. I'm always amazed to see players step out of the batter's box and use the handle end of their bat to knock dirt from their spikes. This is the worst thing for them to do. This seemingly innocent 'house keeping' chore puts small dents in the handle which weakens the wood. Bats should be treated like a finely tuned musical instrument."

Fans watching a game on television might notice that after receiving a walk, certain players, before reaching first base, hand their bat to the batboy. David Chandler said, "Some players will not throw our bats. The bats of MLB players put zeroes at the end of their checks, so they need to take care of their bats."[31]

Finishing

MLB fans might see bats on television or from a stadium seat and marvel at the various shades and different color combinations of the lumber lugged into the batter's box. However, a good-looking finish on a bat is not just about eye appeal. A correct bat finish also helps to make a more durable bat over the long term by keeping out moisture and hardening the surface.

According to *Crack of the Bat*, by Bob Hill, "The finish seals the wood, protects it, makes it stronger and adds a decorative touch."[32] There are many different color schemes available to players now compared to years ago. For example, some players prefer a colored barrel (say, black or gray) with a natural wood color (plain) handle, a colored handle with a plain barrel, a colored handle with a different color barrel, an all-black bat (or all-gray, for example), an all-natural handle and barrel, or any combination of these options.

The two-toned look can be traced back many years. Harry "The Hat" Walker, the 1947 NL batting champion, was visiting the Hillerich & Bradsby factory, looking for the perfect bat. Walker noticed a vat of stain and decided to take a peek. In the vat was a bat, but Walker didn't realize it was there merely to stir the liquid. He pulled the bat from the stain and fiddled with it for a few seconds. Walker thought the half-stained, half-natural bat felt good in his hands. Consequently, Walker started ordering two-toned bats. Today, bats stained in this manner are said to have the "Walker Finish."[33]

Pete Rose preferred an all-black bat during his latter years with the Cincinnati Reds. It is reported that "Charlie Hustle" wiped his bat with rubbing alcohol after each game. This trick showed Rose where his contact points were, and if needed, the opportunity to adjust the next time he was in the batter's box. While Rose used logic on his bat color decision, other players simply choose a color based on aesthetics or superstition. Andy Van Slyke, Pittsburgh center fielder for many years, preferred a rose-colored barrel and a natural handle. The Padres' Tony Gwynn, an eight-time NL batting champion, preferred a black barrel to go with a plain handle.[34]

1947 batting average champion Harry "The Hat" Walker accidentally invented the two-toned bat finish known by his name (National Baseball Hall of Fame and Museum, Cooperstown, N.Y.).

All-black bats have become more commonplace in recent years. Derek Jeter, five-time World Series champion, used an all-black bat while holding down the shortstop position for the New York Yankees. Ken Griffey, Jr., preferred a black bat as well.[35] Yuli Gurriel and Alex Bregman of the Houston Astros and Corey Seager and Justin Turner of the Los Angeles Dodgers are a quartet of players (there were others) who used a black bat during the 2017 World Series.

The finishing or painting/staining process can vary by manufacturer, although a water-based lacquer finish is the industry standard. The steps depend on whether a player requests a plain bat, a lacquer-only finish, or a painted bat either one color or two-toned. At many firms, the process can take four days or more depending on the number of colors on the bat. Each color coat can take 2–8+ hours, and most bats get 2–3 coats.

For a more thorough explanation, the following example outlines the process at one bat-maker.

If a plain bat with no finish is ordered, the bat is hand-sanded on a high-speed, lathe-like machine. The engraving (player's name and bat model number) and trademark (logo) are applied as the last steps.

Some players want only a lacquer finish, and the process is a bit more complicated. First, the entire bat is dipped into a lacquer finish. The bat is then hung vertically, handle up, on a conveyor belt with moderate heat applied for up to 24 hours. Next, the bat is spun on a machine and lightly sanded by hand, like the procedure for a plain bat described above. Following this step, the entire bat is dipped in lacquer for the second time and again hung on the conveyor belt with moderate heat for a maximum of 24 hours. The final step, as with a plain bat, is applying the engraving and trademark.

The most common finishing practice today (and the most labor-intensive) is the painted bat. The process begins by dipping the entire bat in a water-based lacquer finish. After that, the bat is hung on a moving conveyor belt with moderate heat applied for up to 24 hours. If the player requests two tones rather than one color, then one end of the bat (barrel, as an example) is dipped in paint and hung on a conveyor belt with moderate heat for up to 24 hours. The other end of the bat is then dipped in paint and hung on a conveyor belt with moderate heat for up to 24 hours. Where the two colors meet, a distinctive stripe is applied by hand with a paintbrush on another machine called a striper (think lathe again since the bat is rapidly spun). The striped bat is removed from the striper and placed for 10 minutes on a drying rack. After the painting is completed, the bats are moved to a drying room for 24 hours. Then the bats return to a dipping line for a coat of a clear sealer. Once again, the engraving and trademark applications are the last steps.

MLB regulations only permit players to use colored bats that are black (can vary in finish), brown (can't resemble red), or gray (dark but can vary in finish). Two-tone bats are permitted as well as clear or natural-stained bats. Bats, either clear or colored, cannot resemble white. Also, different bat colors are permitted if approved by the Rules Committee of MLB.

Like many rules and regulations, these are exceptions. Pink bats, for example, can be used on Mother's Day to raise awareness for breast-cancer research. The practice began on Mother's Day in 2006 with pink bats sporting the Louisville Slugger logo. Starting on Mother's Day 2014, players were allowed to use pink bats with logos from any MLB-approved manufacturer. The rule change followed a 2013 controversy when Trevor Plouffe (Minnesota Twins) and Nick Markakis (Baltimore Orioles), both sons of breast-cancer survivors, were told they could not, legally, use a pink bat with the logo from their bat manufacturer, MaxBat.[36]

Engraving

Many bat-makers in the 21st century use a laser to engrave the player's name and bat model number on the barrel. Youth groups, corporations (i.e., promotions or bat giveaways), special events (i.e., weddings or birthdays), and so on, might include a name/team/company or date that is laser engraved.

Other methods of engraving didn't change much until recently. For many decades, name, trademark, and the like were "hot branded" on the bat, similar to the branding of cattle. Silk-screening and an electric branding iron were sometimes used in the late 19th century, but today lasers do most of the work, especially with a player's name.[37]

Bat engraving can be traced back well over a century ago. According to *Sweet Spot* by Magee and Shirley, Bud Hillerich was always trying to be one step ahead of his competition. One of his ideas was a marketing scheme to put a player's name on a bat. All he needed was the right player.[38]

Honus Wagner played for Louisville before moving on to the Pittsburgh Pirates, where his career blossomed. By 1905, Wagner, nicknamed the Flying Dutchman, was considered a bona fide superstar in the sport. Since Bud knew the Flying Dutchman (*Sweet Spot* reports the two were old friends), he talked with the shortstop about putting Wagner's name on a bat.[39]

In September 1905, Honus Wagner signed a contract with the Louisville Slugger brand, allowing his signature to be burned onto the bat barrel. This was the first professional sports endorsement of a consumer product. In 1908, Ty Cobb of the Detroit Tigers became the second MLB player to ink a contract as a Louisville Slugger endorser.[40]

Today, literally hundreds of players have signed endorsement deals with dozens of bat-makers. Most players in the 21st century don't receive huge sums of money for signing with a manufacturer. Bat endorsements now, when adjusted for inflation, are not much more than what was paid in the early 1900s. Ty Cobb was offered $75 in 1908; Babe Ruth received

$100 in 1918. The Cobb and Ruth amounts clearly didn't translate to an economic windfall.[41]

Owner David Chandler of Chandler Bats has a unique philosophy on endorsements. He said, "If I don't have a bat endorsement contract with a player, I have to earn their business the old-fashioned way—so it keeps me on my toes and puts the onus on me to do my job, every single day. With a contract, the player is obligated to use your bat. To me, my approach is more pure."[42]

After the bat has been turned, finished, and engraved, the final step for many manufacturers is affixing the logo or trademark. The trademark is either a peel and stick label (maple bats) or engraved. The trademark is placed mid-length on the bat, 90 degrees from the bat's hitting surface. The process of converting a wooden billet into a wooden bat is now complete.

Also, starting in 2009, all MLB bats must be trackable back to the manufacturer. The tracking process can be accomplished via a bat's serial number, production date, or some type of identification mark. The key is that the bat must be trackable back to the bat-maker's production and sales record. The identification symbol can be located on the knob, in the cup, or included with the player name and model number.

The Handle "Dot"

Beginning in the 2010 season, all MLB bat-makers were impacted by the handle dot regulation. This requirement only applied to diffuse-porous woods (maple and birch) with a stained or colored handle finish. A ring-porous wood like ash was not affected.[43]

The clear, unfinished "dot" can be visualized as roughly a quarter-sized area (1-inch diameter circle or diamond-shape) on the handle, 12 inches from the bat knob, and placed on the tangential (face grain) side of the bat.[44] All MLB maple and birch bats with dark-finished handles were required to have this clear dot and subsequently pass an ink or dye test. The test involves placing a small amount of ink in the clear dot and watching it flow with the grain, a process called "bleeding." Since the wood grain of both maple and birch is difficult to see with the naked eye, and since crooked (non-straight) grain was deemed to be one of the main culprits of exploding bats, the ink dot test enabled inspectors to quickly determine the straightness of the grain. Ash bats were not subject to the test because of their highly visible grain.

The dot is created by applying tape or a sticker, like the ones often used to mark prices at garage sales, before the bat handle is finished. After finishing, the sticker is removed and—voila!—a clear dot appears.

Out-the-Door

It often takes a manufacturer a couple of weeks to fulfill an order because of all the steps involved. The bat-making timeline can be shortened to a couple of days for rush orders if all materials are in stock.

Bats are often shipped in cardboard boxes with professionals typically ordering six or a full dozen at a time. MLB teams pay for players' bats. This club gesture is a nice perk for today's major leaguers regardless of their astronomically high income compared to the middle and lower classes.

MLB bat prices have risen from about $1 in 1900 to nearly $200 in the 21st century. The cost of a specific bat can differ for various reasons including end-use, quantity, firm, special order (i.e., customized vs. standard engraving), annual production, etc.

An MLB player in the starting lineup for an entire season might use as many as 150 bats.[45] A notable exception was Hall of Famer Joe Sewell, who compiled 2,226 hits in the AL during the 1920s and 1930s.[46] According to Dan Gutman's book, Sewell used one bat over his entire 14 years in the big leagues.[47] In contrast, Derek Jeter, who used a Louisville Slugger bat during his 20-year New York Yankees career, ordered more than 4,300 bats over this time period.[48] However, all 4,300 bats may not have been used by Jeter, just merely ordered.

Bottom Line

Many steps are required to transform a billet into a MLB bat. Some manufacturers alter the order of the steps to fit their situation or have different procedures for their mill. Regardless, all MLB bat suppliers must adhere to the rules and regulations for major league play.

11

The Future of the Bat
in Major League Baseball

Baseball bats with knobs at the end of the handle have
basically been the same for over 135 years.—Grady Phelan,
ProXR Bats

Baseball has evolved over its long history with modifications to its
rules, increased use of analytics, pitch counts designed to reduce stress
on a pitcher's arm, year-round conditioning and training, and more. However, MLB bats have experienced fewer changes. The few bat innovations
introduced to the sport never became popular with players. Heinie Groh's
bottle bat, the double knob bat endorsed by Nap Lajoie, and Spalding's
mushroom bat are examples.

MLB bats continue to be shaped on a lathe that transforms a billet
into a tapered cylinder with a circular knob at the end. Major league bats
are still crafted from wood found in trees primarily growing in the U.S.
and Canada. Threats to trees, primarily pests, exist, and worries persist
about wood bats breaking without a complete understanding of the characteristics and features of the material carried into the batter's box.

However, time marches on, even for the tradition-rich baseball bat.
A new design was developed in the 21st century that might be the wave
of the future for MLB. Copied after the handle of an axe, the bat innovation has captured the attention of players and bat manufacturers. The axe
handle bat is gaining popularity in all levels of baseball, from tee-ball and
Little League through high school, college, and professional leagues.

In his 1970 book *The Science of Hitting*, Red Sox legend Ted Williams wrote that the act of swinging a bat is similar to swinging an axe.[1]
When hitting a baseball, Williams said, it was important to keep one's
wrists "square and unbroken as they would be at impact when an ax[e] is
swung on a tree." Williams reasoned that to deliver maximum power to
the ball, the batter's swing should avoid wrist-roll *before* bat-ball contact.

The wrist-roll theory was not a new idea for baseball players. However, Williams' axe swing idea, plainly illustrated and clearly stated by perhaps baseball's greatest hitter, reignited the entrepreneurial spirit of innovation.

For generations, baseball players tried different substances and home remedies in a bid to improve their grip. Slathering the bat handle with pine tar, adding specialized grip tape above the knob, and slightly shaving or roughing up the handle are three examples. Also, the idea for an axe handle-shaped baseball bat had likely been in the minds of players, engineers, and others for many years. In 1990, the concept of bat-grip and Williams' theory on bat-swing merged not on a baseball field, but in a suburb in the Empire State.

Near the town of Poughkeepsie, a New York woodworker and lifelong baseball fan was chopping wood with an axe. Bruce Leinert pretended that he was swinging a baseball bat instead of an axe as he struck the tree. (One often thinks about something else when the task at hand is work.) Leinert noticed that his grip on the axe was a more natural fit in his hands than the traditional handle of a bat. After obtaining a piece of ash from a local

Axe-handled bats before going to the lathe for final shaping (author's collection).

sawmill, he built his first axe handle bat prototype in a mere two hours. However, it wasn't until 17 years later, in 2007, that Leinert filed a patent application for his invention.[2]

In 2009, Baden Sports, a Washington state family-owned sporting goods company, signed a 20-year contract with Leinert to license his bat. Baden Sports continued development work on Leinert's invention before marketing the design. The family-owned business used feedback from hitters who tested prototype bats developed with the aid of three-dimensional (3D) models. Baden researchers also studied the tension and torque of tendons in hitters' forearms. Measurements were taken of how the strain of holding a regular bat with a cylindrical handle and round knob affected hitters and their swing. In 2012 Baden Sports felt comfortable enough with their design to market their first bat—named the Axe Bat.[3]

What Is an Axe Handle Bat and How Is It Different?

Baseball bats with knobs on the handle end have basically been the same since the 19th century. Originally, players didn't hold the bat down on the knob. The common practice, before and during the Deadball Era, was to choke up, holding the bat up the handle, often used to improve bat control. Wee Willie Keeler and Ty Cobb are usually portrayed with a choke-up grip. Also, this style of grip with the traditional knob prevented the hands from slipping off the end of the handle. The knob usually did not touch the batter's lower hand during the swing.[4]

In the 21st century, the bat knob is still basically the same—round, symmetrical, and on the end of the handle. The big difference over the decades is how the game is played: from a base to base slap-at-the-ball strategy to today's power style of hitting. MLB players now typically grip the bat on the end of the handle with their palm resting against, or wrapping over, the knob.[5]

Oval-shaped axe handles have been made on a variety of hand tools for hundreds of years. However, it is a relatively new option for a baseball bat.

In comparison to a round handle bat, the Axe Handle bat, as designed and marketed by Baden Sports as the Axe Bat, is different in two ways.[6,7,8] First, the bottom of the Axe Bat is asymmetrical with a flush backside and an oval-shaped knob that extends out into the pinky finger. The oval-shaped handle tapers into a traditional handle between the bottom and top hand. Consequently, the top hand of a player using an Axe Bat

Axe Bat handle designed to improve a hitter's grip (courtesy Axe Bat).

still grips the traditional cylindrical shape. Second, because the knob of an Axe Bat is asymmetrical, the handle will always be held the same way by a hitter. According to Baden Sports, the handle of an Axe Bat doesn't rotate in the hitter's hands, meaning bat-ball contact will always be on the same side of the barrel. This impact surface is called one-sided hitting. Since the manufacturer can predict where the contact will occur, it is possible to design a barrel where the ball hits the densest, most durable bat side.

Gripping and Swinging a Bat

Maintaining a good grip while swinging a bat is important. We've all witnessed, heard descriptions of, or seen pictures of entire bats flying into the stands or dugout. Bats can even slip from your hands in your backyard.

If a bat is gripped too tightly, the tightness inhibits a hitter's arm muscles from helping them during their swing. Loose muscles are fast muscles that result in quicker bat speed.[9]

When gripping a round handle bat, the grip type used by most MLB players is to wrap their fingers around the handle of the bat with the pinky on the knob and the edge of the knob pressing into their palm. This traditional grip allows players to achieve a more neutral wrist angle as they begin their swing and to use their forearm muscles through the swing, resulting in additional bat speed. However, the downside is that some players need a tight grip to keep the bat from shifting in their hands. The extra effort to grip the bat reduces bat speed and can result in hand calluses and blisters.

When the barrel of a bat with a circular knob strikes a ball, the knob vibrates slightly. Over time, this minor movement can cause the tiny hamate bone (located in our lower hands and which attaches muscles to the little finger) to fracture and injure the ulnar nerve. Similarly, a hard or checked swing causes additional pressure on the hamate bone and ulnar nerve. Over time, hamate bone fractures have kept many hitters out of the lineup. Post-surgery recovery after removing bone fragments due to a broken hamate can require six to nine weeks.[10]

The list of MLB players, past and present, who landed on the disabled list due to a broken hamate caused by swinging, is endless. Here are a few names recognizable to baseball fans:

- Dustin Pedroia
- J. D. Martinez
- Giancarlo Stanton
- Ken Griffey, Jr.
- David Ortiz
- Jose Canseco
- Nomar Garciapara
- Pablo Sandoval
- Pedro Alvarez
- Nick Markakis
- Gary Sheffield
- Troy Tulowitzki
- Jose Bautista
- Scott Rolen
- Jed Lowrie
- Jim Thome ... and many more.[11]

Players recovering from a hand injury sometimes experiment with Axe Handle bats because the handle doesn't press into the palm of the lower hand. Chili Davis remarked when he was the hitting coach for the Boston Red Sox, "The whole design [of the Axe Handle bat] is to minimize the bat movement in your hands. You get a grip and the grip is constant throughout your swing and might help minimize hamate injuries and things like that."[12]

What Are the Benefits of Using an Axe Handle Bat?

A 2014 study funded by Baden Sports was conducted by UCLA Engineering Professor Dr. Vijay Gupta, who investigated the ergonomics of Baden's Axe Bat.[13] His study used high-speed cameras and slow-motion analysis of the performance of Division 1 college baseball players using traditional round handle bats compared to the Axe Bat. Dr. Gupta's study summarized the Axe Handle design in six categories[14]:

- **Comfort:** The oval shape of the Axe Handle better matches the contours and angles of the batter's hand. The design increases, and more evenly distributes, the surface area of the grip within the hitter's hand on the bat. The result is a decrease in pressure points between the hand and handle.
- **Improved performance:** Enhanced grip stability leads to reduced vibration of the bat handle [this vibration is an engineering term called "kinematics"].[15] With a traditional handle, the knob of the bat moves into the lower portion of the hand as the bat is swung, pushing the knob into the palm. Furthermore, the batter's swing creates bat handle vibration due to the slight gap between the thumb and index finger of the *bottom hand* [this motion happens so fast even Ted Williams couldn't see it!].

A batter's standard grip on a traditional handle and the resulting bat-knob vibration creates two problems, according to Dr. Gupta. First, the grip area has reduced bat-pressure at the instant bat and palm meet. Second, the bat-grip is more prone to vibration, and thus less control, during the swing. This results in reduced swing performance.

In contrast to a traditional round handle with a knob, the back of an axe handle bat is flush throughout its handle length and without a backside knob. The elimination of the knob resting against the lower edge of the palm creates a more stable grip with less tension in the hands. The palm therefore has substantial contact while swinging an axe handle bat, removing the need to grip the bat as tightly to minimize vibration. This results in increased performance.

- **Increased power to the ball:** An Axe Handle bat creates additional "whip" before striking the ball. With a round handle bat, a gap occurs in the grip between the portion of the palm that is pressed into the knob and the index finger. A traditional round handle requires the *bottom hand* to apply large forces at these two points in order to achieve sufficient grip stability through the swing. An axe handle allows the hand to maintain contact with the bat along the full length of the palm, thus, less force is required to maintain the grip. The reduced tension allows more range of motion in the batter's wrist, achieving more whip with the bat prior to ball contact.
- **Increased bat speed:** When gripping a round handle bat, the wrist angle is less than 90 degrees (acute) and the wrist is almost fully flexed at the onset of the swing. The grip on an axe handle bat creates a wrist angle between 90 and 180 degrees (obtuse). Thus, the wrist is in a more neutral position at the onset of the swing. Also, an Axe Handle bat allows the wrist to move the barrel a greater distance. With 15–20 degrees of additional bat whip and more opportunity to accelerate an axe handle bat, greater bat speed can be generated at the point of contact with the ball. This translates to increased force over a greater swing angle.

Ex-MLB player Chili Davis told *USA Today* about the non-traditional knob on the Axe Handle bat compared to a traditional bat. Davis said, "a lot of guys don't like the knob below their hand and so they put it in their palm. With that bat [Axe Bat], you don't feel as much knob below your hands. You feel like it's more just bat that you're holding ... [consequently] it would increase bat speed."[16]

- **Improved bat control and pain reduction:** When a ball strikes the barrel of a round handle bat, the knob area of the handle moves from the palm surface towards the fingers. The movement is due

The backside of an Axe Bat is flush throughout the handle length and without the traditional knob (courtesy Axe Bat).

147

to bat vibration prior to striking the fingers and rebounding into the palm. With an Axe Handle, the palm conforms to, and remains in contact with, the bat. There is little or no movement of the lower grip prior to, or when, contacting the ball.

- **Reduced injuries to hamate bone and ulnar nerve, and thrown bats:** When a round handle bat is gripped, the knob pushes into the hamate bone and ulnar nerve area of the lower palm (below the pinky finger). During contact with the ball, substantial pressure is applied to the top of the hamate bone and the root of the ulnar nerve. A player can lose control of the bat if the ulnar nerve, which controls grip, is pinched significantly. Also, repeated incidences of high pressure to the palm of the *lower hand* can fracture the hamate bone.[17] Because of the large contact area in the axe handle grip, the palm pressure to the ulnar nerve and hamate bone is reduced. An axe handle bat distributes the pressure over the entire grip. Also, the back side of the handle is flat, so it won't poke a hitter in the palm the way a traditional bat handle does.

When asked about Axe Handle bats and hamate injuries, Chili Davis told *Popular Science* in 2016, "With the round knob, you get big calluses on your hand, big blisters because of that knob moving around in your hand. I know you get used to that; it's what you've grown up with. But it can cause a hamate bone injury. You never know when you're getting it. It just happens as a consequence of the pounding in your hand. This bat [axe handle] minimizes the risk of injury."[18]

Dustin Pedroia of the Boston Red Sox agreed with Davis. After coming off a 2014 season-ending thumb and wrist surgery, Pedroia experimented with an Axe Handle bat the following spring training. Davis said, "He [Pedroia] picked it up.... And he goes, 'This is what I need. I need this knob [Axe Handle]. I can lock my fingers the way I want to, you know?'" Pedroia added, "It just feels good in your hands."[19]

What Is the Future of the Axe Handle Bat?

Baseball players, like many other athletes, are creatures of habit and are resistant to change. When they are hitting well, they want to keep the streak going by taking the same approach in their diet, warmups, and mechanics, continuing to wear something they think brought them the good luck, etc. Maintaining an allegiance to a bat is no different. So why would a ball player switch from their tool of the trade, the round handle bat, to an axe handle bat which looks and feels very different?

Hugh Tompkins, Baden Sports' director of research and development, told *USA Today*, "Hitters [using an Axe Handle bat] are afforded more space to build bat speed and track pitches, are able to transfer more power from the swing to the ball and can control bat position and handle vibration better."[20] Tompkins continued, "Less muscle tension is required to control the bat, leaving more available [muscle] for accelerating the barrel. The increased force distribution in the hand also means that more of the swing force is transferred to the ball versus being wasted in the grip."

Thus, per Baden Sports, the Axe Handle bat minimizes stress on a player's hands, increases bat speed, and delivers more power. However, it takes time to get used to the different grip on the Axe Handle bat as it needs to be held in a set position.[21]

Major league players sometimes suffer general batting-related injuries or specific hamate fractures which may require surgery and several weeks or more to recover. Some players have begun using the Axe Handle bat to keep them off the disabled list a second time. Others experiment with the Axe Bat to avoid being on the list at all.

By the end of the 2017 season, 59 players were using a bat with an axe handle.[22] Those players included Mookie Betts (2018 American League MVP), George Springer (2017 World Series MVP) and Carlos Correa (Houston Astros), Jake Lamb (Arizona Diamondbacks), and Dustin Pedroia (Boston Red Sox).[23] A comparison of Axe Handle versus round knob hitting statistics for 2017 showed a higher batting average (.273 vs. .255), slugging percentage (.463 vs. .422) and on-base plus slugging percentage (.805 vs. .745) for Axe Handle bat use.[24]

George Springer's first full year swinging an Axe Handle bat (2017) produced career-best totals in home runs, RBI, batting average, slugging percentage, and on-base plus slugging percentage. Springer said, "The handle feels very natural, like it was made for my swing, and allows me to make better contact more often. I noticed the improvement immediately after I switched. It takes a little bit of getting used to ... but I got the hang of it and I love it.... I'm going to stick with it."[25]

Chili Davis said, "It will probably end up [spreading] with a player grabbing another player's bat, or a guy with a previous hamate injury that's coming off recovering from hamate surgery, and just saying, 'Hey, here's something, try this.'"[26] Mookie Betts had his own reason for trying an Axe Handle bat. He told a Boston Red Sox beat reporter in 2016, "I started using it because it was something new, figured I'd try it. I started to like it and stuck with it."

Because the Axe Handle bat is available for players from tee-ball all the way through the major leagues, more players will get introduced to it at a young age and grow accustomed to using it as they move to higher levels of organized baseball. As more players become exposed to Axe bats, they will try it to improve their bat speed and exit velocity and to reduce hand injuries.

Another Axe Handle-Like Innovation Is Born

In 2003, six years before Baden Sports bought the Axe Bat design from Bruce Leinert, another out-of-the-blue innovative instant occurred, this time in the Midwest. Grady Phelan was playing in his backyard with his son when he accidentally threw a baseball bat that just missed hitting the boy. Seeing the bat fly by his son's head was all the motivation Phelan needed to design a better grip for the bat. Thus, ProXR Ergonomic Bat Technology was born in St. Louis.[27]

The ProXR design has an oval-shaped knob but not the flush back-side like the Baden Sports Axe Bat. Nevertheless, both firms broke from tradition and developed a new method to grip the bat handle. The design process Phelan used involved many iterations and refinements, including batting cage trials with his son. When Phelan was satisfied with the product, testing began with players including those at his alma mater Kansas University, and hometown Washington University.[28]

During the design process, Phelan had some observations that were in line with Leinert's. Phelan discovered, "[Traditional] bat knobs generate rapid and violent compression in a batter's base gripping hand during the swing." Phelan also found that the massive compression in the palm (bottom gripping hand) caused by a traditional bat knob "is the root cause of almost every thrown bat and ... hamate injury in baseball." Phelan's website has pictures of players' hands with the description, "You can see it in their hands and on every worn batting glove—it's right there in their palm."[29]

Phelan further described the damaging effect of a traditional bat knob. "Whether the knob is rounded or flared, it acts like a speed bump to a batter's swing. After the bat passes the intended point of contact with the ball, the hands have to roll over the knob to complete the swing. It's that roll-over that mashes the knob into the heal [sic] of the hand."[30]

Licensing

Baden Sports owns the patent on their Axe Bat design. They have licensed the design to four MLB approved bat-makers—Victus Sports, Chandler Bats, Dove Tail Bats, and Tucci Lumber. The companies manufacture their own series of bats, but Axe Handle requests are fulfilled using the Axe Bat patented design.[31] Interestingly, the founder of Tucci Lumber was a former first-round draft pick who suffered a devastating hand injury while swinging a bat.

Grady Phelan's ProXR Grip Technology was made available for the 2019 season to MLB-approved Old Hickory bat company.[32] Both ProXR Grip Technology and Baden Sports market their bats to other bat makers not affiliated with MLB.

Bottom Line

Over the years, baseball has evolved with numerous changes since the first professional team took the field in 1869. Bats, a primary tool in a sport known in the U.S. as the National Pastime, have also experienced changes. The modifications and alterations to major league bats have been slow in comparison to the overall game. Who knows what the following years will bring to baseball and the bat? One thing known for certain is that the future cannot be accurately predicted. The axe bat-style handle might or might not be widely adopted by Major League Baseball players. Also, bat-makers, bat manufacturing, trees supplying MLB with wood for bats, and other factors could change as the years go by. Only time will tell.

Appendix:
Pine Tar and Rosin

But there is no joy in Mudville
Mighty Casey has struck out.
—Ernest Lawrence Thayer

MLB bats have always been made of wood. This book has described the ins and outs, and often, the forgotten, overlooked, or unknown aspects, of "Major League Lumber." However, this appendix deals with two other on-field products derived from trees and useful for batters—pine tar and resin. Even though both products can help the batter, the former is primarily associated with the hitter and the latter with the pitcher.

Naval Stores

Pine tar and rosin are in the group of products called naval stores. It seems like a peculiar name, but naval stores is a generic term for all the individual products derived from pine gum, also known as oleoresins. The oleoresins include pitches, turpentine (the basis for rosin), tar and oils.

Naval stores got its name from an early use of these various products for the sailing and boating industry. Today, most naval stores in the U.S. are a by-product of the wood pulping process (for techies this is the sulfate/kraft or alkaline solution process).[1]

According to the Society of American Foresters' *Forestry Handbook*, the total U.S. yearly production of rosin, turpentine, and what is technically called "tall-oil fatty acids" is roughly 1,200 million pounds. Fatty oils plus resin acid and other materials form the basis for tall oil, which can be used to make pine tar.[2]

The Just Bats website says, "For centuries before its use in baseball,

Southern pine marked for Naval Stores collection (bugwood.com).

mariners were using pine tar to help preserve and seal the wood on their vessels. The use of pine tar ensured that these ships lasted the rigors of the water with much more efficiency."[3] Pine tar was also used to protect the rope rigging of these sailing vessels. The rope was also soaked in a liquid form of rosin called pitch. The resin-soaked rope could also be pounded between the planks of ships to make them water tight and to coat hulls for protection from sea worms of tropical waters.[4]

In baseball's infancy, players were always on the lookout for anything that would help them get a better grip on the bat. Since the early players wore woolen uniforms, participated in daytime games in the burning sun, and had many other inconveniences and complaints (some still continuing), palms became perspiration-filled (and always will!). The game's pioneers tried various techniques, many still used today, to get a better grip on the bat. These practices included rubbing dirt on the bat handle, wiping hands and bat with a towel, wiping hands on the uniform, and a host of other techniques they may have learned on the farm.

Even in the 21st century, the bat knob helps to prevent the bat from slipping out of the batter's hand when he swings. Most batters grip the bat so that the knob touches their bottom hand or even wrap their bottom hand around the knob. Also to improve grip, the handle of the bat is often wrapped in string or tape. The Axe Handle is another current innovation designed to improve a player's grip. Max Kay of Axe Bats says a round handle, with a knob was a historical accident. He argues that the knobs were there because lathes could only make symmetrical pieces and were needed initially for turning the wood.[5] However, the most popular method for improving grip is pine tar.

Pine Tar: Source and Manufacture

Do you know how sticky tree sap is? If so, you have a general idea of how sticky pine tar can be.

Pine tar is a tacky substance produced by the high-temperature carbonization of pine wood coming from pine trees, such as Southern yellow pines like longleaf and slash. Specifically, it is formed by rapidly heating, at a high temperature, pine wood with reduced air to prevent the burning of the wood. The destruction of the wood results in various products, two of which are the familiar charcoal and baseball's well-known pine tar.[6] The traditional method of pine tar production only used pine stumps and roots. The tree trunk is the source of most pine tar today.[7]

The U.S. colonies prior to statehood had a commodity Great Britain did not—extensive pine forests. Tar and pitch for maritime use was in such demand that it became an important export for the soon-to-be country.

The early history of North Carolina found it to be a leading producer of supplies for the naval industry's naval stores. Workers who labored in the naval stores industry often went barefoot during the hot summer months and undoubtedly collected tar on their heels. To call someone a "rosin heel" or "tar heel" was to imply they that they worked in a lowly trade.

The North Carolina State University Museum explains, "During the Civil War, North Carolina soldiers flipped the meaning of the term, and turned an epithet into an accolade. They called themselves 'tar heels' as an expression of state pride. Others adopted the term and North Carolina became widely known as the 'Tar Heel State.'"[8]

Pine Tar Uses

In addition to a long history as a wood preservative, pine tar had many colonial era uses. It made a satisfactory hair dressing and once served to "tar and feather" undesirable individuals. Hot tar was also used to stop bleeding and to sterilize wounds and amputations.[9]

Pine tar is used today in soaps, shampoos, and treatments for certain skin conditions like psoriasis, eczema, and rosacea.[10] It is also used by the equine industry for horse care as a natural, antiseptic germicidal treatment on hooves.[11] Pine tar is used as a softening solvent in the rubber industry, for treating and fabricating construction materials, and in special paints. Pine tar use in baseball is strictly a niche application.

Is Pine Tar Legal in Baseball?

Yes and no. For batters, yes. For pitchers, no, as serious fans of the game already know. The explanation given in the 2018 Major League Baseball's Official Baseball Rules is used to elucidate the issue.[12]

For Batters:

Rule 3.02(c): "The bat handle, for not more than 18 inches from its end, may be covered or treated with any material or substance to improve the grip. Any such material or substance that extends past the 18-inch limitation shall cause the bat to be removed from the game."

Rule 3.02 comment: "If pine tar extends past the 18-inch limitation, then the umpire, on his own initiative or if alerted by the opposing team, shall order the batter to use a different bat. The batter may use the bat later in the game only if the excess substance is removed. If no objections are raised prior to a bat's use, then a violation of Rule 3.02(c) on that play does not nullify any action or play on the field and no protests of such play shall be allowed."

Rule Note: "If the umpire discovers that the bat does not conform to (c) above until a time during or after which the bat has been used in play, it shall not be grounds for declaring the batter out, or ejected from the game."

This is *not* the same rule language (as quoted in Chapter 2) that was in place when AL President Lee MacPhail overturned the umpire's ruling in the Kansas City Royals' George Brett "pine tar game." A complete transcript of MacPhail's decision is available at https://www.nytimes.com/1983/07/29/sports/text-of-league-president-s-ruling-in-brett-bat-case.html.

For pitchers: Pitchers are not immune to the rule book regarding pine tar use.

Rule 3.01: "No player shall intentionally discolor or damage the ball by rubbing it with soil, rosin, paraffin, licorice, sand-paper, emery-paper or other foreign substances [such as pine tar]." The penalty is automatic ejection and a 10-game suspension.

Rule 6.02(c)(7) Comment: "The pitcher may not attach anything to either hand, any finger, or either wrist (e.g., Band-Aid, tape, Super Glue, bracelet). The umpire shall determine if such attachment is indeed a foreign substance [e.g., pine tar] for the purpose of Rule 6.02(c)(7), but in no case may the pitcher be allowed to pitch with such attachment to his hand, finger or wrist."

Pitchers sometimes get in trouble with umpires and opposing teams for deliberately putting pine tar on a baseball. Violations with pitchers and baseballs are more likely to occur than violations with batters and bats.

An example of a pitcher willfully using pine tar was former New York Yankees' Michael Pineda, in 2014. MLB.com reported that Pineda broke rule 3.01 when he applied "a foreign substance to the ball" (the rule was numbered 8.02 in 2014 when the incident took place).[13] He was immediately ejected, and suspended for ten games.

As an aside, it is a common occurrence for the official rules of MLB baseball to be amended on a regular basis. For instance, eight changes were made for the 2018 season, but none directly focused on foreign substances like pine tar.

Appendix

Players and Use of Pine Tar

Pine Tar and Bats

Pine tar is used on bat handles by many players in MLB. The practice is so common that it is now taken for granted. Three examples of auctioned bats include a mention of pine tar. The advertisements illustrate the growth of this naval stores product.

Joe Mauer played his entire 15-year career with the Minnesota Twins before retiring at the end of the 2018 season. He earned numerous awards from MLB, including the MVP Award in 2009. He posted a career batting average of .306 and won three batting titles. According to a Vintage Bats advertisement, Mauer consistently applied a concentration of pine tar at the center of the bat just below, and sometimes extending into, the Rawlings "R." The Vintage Bats sales announcement continued by noting that Mauer could often be seen grabbing at the pine tar on the bat to strengthen his grip.[14]

Manny Machado spent the first 96 games of the 2018 season with the Baltimore Orioles before he was traded to the Los Angeles Dodgers. In those 96 games with the O's, Machado batted .315 with 24 home runs and 115 hits. According to Goldin Auction House, a 2018 Machado bat had a heavy coating of pine tar on the upper handle.[15]

Chicago Cubs star Kris Bryant, the 2015 National League Rookie of the Year and 2016 NL MVP, used a number of different bat companies and colors in five seasons playing MLB baseball. The same auction house that offered the Manny Machado bat also offered an all-black, game-used Bryant bat. The bat had a light coating of pine tar on the handle, and there was a mark on the handle that identified the grain.[16]

Pine Tar on Helmets

Pine tar is also used on batting helmets for bat grip. Players sometimes have head-gear that looks old and worn out. What fans see, however, with this disfigured equipment is often pine tar. A MLB batter in need of a better grip simply reaches up to the helmet to get a dab of the sticky stuff. A few players are notorious for this practice.

Manny Ramirez, now retired, was a player who carried huge amounts of pine tar on his helmet. Ramirez donated the filthy-looking helmet to the Hall of Fame.[17]

Craig Biggio, Vladimir Guerrero, Pablo Sandoval, and hundreds of other present and retired MLB batsmen had dirty helmets. Pine tar was the primary reason for the gunk. It enabled players in the batter's box to avoid calling time out (not always granted by the umpire) and going to the on-deck circle to load up with the sticky stuff.[18]

Rosin: Source and Manufacture

Resin, spelled with an "e," is a substance produced from turpentine. Resin is a sticky liquid secreted from coniferous plants like longleaf and slash pines. Resin is produced by heating the liquid resin to separate the terpene components and other materials. One product is the liquid form of rosin, spelled with an "o." After additional processing and when brought to room temperature, solid rosin is formed.[19]

Uses

Rosin is used in a variety of products, most notably as an industrial chemical. A primary chemical application includes the sizing of paper to reduce liquid flow. Rosin is also used in making paints, lacquers, varnishes, hot melt adhesives, printing ink, plastics, linoleum floor covering, and synthetic rubber production. Chewing gum and sporting events (rosin bag), are both minor, but familiar uses for rosin.[20]

Rosin can be in liquid or solid form. The solid form, when crushed, produces powered rosin, the form found at many sporting events. Sports will always be competitive. Sometimes an athlete needs to be equipped with certain tools that help achieve maximum performance. Obstacles like perspiration and moisture hinder peak performance. Rosin is one of the accessories used by athletes to better help them achieve their goals.[21]

The use of powdered rosin in sports is endless. For example, bull riders rub rosin on their rope and glove for additional grip. Ten-pin bowlers use powdered rosin for better ball control. Rosin is often applied to the hands in aerial acrobatics or gymnastics. Climbers use rosin in scaling mountains. And likely, rosin use in sports is most noticeable in baseball.

In baseball, the rosin powder is placed in a small pouch or bag. When this bag is tapped, it releases the powder onto the surface on which it is dusted. The powder has a friction-increasing capacity, called by some a miracle powder. See https://sportsaspire.com/what-is-rosin-bag-how-is-it-used-in-different-sports

Prior to removal for wood pulp, a Southern pine is scarred for resin collection which is made into baseball's familiar rosin (bugwood.com).

Baseball: Legality for Batters and Pitchers

Batters

Batters can use rosin on the bat handle as long as they stay within the 18-inch handle limitation. The same rule applies as any other foreign substance per rule 3.02(c) as cited earlier per pine tar.

Batters also mix rosin with other grip enhancers, like pine tar or dirt, to improve their hitting odds in the batter's box. These two combinations are common.

Players sometimes use their own mixture, not a store-bought product or brand. One example is Evan Gattis. Gattis, a catcher for the 2017 World Series champion Houston Astros, has used a homemade substance he calls "rodeo rub." Gattis told MLB.com that the rub allows him to grip the bat more securely and build calluses more quickly. Speculation is that Gattis' "rodeo rub" contains rosin since, as mentioned earlier, bull riders use the grip enhancer.[22]

Pitchers

Powdered rosin is commonly used by MLB pitchers for better ball control. Use is legal on the hands but not for "dusting" the ball. The Rule 6.02(d) comment contains the no-dusting language for the pitcher.

Interestingly, it wasn't until the early 1930s that rosin use by pitchers was practiced in both the NL and AL. Peter Morris, in *A Game of Inches*, states, "Of all the items in the baseball firmament, the innocuous rosin bag would seem one of the least likely to prompt a heated debate. And yet the rosin bag was at the center of one of baseball's most singular controversies."[23]

The abbreviated story began in the 19th century. In the late 1800s, the rosin bag was not yet placed behind the pitcher. Pitchers discovered that a small amount of rosin on the fingers gave them a better grip on the ball, and consequently started carrying rosin in their back pocket. In 1912, Christy Mathewson confirmed the "rosin-in-pocket" practice.

However, after the 1919 season, foreign substances were banned to prevent "trick pitching," and rosin was considered one of the foreign substances linked to illegal pitches. Since rosin left no mark on the baseball, the rule was deemed essentially unenforceable. Batters were still allowed to use rosin for improving bat grip.

For the 1926 season, umpires started preparing a rosin bag and placing it on the ground behind the pitching mound. The caveat was that pitchers had to request to use the rosin bag. The NL adopted Commissioner Landis' recommendation, but the AL and their president Ban Johnson, did not agree (Landis and Johnson had a long-running feud). Johnson instructed his AL managers to tell pitchers not to request or use the rosin bag. When the 1926 season began, NL pitchers used the rosin bag, but AL pitchers did not.

In 1931, Johnson and his successor both died, and the incoming AL President was in favor of pitchers using rosin on their hands. It was then that the AL joined the NL in allowing all pitchers to use the rosin bag without fear of reprisal.

Players and Use of Rosin

Rosin use by MLB batters is most noticeable when pinch-hitters are asked to bat for the first time in a game. They often slather their bat handle (often in, or near, the on-deck circle) with various items including rosin to improve their grip. The pinch-hitter can use a rosin bag to accomplish this task. The hitter slaps the handle repeatedly and a cloud of white powder can be seen emanating into the air. Who can blame them when there're batting against a flame thrower like Aroldis Chapman or a skillful off-speed pitcher? The last thing any batter wants is a less-than-perfect grip on their lumber.

Of course, general rosin use is most familiar in baseball with pitchers at all levels of play. It is a common sight to see, or hear via radio, that the pitcher is "going to the rosin bag."

Bottom Line

The use of trees in the MLB goes beyond the wooden bat. Pine tar and rosin are two examples of other tree products used in baseball. Along with the bat, items included in the naval stores industry are indispensable to the game.

Chapter Notes

Introduction

1. https://www.poetryfoundation.org/poems/42891/stopping-by-woods-on-a-snowy-evening (accessed March 25, 2018).

2. Technically, tree-covered land does not always fit the definition of "forest." Tree height/size, number of trees per acre, and tree growth, among other measurements, must meet a minimum before the land is classified as "forest."

Chapter 1

1. David Block, *Baseball Before We Knew It: A Search for the Roots of the Game* (Lincoln: University of Nebraska Press, 2005), xvi.

2. John Thorn, *Baseball in the Garden of Eden: The Secret History of the Early Game* (New York: Simon & Schuster, 2011), ix.

3. Charles Leerhsen, *Ty Cobb: A Terrible Beauty* (New York: Simon & Schuster, 2015), 251.

4. Thorn, *Garden of Eden*, xiv, 30, 50–51, 73, 83–84, 106, 118, 133, 312, 320.

5. Josh Leventhal, *A History of Baseball in 100 Objects: A Tour Through the Bats, Balls, Uniforms, Awards, Documents, and Other Artifacts That Tell the Story of the National Pastime* (New York: Black Dog & Leventhal, 2015), 31–37, 47; Lawrence Ritter, *The Story of Baseball, 3d ed.* (New York: Morrow Junior Books, 1999), 9; Beth Hise, *Swinging Away: How Cricket and Baseball Connect* (London: Scala Books, 2010), 39, 62, 64, 99, 123.

6. Leventhal, *A History of Baseball*, 13–14.

7. *Ibid.*, 15.

8. David Block, *Baseball Before We Knew It*, cover. See page 149 for complete reference on calendar.

9. Leventhal, *A History of Baseball*, 14.

10. *Ibid.*, 15.

11. *Ibid.*, 17–18.

12. Hise, *Swinging Away*, 28–30.

13. Leventhal, *A History of Baseball*, 21.

14. Robert Tholkes, Personal communication, January 4, 2019.

15. Thorn, *Garden of Eden*, xiii.

16. Leventhal, *A History of Baseball*, 23.

17. Hise, *Swinging Away*, 25–32.

18. *Ibid.*, 10–13.

19. *Ibid.*, 10.

20. Tholkes, January 4, 2019. George Wright was not the *only* player to play both baseball and cricket, as mentioned in the paragraph's first sentence.

21. Hise, *Swinging Away*, 126–127, 132, 135, 137.

22. https://englishhistory.net/tudor/ (accessed February 10, 2019).

23. Hise, *Swinging Away*, 99; John Odell, ed., *Baseball as America* (Washington: National Geographic Society and Cooperstown, NY: National Baseball Hall of Fame, 2002), 38.

24. https://en.wikipedia.org/wiki/Henry_Chadwick_(writer).

25. Hise, *Swinging Away*, 72–73.

26. Odell, *Baseball as America*, 41.

27. *Ibid.*, 21, 171–172; Hise, *Swinging Away*, 173–174.

28. *Ibid.*, 173.

29. *Ibid.*, 173–174.

30. Odell, *Baseball as America*, 174.

31. Block, *Baseball Before We Knew It*, 13, 33, 326.

32. Leventhal, *A History of Baseball*, 27–29; Odell, *Baseball as America*, 41–43; Hise, *Swinging Away*, 173–176.

33. Leventhal, 29.

34. *Ibid.*, 27–29; Odell, *Baseball as America,* 41–43; Hise, *Swinging Away,* 173–176.

35. Block, *Baseball Before We Knew It,* xv, 161.

36. *Ibid.*, 156, 157.

37. Thorn, *Garden of Eden*, 59, 135, 184. Thorn states in 2011 that the original game of *town ball*, played by the Olympic Ball Club of Philadelphia and organized in 1833, vanished by 1884. Town ball, as played across the country even in the 21st century, is known by some as a collection of old-fashioned ball games.

38. https://ourgame.mlblogs.com/the-bat-and-ball-a-distinct-game-or-a-generic-term-ebfdc19df329 (accessed April 11, 2017).

Chapter 2

1. "Aladdin had ... his bat." Quote from Ted Williams and Jim Prime, *Ted Williams' Hit List* (Toronto: Stoddart, 1996), 5.

2. Beth Hise, *Swinging Away: How Cricket and Baseball Connect* (London: Scala Books, 2010), 10, 48.

3. John Odell, ed., *Baseball as America* (Washington: National Geographic Society and Cooperstown, NY: National Baseball Hall of Fame, 2002), 260–61.

4. Bernie Mussill, "The Baseball Bat: From the First Crack to the Clank," *Old-tyme Baseball News* 2 (1998), 21–25.

5. Stuart Miller, *Good Wood: The Story of the Baseball Bat* (Chicago: ACTA Publications, 2011), 83.

6. Josh Leventhal, *A History of Baseball in 100 Objects: A Tour Through the Bats, Balls, Uniforms, Awards, Documents, and Other Artifacts That Tell the Story of the National Pastime* (New York: Black Dog & Leventhal, 2015), 201.

7. Miller, *Good Wood,* 84.

8. Robert Adair, *The Physics of Baseball,* 3d ed. (New York, Perennial, 2002), 114, 138; *The Baseball Encyclopedia,* 8th edition (New York: Macmillan, 1990), 1401–1402.

9. Adair, *The Physics of Baseball,* 114, 138.

10. *Ibid.* 114.

11. Dan Gutman, *Banana Bats & Ding-Dong Balls: A Century of Unique Baseball Inventions* (New York: Macmillan, 1995), xviii. Bats had been made earlier than 1884, but none developed wide-scale popularity like the Louisville Slugger brand.

12. Steve Rushin, *The 34-Ton Bat* (New York: Little, Brown, 2013), 60.

13. Ken Burns, *Baseball: A Film by Ken Burns,* episode 1, "First Inning: Our Game," directed by Ken Burns, written by Geoffrey C. Ward, Burns, PBS, 1994.

14. Gutman, *Banana Bats,* 7; Miller, *Good Wood,* 84.

15. Bob Hill, *Crack of The Bat: The Louisville Slugger Story* (Champaign, IL: Sports Publishing, 2002), 7; Gutman, *Banana Bats,* 7. Second growth is a forest that grows up after a disturbance and leads to trees being replaced. In the case of ash, the tree replacement is typically from seed of nearby trees.

16. https://connect.xfinity.com/appsuite/api/mail/Advertisement%20for%20Bats%201895%20Spalding%20Guide.jpg?action=attachment&folder=default0%2FINBOX&id=497803&attachment=9&user=2&context=10135375&decrypt=&sequence=1&delivery=view (accessed March 3, 2019).

17. John Thorn, "A Peek into the Pocket-book," Our Game, April 19, 2016, https://ourgame.mlblogs.com/a-peek-into-the-pocket-book-a9bd03dfe31d (accessed May 1, 2017).

18. David Magee and Philip Shirley, *Sweet Spot: 125 Years of Baseball and The Louisville Slugger* (Chicago: Triumph Books, 2009), 8.

19. Leventhal, *A History of Baseball in 100 Objects,* 2015; Adair, *The Physics of Baseball,* 130.

20. Scott Drake, vice president of business operations for baseball bat manufacturer PFS Teco, personal communication, April 5, 2017.

21. Leventhal, *A History of Baseball in 100 Objects,* 37, 73. The NABBP was replaced by the National Association of Professional Base Ball Players (NA) in 1871. In 1876, the National League of Professional Base Ball Clubs was formed, and it still exists today.

22. Leventhal, 37, 203.

23. Miller, *Good Wood*, 84.

24. Magee and Shirley, *Sweet Spot*, 22.

25. Gutman, *Banana Bats*, 10; Miller, *Good Wood*, 84.

26. Leventhal, *A History of Baseball in 100 Objects*, 203.

27. Tom Lepperd, ed. *Official Baseball Rules: 2018 Edition* (New York: Office of the Commissioner of Baseball, 2018), 5 (MLB rule 3.02 a).

28. Gutman, *Banana Bats*, 26.

29. Miller, *Good Wood*, 89.

30. Tom Lepperd, ed. *Official Baseball Rules: 2018 Edition* (New York: Office of the Commissioner of Baseball, 2018), 5 (MLB rule 3.02[c]).

31. Peter Morris, *A Game of Inches: The Story Behind the Innovations That Shaped Baseball* (Chicago: Ivan R. Dee, 2010), 288.

32. Filip Bondy, *The Pine Tar Game: The Kansas City Royals, the New York Yankees, and Baseball's Most Absurd and Entertaining Controversy* (New York: Scribner, 2015), 5.

33. Morris, *A Game of Inches*, 288.

34. *Ibid.*

35. Bondy, 4.

36. Bruce Slutsky, "July 24, 1983: The Pine Tar Game" https://sabr.org/games proj/game/july-24-1983-george-brett-pine-tar-game#_edn6 (accessed March 10, 2019); Bondy, 4–6, 144–45, 148, 162–63.

37. Lepperd, *Official Baseball Rules 2018*, 5–6.

38. Hill, *Crack of the Bat*, 4–6.

39. Lawrence Ritter, *The Story of Baseball*, 3d ed. (New York: Morrow Junior Books, 1999), 26–27.

40. Adair, *The Physics of Baseball*, 114.

41. Hill, *Crack of the Bat*, 6; Miller, *Good Wood*, 22–23.

42. Charles Leerhsen, *Ty Cobb: A Terrible Beauty* (New York: Simon & Schuster, 2015), 36.

43. Leerhsen, 96.

44. Hill, *Crack of the Bat*, 10; Miller, *Good Wood*, 84; Leerhsen, *Ty Cobb*, 201, 324, 361. In *Sweet Spot*, Magee and Shirley note that the first bat order Cobb placed for his Louisville Slugger was 32 ounces, and that Cobb got most of his hits with a Louisville Slugger.

45. Miller, *Good Wood*, 84.

46. *Ibid.*, 21–22.

47. *Ibid.*

48. Ritter, *The Story of Baseball*, 26, 28; Morris, *A Game of Inches*, 271–279; "Spitball," Baseball Reference Bullpen, https://www.baseball-reference.com/bullpen/Spitball, (accessed August 22, 2018); Jimmy Stamp, "A Brief History of the Baseball," *Smithsonian*, June 28, 2013. https://www.smithsonianmag.com/arts-culture/a-brief-history-of-the-baseball-3685086/, (accessed March 9, 2019).

49. Ritter, 86; Leventhal, *A History of Baseball in 100 Objects*, 197.

50. Hill, *Crack of the Bat*, 11.

51. Miller, *Good Wood*, 21 or 86.

52. *Ibid.*, 7 or 21.

53. Adair, *The Physics of Baseball*, 115.

54. Leerhsen, *Ty Cobb*, 307.

55. Adair, *The Physics of Baseball*, 105–106.

56. Ron Selter and Phil Lowry, personal correspondence, August 25, 2018; Curt Smith, *Storied Stadiums: Baseballs History Through Its Ballparks* (New York: Carroll & Graf, 2001), 123. Thanks also to an anonymous reviewer of an earlier chapter draft.

57. Leerhsen, *Ty Cobb*, 308.

58. Leventhal, *A History of Baseball in 100 Objects*, 194.

59. Leehrsen, 308.

60. "Ted Williams," Baseball Reference, https://www.baseball-reference.com/players/w/willite01.shtml (accessed August 19, 2018).

61. Magee and Shirley, *Sweet Spot*, 68; Ritter, *The Story of Baseball*, 117.

62. "Ted Williams," Baseball Reference.

63. Ritter, *The Story of Baseball*, 54.

64. "Ted Williams," Baseball Reference.

65. Ted Williams, *My Turn at Bat: The Story of My Life* (New York, Simon and Schuster, 1969), 54.

66. Williams, 54–55, 109.

67. Williams, 55; Magee and Shirley, *Sweet Spot*, 71.

68. Gutman, *Banana Bats*, 33; Magee and Shirley, 71.

69. Magee and Shirley, 64, 68.

70. *Ibid.*, 68; Miller, *Good Wood*, 13.

71. Paul Mittermeyer, "Eddie Collins," SABR Biography Project, http://sabr.org/bioproj/person/c480756d (accessed June 13, 2017).

72. Magee and Shirley, *Sweet Spot,* 29.

73. *Ibid.,* 29.

74. Miller, *Good Wood,* 87.

75. https://www.baseball-reference.com/players/m/mccarti01.shtml (accessed November 28, 2018).

76. Tim McCarver and Danny Peary, *Tim McCarver's Baseball for Brain Surgeons and Other Fans,* 1998 (New York: Random House, 1998), 175.

77. Adair, *The Physics of Baseball,* 115 (Aaron's bat); Hill, *Crack of the Bat,* 10 (Carew's bat).

78. Miller, *Good Wood,* 23.

79. *Ibid.,* 55.

80. "Bryce Harper's Bat"; "Mike Trout's Bat"; "Kris Bryant's Bat"; Bat Digest, https://www.batdigest.com/mlbbats (accessed September 1, 2018); "Joe Mauer," Vintage-Bats.com, http://www.vintagebats.com/feature_page-JoeMauer.htm (accessed August 4, 2017).

81. Adair, *The Physics of Baseball,* 113.

82. Magee and Shirley, *Sweet Spot,* 128.

83. Miller, *Good Wood,* 53–54.

84. *Ibid.,* 91.

85. Tim Newcomb, "Facts About Floors: Detailing the Process Behind NBA Hardwood Courts," *Sports Illustrated,* December 2, 2015, https://www.si.com/nba/2015/12/02/nba-hardwood-floors-basketball-court-celtics-nets-magic-nuggets-hornets (accessed June 26, 2017).

86. Miller, *Good Wood,* 91–92; Stephen Canella, "Good Wood," *Sports Illustrated,* March 25, 2002, https://www.si.com/vault/issue/703412/108/2 (accessed November 27, 2017).

87. Scott Drake, personal correspondence; Everett Rogers, *Diffusion of Innovations,* 3d ed. (New York: Free Press, 1983).

88. Scott Drake, personal correspondence.

89. Miller, *Good Wood,* 91–93.

90. "Asian Longhorned Beetle: Annotated Host List," U.S. Department of Agriculture, January 2015, https://www.aphis.usda.gov/plant_health/plant_pest_info/asian_lhb/downloads/hostlist.pdf (accessed August 26, 2018).

91. In 1989, Peter Gammons wrote in *Sports Illustrated:* "Like it or not, the crack of the bat is inevitably being replaced by a ping. By the turn of the century even the majors will probably have put down the lumber and picked up the metal." Gammons, "End of an Era," *Sports Illustrated,* July 24, 1989.

Chapter 3

1. John Feinstein, 2003, *Open* (Boston: Little, Brown), vii.

2. https://history.state.gov/milestones/1801-1829/louisiana-purchase (accessed January 12, 2018).

3. Dan Gutman, *Banana Bats & Ding-Dong Balls: A Century of Unique Baseball Inventions* (New York: Macmillan, 1995), xviii–xix, 2.

4. David Magee and Philip Shirley, *Sweet Spot: 125 Years of Baseball and The Louisville Slugger* (Chicago: Triumph Books, 2009), 11, 145.

5. Gutman, *Banana Bats,* 2; Stuart Miller, *Good Wood: The Story of the Baseball Bat* (Chicago: ACTA Publications, 2011), 107; Magee and Shirley, *Sweet Spot,* 9.

6. Magee and Shirley, 11.

7. Gutman, *Banana Bats,* 2–3.

8. *Ibid.,* 3.

9. *Ibid.*

10. *Ibid.,* 4.

11. Magee and Shirley, *Sweet Spot,* 15.

12. *Ibid.,* 34, 38–39.

13. *Ibid.,* 28–29, 34, 38–39.

14. *Ibid.,* 39.

15. *Ibid.*

16. *Ibid.,* 40–41.

17. *Ibid.,* 54. Also according to this source and page, Babe Ruth liked to spend his winters in Florida playing golf. So did Bud Hillerich. Bud liked providing clubs to ball players like Ruth, who often played with Hillerich & Bradsby's PowerBilt clubs during the off-season.

18. *Ibid.,* 45. Although Ruth led the AL in 1918 with 11 home runs, he was used primarily as a pitcher with the Red Sox.

19. *Ibid.* Ruth was the first player to order a Louisville Slugger with a knob at the handle end; thus he is often given partial credit for developing the modern baseball bat.

20. Steve Rushin, *The 34-Ton Bat* (New York: Little, Brown, 2013), 56–57.

21. Louisville Slugger Museum and

Factory, "From butter churns to baseball bats, https://www.sluggermuseum.com/about-us/our-history (accessed March 3, 2019).

22. Rushin, *The 34-Ton Bat*, 60.

23. Magee and Shirley, *Sweet Spot*, 59.

24. Stuart Miller, *Good Wood*, 114.

25. Rick Wolff, ed., *The Baseball Encyclopedia, 8th ed.* (New York: Macmillan, 1990). 57, 2217, 2567. Spalding's 1875 pitching record came before the formation of the NL or AL.

26. John Odell, ed., *Baseball as America* (Washington, D.C.: National Geographic Society and Cooperstown, NY: National Baseball Hall of Fame, 2002), 171–172; https://www.baseball-reference.com/players/s/spaldal01.shtml (accessed September 16, 2017).

27. John Thorn, *Baseball in the Garden of Eden: The Secret History of the Early Game* (New York: Simon & Schuster, 2011), xv–xvi.

28. http://www.spalding.com/about-spalding.html (accessed September 12, 2017).

29. http://www.antiquefootball.com/wright_ditson.htm (accessed September 20, 2017).

30. http://www.spalding.com/about-spalding.html (accessed September 12, 2017).

31. Magee and Shirley, *Sweet Spot*, 22.

32. Beth Hise, *Swinging Away: How Cricket and Baseball Connect* (London: Scala Books, 2010), 46–47.

33. http://www.post-gazette.com/sports/pirates/2017/08/11/pie-traynor-bat-mears-auctions-pirates-memorabilia/stories/201708110113 (accessed January 4, 2018).

34. Hise, *Swinging Away*, 125–130; Odell, *Baseball as America*, 178.

35. National Baseball Hall of Fame, http://baseballhall.org/hall-of-famers/wright-george (accessed August 30, 2019).

36. Rick Wolff, *The Baseball Encyclopedia*, 57, 1616, 2570.

37. Hise, *Swinging Away*, 130, 132; http://www.antiquefootball.com/wright_ditson.htm (accessed September 20, 2017).

38. https://wrightandditson.com/history/ and http://www.antiquefootball.com/wright_ditson.htm (accessed Sep-

tember 20, 2017). According to the latter website, George Wright and Henry Ditson had *separate* businesses during the 1870s. While publications often list 1871 as the company's founding, 1880 was the first time the Boston business directory listed the name of "Wright & Ditson."

39. http://www.woodtennis.com/WaD.html; http://www.antiquefootball.com/wright_ditson.htm (accessed September 20, 2017).

40. Gutman, *Banana Bats*, 15; Wolff, *The Baseball Encyclopedia*, 1121–1122; http://www.antiquefootball.com/wright_ditson_p3.htm (accessed September 24, 2017).

41. https://www.baseball-reference.com/bullpen/A.J._Reach_Company (accessed October 3, 2017).

42. Bernie Mussill, "The Baseball Bat: From the First Crack to the Clank," *Old-tyme Baseball News* 2 (1998), 21.

43. https://www.baseball-reference.com/teams/ATH/1871.shtml (accessed February 20, 2019).

44. *The Baseball Encyclopedia*, 8th edition, doesn't list Reach as a player because his career started and ended before the formation of the National League.

45. Magee and Shirley, *Sweet Spot*, 23.

46. Josh Leventhal, *A History of Baseball in 100 Objects: A Tour Through the Bats, Balls, Uniforms, Awards, Documents, and Other Artifacts That Tell the Story of the National Pastime* (New York: Black Dog & Leventhal, 2015), 60. Spalding purchased the A. J. Reach company in 1889 per Gutman, *Banana Bats*, 17.

47. https://www.baseball-reference.com/bullpen/A.J._Reach_Company (accessed October 3, 2017).

48. Rushin, *The 34-Ton Bat*, 94.

49. https://www.baseball-reference.com/bullpen/A.J._Reach_Company (accessed January 4, 2018).

50. http://www.ebay.com/bhp/reach-baseball (accessed October 10, 2017).

51. https://www.ebth.com/items/1437536-a-j-reach-bing-miller-baseball-bat (accessed October 10, 2017); Wolff, *The Baseball Encyclopedia*, 1235.

52. http://shiawasseehistory.com/zimmerman.html (accessed October 10, 2017); Magee and Shirley, *Sweet Spot*, 23.

53. https://www.sportscollectorsdaily.com/peck-and-snyder-the-company/ (accessed November 6, 2017).
54. Gutman, *Banana Bats*, 6.
55. https://www.sportscollectorsdaily.com/peck-and-snyder-the-company/ (accessed November 6, 2017).
56. http://keymancollectibles.com/bats/pontiacturningcobaseballbat.htm (accessed November 7, 2017).
57. http://keymancollectibles.com/bats/pontiacturningcobaseballbat.htm (accessed November 7, 2017).
58. http://keymancollectibles.com/bats/pontiacturningcobaseballbat.htm (accessed November 7, 2017); Wolff, *The Baseball Encyclopedia*, 764, 1062; 1121.
59. http://www.dugouttreasures.com/productDetail.cfm?sID=8&prodID=279 (accessed November 7, 2017); Wolff, 764–765.
60. Mussill, *The Baseball Bat*, 23.
61. *Ibid.*
62. Wolff, *The Baseball Encyclopedia*, 19, 936, 1408–1409.
63. https://goldenauctions.com/1930_1938_Lou_Gehrig_Hanna_Batrite_Bat___MEARS_A5_-LOT18223.aspx (accessed November 10, 2017).
64. https://www.sportscollectorsdaily.com/new-gehrig-bat-uncovered-was-used-as-homeowners-protection/ (accessed November 10, 2017).
65. https://sports.ha.com/itm/baseball-collectibles/bats/1930-eddie-collins-game-used-bat/a/7051-81428.s (accessed November 9, 2017); Wolff, *The Baseball Encyclopedia*, 786–787.
66. Gutman, *Banana Bats*, 26.

Chapter 4

1. http://www.nytimes.com/2013/05/26/sports/baseball/remembering-the-major-leaguers-who-died-in-world-war-ii.html (accessed January 14, 2018).
2. Stuart Miller, *Good Wood: The Story of the Baseball Bat* (Chicago: ACTA Publications, 2011), 114; David Magee and Philip Shirley, *Sweet Spot: 125 Years of Baseball and The Louisville Slugger* (Chicago: Triumph Books, 2009), 83, 90; 96–97.
3. https://www.baseball-reference.com/leaders/HR_careet.shtml (accessed August 25, 2017); Magee and Shirley, *Sweet Spot*, 76.
4. *Ibid.*, 92, 104.
5. https://www.mlb.com/news/louisville-slugger-retires-p72-bat-model-in-honor-of-derek-jeter/c-96195366 (accessed August 25, 2017).
6. Magee and Shirley, *Sweet Spot*, 148.
7. https://www.bizjournals.com/louisville/news/2015/03/23/wilson-sporting-goods-acquires-rights-to.html (accessed January 13, 2018); http://powerbilt.com/about-powerbilt-golf (accessed September 2, 2017).
8. https://www.newyorkupstate.com/news/2016/05/things_you_probably_didnt_know_were_invented_in_upstate_new_york.html; Jacob Pucci, undated, *"29 things you probably didn't know were invented in Upstate New York,"* May 2016.
9. Sean Kirst, "Cut from a family tree: Kren bats, used by legends, once made in Syracuse," *Syracuse Post-Standard*, October 25, 1995, http://www.syracuse.com/kirst/index.ssf/1995/10/cut_from_a_family_tree_kren_bats_used_by_baseball_legends_once_made_in_syracuse.html (accessed March 3, 2019).
10. *Ibid.*
11. *Ibid.*
12. Bernie Mussill, "The Baseball Bat: From the First Crack to the Clank," *Old-tyme Baseball News* 2 (1998), 24.
13. *Ibid.*
14. Steve Rushin, *The 34-Ton Bat* (New York: Little, Brown, 2013), 61–62; Mussill, 24.
15. Rick Wolff, *The Baseball Encyclopedia* (New York: Macmillan, 1990), 1529, 2189.
16. Miller, *Good Wood*, 41.
17. Rushin, *The 34-Ton Bat*, 61–62; Miller, 41.
18. www.foxsports.com/mlb/story/willie-mays-san-francisco-giants-600-career-homers-say-hey-kid-hall-of-fame-mvp-092215 (accessed November 22, 2017).
19. *Ibid.*
20. https://www.baseball-reference.com/bullpen/1977_World_Series (accessed March 9, 2019); Miller, *Good Wood*, 49–50, 118.
21. Miller, 49.

22. *Ibid.*, 50.

23. *Ibid.*

24. Richard Perez-Pena, "This Factory's Bats are Going, Going, Gone; As Home of McGwire's 'Big Stick,' Struggling Upstate Town Gets a Lift." *New York Times*, April 25, 1999, http://www.nytimes.com/1999/04/25/nyregion/this-factory-s-bats-are-going-going-gone-home-mcgwire-s-big-stick-struggling.html

25. *Ibid.*

26. *Ibid.*

27. Miller, 118; https://www.markewtwatch.com/story/rawlings-holder-angry-over-k2-pact-nintendo-in-buyout; https://en.wikipedia.org/wiki/K2_Sports (accessed March 18, 2018).

28. https://www.baseball-reference.com/players/m/mauerjo01.shtml (accessed on December 13, 2017).

29. https://www.baseball-reference.com/postseason/ (accessed on December 13, 2017).

30. Miller, *Good Wood*, 178; Rushin, *The 34-Ton Bat*, 67–68.

31. Magee and Shirley, *Sweet Spot*, 96–97.

32. *Ibid.*, 97–99.

33. *Ibid.*, 99, 106.

34. https://www.spaldingequipment.com/about.aspx; https://en.wikipedia.org/wiki/Spalding_(sports_equipment); http://www.spalding.com/about-spalding.html (accessed December 17, 2017).

35. http://www.news-press.com/story/sports/mlb/2014/03/22/bat-makers-look-to-hit-home-runs-with-players/6723579/ (accessed January 7, 2017).

36. Miller, *Good Wood*, 119–121; Stephen Cannella, "Against the Grain," *Sports Illustrated*, March 25, 2002, 87.

37. Miller, 121.

38. *Ibid.*

39. *Ibid.*, 122.

40. Cannella, 86.

41. *Ibid.*, 86–87.

42. https://www.cbsnews.com/news/marucci-bats-a-hit-with-pro-baseball-players/ (accessed March 9, 2019).

43. https://www.si.com/more-sports/2011/03/10/marucci-bats (accessed March 19, 2018).

44. Jack Marucci telephone interview, November 6, 2017.

45. Joe Lemire, "Marucci bats got from tool shed to clubhouse one convert at a time," *Sports Illustrated*, March 10, 2011. https://www.si.com/more-sports/2011/03/10/marucci-bats (accessed March 19, 2018).

46. *Ibid.*

47. *Ibid.*

48. Marucci interview.

49. Miller, *Good Wood*, 129; Lemire, "Marucci bats."

50. Miller, 129; Lemire, "Marucci bats."

51. Miller, 129–130; Marucci interview.

52. Miller, 130; https://maruccisports.com/about/ (accessed December 29, 2017).

53. Marucci interview, https://maruccisports.com/about/ (accessed December 30, 2017)

54. Joe Lemire, "Marucci bats"; Miller, 130.

55. Josh Norris, "Maruccci Sports Acquires Victus Sports," *Baseball America*, February 17, 2017; https://www.baseballamerica.com/business/marucci-sports-acquires-victus-sports/ (accessed December 31, 2017).

Chapter 5

1. R. Bruce Hoadley, *Understanding Wood* (Newtown, CT: Taunton Press, 2000), 7.

2. Frank Lloyd Wright, "In the Cause of Architecture: Wood," *The Architectural Record*, May 1928.

3. *Independent Sawmill & Woodlot*, April 2016, No. 144, 32–37.

4. *Ibid.*, 32.

5. *Ibid.*

6. *Ibid.*

7. Jim L. Bowyer, Rubin Shmulsky, and John Haygreen, *Forest Products and Wood Science: An Introduction*, 5th ed. (Ames, IA: Blackwell, 2007).

8. *Independent Sawmill & Woodlot*, April 2016, No. 144, 34.

9. John B. Sharp, *Wood Identification: A Manual for the Non-Professional* (Knoxville, TN: University of Tennessee, Agricultural Extension Service Publication 1389, 1990), 10; Hoadley, *Understanding Wood*, 11.

10. Jim Bowyer, personal communication, February 10, 2017.

11. *Independent Sawmill & Woodlot*, April 2016, No. 144, 34.

12. Hoadley, *Understanding Wood*, 16.

13. *Ibid.*, 14–15.

14. For the sake of simplicity, vessels will be referred to as pores for the remainder of this chapter.

15. For a discussion of vessels (pores), see Hoadley, 21.

16. Hoadley, 10.

17. John B. Sharp, *Wood Identification*, 10; Hoadley, 11.

18. http://www.woodbat.org/woodbat. pdf (accessed November 17, 2018); *Independent Sawmill & Woodlot*, April 2016, No. 144, 32–37.

19. David Magee and Phillip Shirley, *Sweet Spot: 125 Years of Baseball and The Louisville Slugger* (Chicago, Triumph Books, 2009), 68.

20. Stuart Miller, *Good Wood: The Story of the Baseball Bat* (ACTA Publications, Chicago, 2011), 20.

21. Miller, 13.

22. Filip Bondy, *The Pine Tar Game: The Kansas City Royals, the New York Yankees, and Baseball's Most Absurd and Entertaining Controversy* (New York: Scribner, 2015), 1.

23. Tim McCarver and Danny Peary, *Tim McCarver's Baseball for Brain Surgeons and Other Fans* (USA: Random House, 1998), 175.

24. Miller, *Good Wood*, 20.

25. *Ibid.*

26. U.S. Department of Agriculture, *Wood Handbook: Wood as an Engineering Material*, Forest Products Laboratory, General Technical Report FPL-GTR-113, Madison, WI: U.S. Department of Agriculture, 1999, 3–11, Table 4-3a, 4-8, 4-5a.

27. Hoadley, *Understanding Wood*, 14.

28. Bowyer, Shmulsky, and Haygreen, *Forest Products and Wood Science*, 201, 204, 236–239. (Ex: A block containing 50 percent void volume will resist crushing to a greater extent than a block with 75 percent void volume.)

29. Hoadley, *Understanding Wood*, 14.

30. Balsa is classified as a hardwood because it is a deciduous (broadleaf) tree. However, as an illustration, Southern yellow pine and Western larch are evergreen (needleleaf) trees and thus classified as softwoods even though both species have a higher density than balsa.

31. Stuart Miller, *Good Wood: The Story of the Baseball Bat* (Chicago: ACTA Publications, 2011), 92–93.

32. A. J. Panshin and Carl de Zeeuw, *Textbook of Wood Technology, Volume 1* (New York: McGraw-Hill, 1970), 4.

33. Bowyer, Shmulsky, and Haygreen. *Forest Products and Wood Science*, 204–211; personal communication with Dr. Jim Bowyer, February 10, 2017.

34. Robert Adair, *The Physics of Baseball, 3d ed.* (New York, Perennial, 2002), 114.

35. *Ibid.*

36. Bowyer et al., *Forest Products and Wood Science*, 171, 175.

37. https://www.nytimes.com/2012/09/25/sports/baseball/for-ichiro-suzuki-respect-for-bats-is-key-to-hitting.html; https://www.agedwoods.com/the-baseball-bat/; https://en.wikipedia.org/wiki/Baseball_bat (all sites accessed March 9, 2019).

38. Bowyer, et al., *Forest Products and Wood Science*, 242.

39. *Ibid.*, 167–168, 170, 175. Moisture content is based on freshly cut lumber that is completely void of water, which is termed oven-dry weight.

40. Miller, 137.

41. Bruce Hoadley, *Understanding Wood*, 12; John Sharp, *Wood Identification*, 8; A. J. Panshin and Carl de Zeeuw, *Textbook of Wood Technology, Volume 1* (New York: McGraw-Hill, 1970), 396.

42. https://sabr.org/research/properties-baseball-bats (accessed November 19, 2018).

43. Ted Williams, *My Turn at Bat: The Story of My Life (as told to John Underwood)* (New York: Simon and Schuster, 1969), 140.

44. Dan Gutman, *Banana Bats & Ding-Dong Balls: A Century of Unique Baseball Inventions* (New York: Macmillan, 1995), 34.

45. Adair, *Physics of Baseball*, 79–80.

46. Jim Collins, *The Last Best League: One Summer, One Season, One Dream* (Boston: De Capo Press, 2005), 86–87.

47. Williams, *The Science of Hitting*, 54–55.

48. *Ibid.*

49. https://www.phoenixbats.com/blog/difference-ash-maple-bats/; https://rundown.maruccisports.com/2015/07/08/maple-vs-ash/ (both sites accessed December 1, 2018).

50. Adair, *Physics of Baseball*, 114; *The Baseball Encyclopedia*, 8th edition, 1401, 1402; **https://maruccisports.com/the-rundown/maple-vs-ash/** published July 7, 2015 (accessed August 1, 2017).

51. https://www.nytimes.com/2007/07/12/sports/12iht-BATS.1.66 26195.html (accessed December 6, 2018).

52. *Ibid.*

Chapter 6

1. http://www.mlb.com/pa/pdf/health_advisory_120908.pdf; Technical Note http://www.woodbat.org/woodbat.pdf (both sites accessed October 11, 2018).

2. *Ibid.*

3. *Ibid.*

4. Wood and Wood Products, "Batting a Thousand," August 2008, 9.

5. https://www.sciencedirect.com/science/article/pii/S1877705812017183 (accessed November 12, 2018).

6. http://www.mlb.com/pa/pdf/health_advisory_120908.pdf; Technical Note http://www.woodbat.org/woodbat.pdf (both sites accessed on October 11, 2018).

7. http://www.mlb.com/pa/pdf/health_advisory_120908.pdf (accessed on October 11, 2018).

8. *Ibid.*

9. https://www.sciencedirect.com/science/article/pii/S1877705812017183 (accessed November 12, 2018).

10. http://www.mlb.com/pa/pdf/health_advisory_120908.pdf (accessed on October 11, 2018).

11. *Ibid.*

12. *USA Today*, May 25, 2005, 1C–2C.

13. *Ibid.*

14. https://www.livescience.com/2699-science-breaking-baseball-bats.html (accessed October 18, 2018).

15. https://www.yahoo.com/news/mlb-rules-cause-maple-bat-051500525--mlb.html (accessed October 19, 2018).

16. *Ibid.*

17. https://www.mlb.com. (accessed March 1, 2010.)

18. https://www.mlb.com/news/c-36046676/print (accessed November 2, 2018).

19. High-density maple correlated to .0245 lbs./cubic inch or higher mass to volume ratio, whereas a lower number translated to low-density maple (i.e., a weaker bat).

20. Telephone conversation with Scott Drake, April 18, 2018.

21. *Ibid.*

22. *Ibid.*

23. https://www.nytimes.com/2013/07/26/us/science-lowers-shattering-risk-at-home-plate.html?rref=collection%2Fbyline%2Ffelicity-barringer&action=click&contentCollection=undefined&region=stream&module=stream_unit&version=search&contentPlacement=1&pgtype=collection; https://www.reuters.com/article/us-usa-baseball-bats/unshattered-record-pro-baseball-bats-now-break-50-percent-less-usda-says-idUSBRE96B11320130713; https://www.bostonglobe.com/sports/2015/06/08/fenway-incident-puts-scrutiny-back-maple-bats/DTSOKWj3kR6621Fevq9wnN/story.html; https://www.chronicle.com/article/University-Scientists-Go-Extra/125223 (all sites accessed October 29, 2018).

24. https://www.chronicle.com/article/University-Scientists-Go-Extra/125223 (accessed October 30, 2018).

25. https://onwisconsin.uwalumni.com/on_alumni/bat-man/ (accessed October 31, 2018).

26. *Ibid*; https://www.mlb.com/news/c-36046676/print; http://www.espn.com/mlb/story/_/id/7275006/canadian-manufacturer-board-mlb-low-density-maple-bat-ban (accessed October 31, 2018).

27. https://www.mlb.com/news/c-36046676/print (accessed October 31, 2018). Note: The Timber Engineering Company (TECO) merged in 2015 with PFS (Product Fabrication Service Corporation) to form PFS TECO.

28. https://www.mlb.com/news/c-36046676/print (accessed October 31, 2018).

29. Many times the drop in youth bats

will be advertised in ounces, such as minus 3 oz.

30. https://www.sbnation.com/2012/2/29/2829452/new-rule-rookies-maple-bat-density (accessed November 5, 2018).

31. Miller, *Good Wood,* 95.

32. https://www.sbnation.com/2012/2/29/2829452/new-rule-rookies-maple-bat-density (accessed November 2, 2018).

33. http://www.espn.com/mlb/story/_/id/7275006/canadian-manufacturer-board-mlb-low-density-maple-bat-ban (accessed November 12, 2018).

34. https://www.nytimes.com/2013/07/26/us/science-lowers-shattering-risk-at-home-plate.html (accessed November 12, 2018).

35. https://www.sbnation.com/2012/2/29/2829452/new-rule-rookies-maple-bat-density (accessed November 4, 2018). Note: The Jason Rosenberg blog can be found at http://itsaboutthemoney.blogspot.com/2018/ (accessed November 4, 2018).

36. https://www.nytimes.com/2013/07/26/us/science-lowers-shattering-risk-at-home-plate.html (accessed November 6, 2018).

37. *Ibid.*

38. *Ibid.*

39. https://www.bostonglobe.com/sports/2015/06/08/fenway-incident-puts-scrutiny-back-maple-bats/DTSOKWj3kR6621Fevq9wnN/story.html (accessed November 7, 2018).

40. *Ibid.*

41. https://www.foxsports.com/mlb/story/ash-may-not-be-solution-to-baseballs-maple-bat-problem-092110 (accessed November 10, 2018).

42. https://www.bostonglobe.com/sports/2015/06/08/fenway-incident-puts-scrutiny-back-maple-bats/DTSOKWj3kR6621Fevq9wnN/story.html (accessed November 7, 2018).

Chapter 7

1. http://www.historynet.com/president-william-mckinley-assassinated-by-an-anarchist.htm; www.eyewitnesstohistory.com/mckinley.htm (both sites accessed March 24, 2018).

2. *Ibid.*

3. http://www.historynet.com/president-william-mckinley-assassinated-by-an-anarchist.htm (accessed March 24, 2018).

4. *Forest Products Journal,* January 1995, 18.

5. The one-third estimate does not include trees in urban areas such as along streets, parks, cemeteries, and so forth.

6. Douglas MacCleery, "Resiliency: The Trademark of American Forests," *Forest Products Journal* 45:1 (1995): 1–22.

7. *Ibid.* For a detailed description of U.S. forests, see entire volume of Douglas MacCleery, *American Forests: A History of Resiliency and Recovery* (Forest History Society, 2011), 70.

8. MacCleery, *Resiliency,* 23–25.

9. https://en.wikipedia.org/wiki/Theodore_Roosevelt (accessed March 22, 2018). Also, see link for more information on Theodore Roosevelt.

10. Candice Millard, *The River of Doubt: Theodore Roosevelt's Darkest Journey* (New York: Broadway Books, 2005), 22–25.

11. Char Miller, *Journal of Forestry* 114:1 (2016): 75–76.

12. James Buckley, *America's Classic Ballparks* (San Diego: Thunder Bay Press, 2013), 15.

13. http://mlb.mlb.com/mlb/history/postseason/mlb_ws_recaps.jsp?feature=1909 (accessed March 1, 2019).

14. MacCleery, *Resiliency,* 22, 26–28.

15. Wolff, *The Baseball Encyclopedia,* 964, 1779; MacCleery, 26–28.

16. MacCleery, 29–46.

17. www.dovetailinc.org/report_pdfs/2012/dovetailusforests0312.pdf Dovetail/Bratkovich, 3–4.

18. https://www.fia.fs.fed.us/program-features/rpa/docs/2017RPAFIATABLESFINAL_050918.pdf; https://usforests.maps.arcgis.com/apps/Cascade/index.html?appid=d80a4ffed7e044219bbd973a77bea8e6 (both sites accessed December 14, 2018).

19. https://www.fia.fs.fed.us/program-features/rpa/docs/2017RPAFIATABLESFINAL_050918.pdf; https://usforests.maps.arcgis.com/apps/Cascade/index.html?app

id=d80a4ffed7e044219bbd973a77bea8e6 (both sites accessed December 14, 2018).

20. https://www.fia.fs.fed.us/program-features/rpa/docs/2017RPAFIATABLES FINAL_050918.pdf (accessed December 11, 2018). The Pacific Coast region had a decline of timber growing stock of less than 2 percent from 1953 to 2017.

21. *Ibid.* Also, Southern and West Coast states have been impacted, to the detriment of their forestland, by urban expansion and development into forested areas. See http://www.dovetailinc.org/report_pdfs/2012/dovetailusforests0312.pdf (accessed December 11, 2018), 5.

22. William Harlow and Ellwood Harrar, *Textbook of Dendrology, 5th ed.* (New York: McGraw-Hill, 1969), 6, 445.

23. Green, black, blue, and Oregon ash all have two or more properties that are substandard when compared to white ash. These properties include density, impact bending strength, distribution, and tree form (straightness of trunk, which is the prime baseball bat location on the tree). For additional information, see Harlow and Harrar, 442–450, and *Wood Handbook*, Table 4-3a. (The latter can be found at: https://www.fpl.fs.us/documnts/fplgtr/fpl_gtr190.pdf.)

24. Harlow and Harrar, *Textbook of Dendrology,* 442–450.

25. *Ibid.,* 445; Luppold and Pugh, *Forest Products Journal,* 60–61. Note: Tree width or diameter is measured 4½ feet from the ground.

26. https://www.fs.fed.us/nrs/pubs/ru/ru_fs132.pdf (accessed December 19, 2018).

27. https://www.fs.fed.us/nrs/pubs/ru/ru_fs170.pdf (accessed December 20, 2018).

28. Harlow and Harrar, *Textbook of Dendrology,* 445–446.

29. Gutman, *Banana Bats,* 27; and Harlow and Harrar, 446.

30. Harlow and Harrar, 445; Luppold and Pugh, *Forest Products Journal,* 60–61.

31. https://www.fs.fed.us/nrs/pubs/ru/ru_fs132.pdf (accessed December 19, 2018).

32. https://www.fs.fed.us/nrs/pubs/ru/ru_fs170.pdf (accessed December 20, 2018).

33. Harlow and Harrar, *Textbook of Dendrology,* 266.

34. *Ibid.,* 405–407.

35. *Ibid.,* 407.

36. The winged fruit of red (*Acer rubrum*) and silver (*Acer saccharinum*) maples drop from the trees in the spring.

37. The species and geographical distribution of birch in North America is confined to birch *trees,* not *shrubs.*

38. It is not uncommon for trees to produce large seed crops approximately every three+ years.

39. https://www.fs.fed.us/nrs/pubs/ru/ru_fs170.pdf (accessed December 20, 2018).

40. Black birch also produces wintergreen oil, as do other plants like the evergreen shrub and teaberry (*Gaultheria procumbens*).

41. https://www.giss.nasa.gov/research/news/20170118/; https://www.fs.fed.us/nrs/news/review/review-vol11.pdf (both sites accessed December 26, 2018).

42. https://www.fs.fed.us/nrs/news/review/review-vol11.pdf (accessed December 26, 2018).

43. http://advances.sciencemag.org/content/3/5/e1603055; https://www.nrs.fs.fed.us/pubs/jrnl/2009/nrs_2009_woodall_001.pdf. Both are examples of published studies. (Both sites accessed on December 23, 2018.)

44. https://www.nrs.fs.fed.us/pubs/jrnl/2009/nrs_2009_woodall_001.pdf (accessed December 26, 2018).

Chapter 8

1. Jessica Simons, *Sawmill & Woodlot Magazine,* January 2007; 2016 personal communication.

2. Much of this paragraph is adapted from the Forest History article Robert Haack, Yuri Baranchikov, Leah Bauer, and Therese Poland, "Emerald Ash Borer Biology and Invasion History" in *Biology and Control of Emerald Ash Borer,* eds. Roy G. Van Driesche and Richard C. Reardon (Washington, D.C.: USDA Forest Service, 2015) 1–13. https://www.fs.fed.us/foresthealth/technology/pdfs/

FHTET-2014-09_Biology_Control_EAB.pdf (accessed January 20, 2019).

3. Joseph Beckwith, USDA-APHIS (Webinar, "National Perspective on EAB").

4. Jessica Simons, email on September 28, 2017.

5. http://www.syracuse.com/kirst/index.ssf/2014/10/at_world_series_time_in_dolgeville_baseball_history_has_turned_on_this_plant.html (accessed January 25, 2017).

6. Interestingly, and unknown by most, is that an EAB-infested ash still contains usable wood. Since the EAB kills its host by working just underneath the bark layer of a tree, the wood is undamaged. In the short-term (up to 1–2 years), dead or dying trees can still be made into products like cabinets, flooring, and baseball bats. Of course, EAB puts the future sustainability of any industry that uses ash trees at risk.

7. As of 2017, The Nature Conservancy had many initiatives and partners in its "Do Not Move Firewood" campaign. Its website serves as a hub for national information on firewood movement. https://www.nature.org/ourinitiatives/habitats/forests/explore/firewood-buy-it-where-you-burn-it.xml and https://www.dontmovefirewood.org/about/ (accessed April 26, 2017).

8. Stuart Miller, *Good Wood: The Story of the Baseball Bat* (Chicago: ACTA Publications, 2011), 98.

9. Dave Boyt, "Invasive Bugs," *Sawmill & Woodlot.* May/June 2016, 11–14. The reference to PSU and the range of EAB in 2016 is from Matt Swayne, "Invasion!" *Penn State Ag Science* 18 (Fall/Winter 2016).

10. https://www.aphis.usda.gov/plant_health/plant_pest_info/asian_lhb/downloads/response-guidelines.pdf (accessed January 31, 2017).

11. Swayne, 18.

12. https://www.aphis.usda.gov/aphis/resources/pests-diseases/asian-longhorned-beetle/About-ALB (accessed January 27, 2017).

13. Steven Katovich, Forest Entomologist, USDA Forest Service, St. Paul, MN. Personal communication on March 6, 2017.

14. Dennis Haugen, Forest Entomologist, USDA Forest Service, St. Paul, MN. Personal communication on March 2, 2017. The goal for ALB is "eradication," thus removing infested trees if possible; for EAB (which is beyond eradicating in North America), the goal is "management," although it has not been very successful to date.

15. http://www.uvm.edu/~albeetle/management/eradicationmgt.html (accessed January 31, 2017).

16. Dave Boyt, "Invasive Bugs," *Sawmill & Woodlot* (May/June 2016), 14.

17. *Ibid.*, 11–14.

18. *Ibid.*, 14.

19. *Ibid.*, 11–12.

20. Charles Becker, "The Invasives are Coming," *Sawmill & Woodlot* (Dec./Jan. 2007), 18.

21. www.whatproswear.com (accessed June 15, 2016.) The Trumbo bat was a PS 27:1 model.

22. http://www.trinitybatco.com/wood-types/ (accessed February 3, 2017)

23. Scott Drake, personal communication, January 4, 2017.

24. https://www.birchbats.com/why-swing-birch.php (accessed February 3, 2017).

25. https://www.maxbats.com/blog/differences-maple-bats-birch-bats/ (accessed February 2, 2017).

26. https://www.aphis.usda.gov/plant_health/plant_pest_info/asian_lhb/downloads/hostlist.pdf (accessed March 12, 2017).

Chapter 9

1. Magee and Shirley, *Sweet Spot: 125 Years of Baseball and The Louisville Slugger* (Chicago: Triumph Books, 2009), 135.

2. In simple terms, a logger cuts trees and builds trails to move the wood out of the forest. Foresters manage forests to meet ownership goals.

3. Collin Miller interview, November 10, 2017. LTP was originally organized in 1994; the billet entity was founded in 2009.

4. http://www.leatherstockinghandsplits.com/about-us.aspx (accessed January 23, 2018).

5. Collin Miller interview, November 10, 2017.

6. *Ibid.*

7. *Ibid.*

8. Bob Hill, *Crack of the Bat: The Louisville Slugger Story* (Champaign, IL: Sports Publishing, 2002), 108.

9. Collin Miller interview, November 10, 2017.

10. Magee and Shirley, *Sweet Spot*, 80.

11. Collin Miller interview, November 10, 2017.

12. Magee and Shirley, *Sweet Spot*, 80.

13. Collin Miller interview, November 10, 2017.

14. Stuart Miller, *Good Wood: The Story of the Baseball Bat* (Chicago: ACTA Publications, 2011), 134.

15. Jack Marucci, Personal interview, November 6, 2017.

16. Hill, *Crack of the Bat*, 108. One board foot of wood is 144 cubic inches.

17. Collin Miller interview, November 10, 2017.

18. Miller, *Good Wood*, 133; Collin Miller interview.

19. Miller interview, November 10, 2017.

20. *Ibid.*

21. *Ibid.*

22. *Ibid.*

23. *Ibid.*

24. *Ibid.*

25. *Ibid.*

26. *Ibid.*

27. *Ibid.*

28. *Ibid.*

29. *Ibid.*

30. Hill, *Crack of the Bat*, 114.

31. Miller interview, November 10, 2017.

32. *Ibid.*

33. *Ibid.*

34. *Ibid.*; Hill, *Crack of the Bat*, 114.

35. Hill, *Crack of the Bat*, 114.

36. http://factsheets.okstate.edu/documents/fapc-146-fundamental-aspects-of-kiln-drying-lumber/ (accessed January 30, 2018).

37. Collin Miller interview, November 10, 2017.

38. Peter Morris, *A Game of Inches: The Story Behind the Innovations That Shaped Baseball* (Chicago: Ivan R. Dee, 2010), 284.

39. http://www.vacdry.com; http:// factsheets.okstate.edu/documents/fapc-146-fundamental-aspects-of-kiln-drying-lumber/ (accessed January 30, 2018).

40. https://www.americanwood technology.com/vacuum-kiln-plants/ (accessed January 30, 2018).

41. https://www.fpl.fs.fed.us/documents/fplgtr/fplgtr118.pdf (accessed January 31, 2018).

42. Collin Miller interview, November 10, 2017.

43. *Ibid.*

44. *Ibid.*

45. *Ibid.*

46. *Ibid.*

47. *Ibid.*

48. *Ibid.*

49. *Ibid.*

Chapter 10

1. Dave Chandler of Chandler Bats, Personal interview, April 4, 2018.

2. The handling of billets upon arrival at the bat-making factory can vary between manufacturers, but the process is generally as described in the text.

3. https://www.mlb.com/news/lighter-bat-means-farther-homers-for-stanton/c-61118846 (accessed February 6, 2019).

4. William Jaspersohn, *Bat, Ball, Glove: The Making of Major League Baseball Gear* (Boston: Little, Brown, 1989), 73–77; Bob Hill, *Crack of the Bat: The Louisville Slugger Story* (Champaign, IL: Sports Publishing, 2002), 120–125.

5. Stuart Miller, *Good Wood: The Story of the Baseball Bat* (Chicago: ACTA Publications, 2011), 134–135.

6. *Ibid.*, 135.

7. Tom Lepperd ed., *Official Baseball Rules* (New York: Office of the Commissioner of Baseball, 2018), 5.

8. Stuart Miller, *Good Wood*, 88.

9. Dan Gutman, *Banana Bats & Ding Dong Balls: A Century of Unique Baseball Inventions* (New York: Macmillan, 1995), 26.

10. Bernie Mussill, "The Baseball Bat: From the First Crack to the Clank," *Oldtyme Baseball News* 2 (1998): 25.

11. Robert Adair, *The Physics of Base-*

ball, 3d ed. (New York: Perennial, 2002), xv.

12. *Ibid.*, 120–121, 136.

13. Robert Watts and A. Terry Bayhill, *Keep Your Eye on the Ball: The Science and Folklore of Baseball* (New York: W. H. Freeman, 1991).

14. http://sabr.org./research/properties-baseball-bats, 8.

15. Adair, *The Physics of Baseball*, 119–120.

16. Jaspersohn, *Bat, Ball, Glove*, 76.

17. Miller, *Good Wood*, 135; Hill, 125; Jaspersohn, 76.

18. Ted Williams, *My Turn at Bat: The Story of My Life* (New York: Simon and Schuster, 1969), 54, 173; Hill, *Crack of the Bat*, 54.

19. Miller, *Good Wood*, 27.

20. "Boning or ... for decades." A patent, awarded to the Hillerich & Bradsby Co. (at the time the J. F. Hillerich & Sons firm), was granted in 1902, for the purpose of hardening the surface of the bat. See https://text-message.blogs.archives.gov/2015/04/03/baseball-patents/ (accessed on April 19, 2018).

21. Miller, *Good Wood*, 27.

22. *Ibid.*

23. *Ibid.*, 135.

24. *Ibid.*, 27–28.

25. *Ibid.*, 28.

26. George Diaz, "Player's Best Friend? How About His Bat?" *Chicago Tribune,* May 1, 1988. https://www.chicagotribune.com/news/ct-xpm-1988-05-01-8803130672-story.html (accessed March 9, 2019).

27. Miller, *Good Wood*, 27.

28. Adair, *The Physics of Baseball*, 82.

29. Miller, *Good Wood*, 27.

30. Dave Chandler of Chandler Bats, interview April 4, 2018.

31. *Ibid.*

32. Hill, *Crack of the Bat*, 126.

33. Miller, *Good Wood*, 30–31.

34. *Ibid.*, 31–32.

35. Hill, *Crack of the Bat*, 126, 128–129.

36. Lepperd, ed., *Official Baseball Rules 2018*, 5; https://www.foxsports.com/mlb/story/after-dropping-ball-on-pink-bats-last-year-mlb-moves-to-get-it-right-050714 (accessed March 9, 2019); https://en.wikipedia.org/wiki/Pink_bat (accessed May 16, 2018).

37. Jaspersohn, *Bat, Ball, Glove*, 79.

38. Magee and Shirley, *Sweet Spot*, 25.

39. *Ibid.*

40. *Ibid.* Note: Eddie Collins and Home Run Baker were other early bat signees by Louisville Slugger (Miller, *Good Wood*, 2011), 111.

41. Miller, 111; Magee and Shirley, 25, 45, 135.

42. Dave Chandler interview, April 4, 2018.

43. Diffuse-porous and ring-porous wood species were discussed in Chapter 5.

44. The tangential side of a bat was discussed in Chapter 5.

45. https://www.nytimes.com/1999/04/25/nyregion/this-factory-s-bats-are-going-going-gone-home-mcgwire-s-big-stick-struggling.html (accessed April 26, 2018).

46. https://www.baseball-reference.com/players/s/seweljo01.shtml (accessed September 14, 2018).

47. Gutman, *Banana Bats*, 18.

48. https://www.sportsbusinessdaily.com/Daily/Issues/2017/05/10/Marketing-and-Sponsorship/Louisville-Slugger-Jeter.aspx (accessed April 25, 2018).

Chapter 11

1. Ted Williams and John Underwood, *The Science of Hitting* (New York: Simon & Schuster, 1970), 42.

2. https://www.poughkeepsiejournal.com/story/sports/recreational/2018/04/25/dover-mans-axe-bat-invention-gains-major-league-following/549446002/; J. Beckham, Baseball Bat with an Axe Handle Brings More Power, Fewer Injuries. Wired, 2014. https://www.wired.com/2014/08/axe-bat/ (both sites accessed November 21, 2018).

3. *Ibid.*; https://axebat.com/blogs/news/from-the-lab-creating-the-perfect-handle; https://www.masslive.com/redsox/index.ssf/2016/05/dustin_pedroia_mookie_betts_us.html#incart_river_index (both sites accessed January 7, 2019).

4. https://proxr.com/the-knob/ (accessed January 4, 2019).

5. *Ibid.*

6. "3 things to know about axe bat reviews." The baseball bat review site.

https://www.baseballbatreviews.org/bbcor-bats/axe-bat-reviews/ (accessed November 21, 2018).

7. Vijay Gupta, "Biomechanical study of the new axe handle baseball bats and comparison with standard round knob bats." Baden Sports, 2014. https://cdn.shopify.com/s/files/1/0134/8092/t/5/assets/AXE_Bat_Study_4_10_14.pdf (accessed November 21, 2018).

8. Axebat. "Why the axe handle is better." https://axebat.com/pages/technology (accessed November 21, 2018).

9. "The grip—It starts with the hands." Be a Better Hitter. https://www.beabetterhitter.com/the-grip-it-starts-with-the-hands/ (accessed November 21, 2018).

10. Grady Phelan, "Baseball's broken hamate plague." ProXR Information. http://proxr.com/baseballs-broken-hamate-plague/ (accessed November 21, 2018).

11. *Ibid.*, (accessed January 5, 2019).

12. Jen McCaffrey, "Dustin Pedroia, Mookie Betts using Axe Bat to prevent injury, improve swing and offense." MassLive. https://www.masslive.com/redsox/index.ssf/2016/05/dustin_pedroia_mookie_betts_us.html (accessed November 21, 2018).

13. Vijay Gupta, "Biomechanical study of the new axe handle baseball bats and comparison with standard round knob bats." Baden Sports. https://cdn.shopify.com/s/files/1/0134/8092/t/5/assets/AXE_Bat_Study_4_10_14.pdf (accessed November 21, 2018).

14. Note: The six categories pertained to Baden Sports' patented Axe Bat. Dr. Gupta's study did not investigate the ProXR patented design, although many features are the same as the Axe Bat.

15. Note: Performance is defined broadly as relating to swing kinematics and handle effects, such as swing efficiency, ability to meet pitches effectively, and added swing force due to comfort.

16. Ted Berg, "Dustin Pedroia is on a hot streak with an odd-looking bat designed to help hitters." *USA Today.* https://ftw.usatoday.com/2015/06/boston-red-sox-dustin-pedroia-axe-bat-knob-mlb (accessed November 21, 2018).

17. Note: Hamate bone fractures have sent dozens of MLB players to the disabled list.

18. K. Hilton, "How an axe-handle bat is going to take over baseball." *Popular Science.* https://www.popsci.com/how-an-axe-handled-bat-is-going-to-take-over-baseball (accessed November 21, 2018).

19. https://ftw.usatoday.com/2015/06/boston-red-sox-dustin-pedroia-axe-bat-knob-mlb (accessed January 7, 2019).

20. Ted Berg, "Dustin Pedroia is on a hot streak with an odd-looking bat designed to help hitters." *USA Today.* https://ftw.usatoday.com/2015/06/boston-red-sox-dustin-pedroia-axe-bat-knob-mlb (accessed November 21, 2018).

21. Grant McAuley, "Axe handle bat new weapon of choice for Braves' Swanson." Radio.com https://929thegame.radio.com/articles/axe-handle-bat-new-weapon-choice-braves-swanson (accessed November 21, 2018).

22. "Should I be swinging an axe bat?" BaseballMonkey Blog, 2018. http://blog.baseballmonkey.com/should-i-be-swinging-an-axe-bat/ (accessed November 21, 2018).

23. T. Booth, "Get a grip: Axe Bat is trying to revolutionize baseball bats." *Associated Press.* https://www.denverpost.com/2018/04/25/axe-handle-bats-major-league-baseball/ (accessed November 21, 2018).

24. "Should I be swinging an axe bat?" BaseballMonkey Blog, 2018. http://blog.baseballmonkey.com/should-i-be-swinging-an-axe-bat/ (accessed November 21, 2018).

25. https://www.poughkeepsiejournal.com/story/sports/recreational/2018/04/25/dover-mans-axe-bat-invention-gains-major-league-following/549446002/ (accessed January 6, 2019); https://axebat.com/blogs/news/all-star-mvp-george-springer-partners-with-axe-bat) (accessed January 7, 2019).

26. Ted Berg, "Dustin Pedroia is on a hot streak with an odd-looking bat designed to help hitters." *USA Today.* https://ftw.usatoday.com/2015/06/boston-red-sox-dustin-pedroia-axe-bat-knob-mlb (accessed November 21, 2018).

27. https://proxr.com/about/ (accessed January 3, 2019); http://proxr.com/wp-

content/uploads/2017/05/Jay-Williamson-Joins-ProXR-Board-5_24_17.pdf (accessed January 4, 2019).

28. http://tedquarters.net/2010/09/07/qa-with-grady-phelan-bat-inventor/; http://proxr.com/wp-content/uploads/2010/03/KUAlumniGrady BatRevisedT.jpg (both sites accessed January 7, 2019).

29. https://proxr.com/about/ (accessed January 3, 2019).

30. *Ibid.*

31. Axe Bat Team. Axe Bat U.S. Personal communication, November 8, 2018.

32. https://proxr.com; https://www.poughkeepsiejournal.com/story/sports/recreational/2018/04/25/dover-mans-axe-bat-invention-gains-major-league-following/549446002/ (both sites accessed January 6, 2019).

Appendix

1. Jim Bowyer, et al. *Forest Products and Wood Science: An Introduction,* 5th ed. (Ames, IA: Blackwell, 2007), 126, 435.

2. Karl F. Wenger, ed., *Forestry Handbook: Second Edition* (New York: John Wiley & Sons, 1984), 628; Peter Koch, *Utilization of the Southern Pines Volume 2* (Washington, DC: United States Department of Agriculture—Forest Service, Agriculture Handbook—420, 1486; https://www.merriam-webster.com/dictionary/tar%20oil; https://www.puuvene.net/phuhta/artikkelit/tar.html (both sites accessed March 13, 2019).

3. https://blog.justbats.com/what-is-pine-tar-what-does-pine-tar-do (accessed February 15, 2019).

4. https://www.nps.gov/mocr/learn/historyculture/upload/Naval-Stores.pdf (accessed March 13, 2019).

5. Miller, *Good Wood*, 105; https://www.baseball-reference.com/bullpen/Bat (accessed February 18, 2019).

6. https://blog.justbats.com/what-is-pine-tar-what-does-pine-tar-do, https://en.wikipedia.org/wiki/Pine_tar; http://digg.com/2014/what-is-pine-tar-and-why-is-it-illegal-in-baseball (accessed February 15, 2019).

7. https://en.wikipedia.org/wiki/Pine_tar (accessed February 15, 2019).

8. https://museum.unc.edu/faqs (accessed March 13, 2019).

9. https://www.nps.gov/mocr/learn/historyculture/upload/Naval-Stores.pdf (accessed March 13, 2019).

10. http://digg.com/2014/what-is-pine-tar-and-why-is-it-illegal-in-baseball (accessed February 15, 2019).

11. https://www.muddyandinca.com/pine-tar-reg.html?gclid=EAIaIQobChMI2I-Pqpm-4AIVE4TICh2IAAYOEAQYBSABEgJXj_D_BwE (accessed February 15, 2019).

12. Lepperd, Tom, ed. *Official Baseball Rules: 2018 Edition* (New York: Office of the Commissioner of Baseball, 2018).

13. https://www.mlb.com/news/yankees-right-hander-michael-pineda-ejected-for-having-pine-tar-on-neck/c-73145346; Bryan Hoch, "Pineda ejected for having pine tar on neck," mlb.com, April 24, 2014 (accessed March 15, 2019).

14. http://www.vintagebats.com/feature_page-JoeMauer.htm (accessed February 18, 2019).

15. https://goldinauctions.com/2018_Manny_Machado_Game_Used_Rawlings_MY13_Pro_Mod-lot47031.aspx (accessed February 18, 2019).

16. https://goldinauctions.com/2018_Kris_Bryant_Game_Used___Signed_Victus_Pro_Mod-lot46791.aspx (accessed February 18, 2019).

17. https://www.lavidabaseball.com/manny-ramirez-helmet-hall-of-fame/ (accessed March 15, 2019) (accessed January 2019).

18. https://mlblogsmoresplashhits.wordpress.com/2013/04/09/have-you-ever-wondered-whats-up-with-all-that-gunk-on-pablo-sandovals-helmet/ (accessed March 15, 2019).

19. Rashmi Sunder, "What Is a Rosin Bag and How Is It Used in Different Sports?" SportsAspire. February 26, 2018. https://sportsaspire.com/what-is-rosin-bag-how-is-it-used-in-different-sports https://sportsaspire.com/what-is-rosin-bag-how-is-it-used-in-different-sports (accessed March 15, 2019).

20. Jim Bowyer, et al. *Forest Products and Wood Science,* 5th edition, 435; Karl Wenger, *Forestry Handbook*, 628.

21. Rashmi Sunder, "What Is a Rosin Bag and How Is It Used in Different Sports?" SportsAspire. February 26, 2018. https://sportsaspire.com/what-is-rosin-bag-how-is-it-used-in-different-sports (accessed March 15, 2019).

22. Quinn Roberts, "Growing number of hitters ditching batting gloves," mlb. com, July 16, 2015. https://www.mlb.com/news/growing-number-of-hitters-ditch-batting-gloves/c-136913172 (accessed March 15, 2019).

23. Peter Morris, *A Game of Inches: The Story Behind the Innovations That Shaped Baseball* (Chicago: Ivan R. Dee, 2010), 309–312.

Bibliography

Interviews

Charles Blinn (professor and extension specialist, Department of Forest Resources, University of Minnesota), August 4, 2018.

Jim Bowyer (retired professor of bioproducts and biosystems engineering, University of Minnesota), February 10, 2017.

David Chandler, (founder, Chandler Bats), April 4, 2018.

Greg Connor (painter and finisher, BWP Bats) and Josh Johnson (vice president, BWP Bats), September 12, 2018, and September 14, 2018.

Scott Drake (vice president of business operations, PFS Teco, January 4, 2017), April 5, 2017, and April 18, 2018.

Roland Hernandez (wood scientist and former baseball bat manufacturer), January 31, 2019.

Matt Kent (owner, Leatherstocking Hand-Split Billet Co.) and Dave Rama (sales director, Leatherstocking Hand-Split Billet Co.), November 10, 2017, and June 1, 2018.

James Lewis (historian, Forest History Center), March 8, 2019.

Phil Lowry (baseball historian), August 25, 2018.

Jack Marucci (founder, Marucci Sports), November 6, 2017, and February 21, 2019.

Collin Miller (New York City Watershed forester), November 10, 2017, and February 25, 2019.

Ron Selter (baseball historian), August 25, 2018.

Jessica Simons (forester and owner, Verdant Stewardship, November 22, 2016), April 10, 2017 and September 28, 2017.

Stew Thornley (official scorer, Minnesota Twins), December 6, 2018.

Rick Wriskey (retired forester, City of New Brighton, Minnesota), July 22, 2017.

Books and Articles

"1977 World Series." Baseball-reference.com, January 15, 2018. Accessed March 9, 2019. https://www.baseball-reference.com/bullpen/1977_World_Series .

2018 Manny Machado Game Used Rawlings MY13 Pro Model Bat. Goldin Auctions. Accessed February 18, 2019. https://goldinauctions.com/2018_Manny_Machado_Game_Used_Rawlings_MY13-Pro_Mod-lot47031.aspx.

2018 Kris Bryant Game Used & Signed Victus Pro Model Bat. Goldin Auctions. Accessed February 18, 2019. https://goldinauctions.com/2018_Kris_Bryant_Game_Used__Signed_Victus_Pro_Mod-lot46791.aspx.

1930 Eddie Collins Game Used Bat. Accessed November 9, 2017. https://sports.ha.com/itm/baseball-collectibles/bats/1930-eddie-collins-game-used-bat/a/7051-81428.s.

Bibliography

1930–1938 Lou Gehrig Hanna Batrite Bat. Goldin Auctions. Accessed November 10, 2017. https://goldinauctions.com/1930_1938_Lou_Gehrig_Hanna_Batrite_Bat___ MEARS_A5_-LOT18223.aspx.

"About." DontMoveFirewood.org. Accessed August 26, 2018. https://www.dont movefirewood.org/about.

"About Spalding Equipment." Accessed December 17, 2017. https://www.spalding equipment.com/about.aspx.

"About Us." Leatherstocking Hand-Split Billet Company. Accessed January 23, 2018. http://www.leatherstockinghandsplits.com/about-us.aspx.

Adair, Robert. *The Physics of Baseball.* 3d ed. New York: Perennial, 2002.

"A. J. Reach, Bing Miller Baseball Bat." Accessed October 10, 2017. https://www.ebth. com/items/1437536-a-j-reach-bing-miller-baseball-bat.

"A. J. Reach Company." Baseball-reference.com. Accessed October 3, 2017. https:// www.baseball-reference.com/bullpen/A.J._Reach_Company.

Albright, Thomas A. *Forests of Pennsylvania, 2016. Resource Update FS-132.* Newtown Square, PA: U.S. Department of Agriculture, Forest Service, Northern Research Station. Accessed December 19, 2018. https://www.fs.fed.us/nrs/pubs/ru/ru_fs132.pdf.

_____.*Forests of New York, 2016. Resource Update FS-141.* Newtown Square, PA: U.S. Department of Agriculture, Forest Service, Northern Research Station. Accessed December 20, 2018. https://www.fs.fed.us/nrs/pubs/ru/ru_fs141.pdf.

_____. *Forests of New York, 2017. Resource Update FS-170.* Newtown Square, PA: U.S. Department of Agriculture, Forest Service, Northern Research Station. Accessed December 20, 2018. https://www.fs.fed.us/nrs/pubs/ru/ru_fs170.pdf.

Allen, John. "Bat Man." *On Wisconsin,* Fall 2011. Accessed October 31, 2018. https:// onwisconsin.uwalumni.com/on_alumni/bat-man/.

Alverez, Mila. "*Who Owns America's Forests?*" U.S. Endowment for Forestry and Communities, 2017. Accessed December 14, 2018. https://usforests.maps.arcgis. com/apps/Cascade/index.html?appid=d80a4ffed7e044219bbd973a77bea8e6.

Andrews, Kacky. "*Our Initiatives, Habitats, Forests, Explore, Firewood...*" The Nature Conservancy. Accessed April 26, 2017. [The Nature Conservancy website serves as a hub for national information on firewood movement.] https://www.nature. org/ourinitiatives/habitats/forests/explore/firewood-buy-it-where-you-burn-it. xml and https://www.dontmovefirewood.org/about/. Accessed on April 26, 2017.

"Asian Longhorned Beetle: Annotated Host List." U.S. Department of Agriculture, January 2015. Accessed August 26, 2018. https://www.aphis.usda.gov/plant_health/ plant_pest_info/asian_lhb/downloads/hostlist.pdf.

"Asian Longhorned Beetle Eradication." University of Vermont. Accessed January 31, 2017. http://www.uvm.edu/~albeetle/management/eradicationmgt.html.

Associated Press. "Maple Bat Maker OK with MLB Ban." ESPN, November 23, 2011. http://www.espn.com/mlb/story/_/id/7275006/canadian-manufacturer-board-mlb-low-density-maple-bat-ban.

Axe Bat. "From the Lab: Creating the Perfect Handle." Axe Bat, February 1, 2015. Accessed January 7, 2019. https://axebat.com/blogs/news/from-the-lab-creating-the-perfect-handle.

_____. "Why the Axe Handle Is Better." Axe Bat, accessed November 21, 2018. https://axebat.com/pages/technology.

Axe Bat Admin. "All Star MVP George Springer Partners with Axe Bat." Axe Bat, December 14, 2017. Accessed January 7, 2019. https://axebat.com/blogs/news/all-star-mvp-george-springer-partners-with-axe-bat.

Bibliography

Axe Bat Review Team. "Axe Bat Reviews." Baseball Bat Reviews, 2018. Accessed November 21, 2018. https://www.baseballbatreviews.org/bbcor-bats/axe-bat-reviews/.

Bahr, Chris. "Willie Mays Becomes Second Player with 600 Homers." Fox Sports, September 22, 2015. Accessed November 22, 2017. www.foxsports.com/mlb/story/willie-mays-san-francisco-giants-600-career-homers-say-hey-kid-hall-of-fame-mvp-092215.

Baker, Billy. "Fenway Incident Puts Scrutiny Back in Maple Bats." *Boston Globe*, June 9, 2015. Accessed October 29, 2018. https://www.bostonglobe.com/sports/2015/06/08/fenway-incident-puts-scrutiny-back-maple-bats/DTS OKWj3kR6621Fevq9wnN/story.html.

Barringer, Felicity. "Science Lowers Shattering Risk at Home Plate." *New York Times*, July 26, 2013. Accessed October 29, 2018. https://www.nytimes.com/2013/07/26/us/science-lowers-shattering-risk-at-home-plate.html?rref=collection%2Fbyline%-2Ffelicity-barringer&action=click&contentCollection=undefined&region=stream &module=stream_unit&version=search&contentPlacement=1&pgtype=collection

Baseball: A Film by Ken Burns, Episode 1, "First Inning: Our Game." Directed by Ken Burns, written by Geoffrey C. Ward, Burns, PBS, 1994.

Basken, Paul. "University Scientists Go Extra Innings to Help Baseball Solve Breaking Bats." *Chronicle of Higher Education,* November 1, 2010. Accessed October 30, 2018. https://www.chronicle.com/article/University-Scientists-Go-Extra/125223.

"Bat." Baseball-reference.com, April 25, 2018. Accessed February 18, 2019. https://www.baseball-reference.com/bullpen/Bat.

Bat Digest. "Whose MLB Baseball Bat You Looking For?" Accessed December 6, 2018. https://www.batdigest.com/mlb-bats/ .

Beckham, J. "Baseball Bat with an Axe Handle Brings More Power, Fewer Injuries." *Wired*, August 8, 14. Accessed May 23, 2016.

___. "Dustin Pedroia, Mookie Betts Using Axe Bat to Prevent Injury, Improve Swing and Offense." *Wired*, May 23, 2016. Accessed November 21, 2018. https://www.wired.com/2014/08/axe-bat/.

Beckwith, Joseph. Webinar. National Population Manager, United States Department of Agriculture—Animal and Plant Health Inspection Service. "National Perspective on EAB." December 13, 2016. http://www.emeraldashborer.info/eabu.php.

Berg, Ted. "Dustin Pedroia Is on a Hot Streak with an Odd-Looking Bat Designed to Help Hitters." *USA Today*, Accessed November 21, 2018. https://ftw.usatoday.com/2015/06/boston-red-sox-dustin-pedroia-axe-bat-knob-mlb.

_____. "Q&A with Grady Phelan, Bat Inventor." *Tedquarters*, September 7, 2010. Accessed January 7, 2019. http://tedquarters.net/2010/09/07/qa-with-grady-phelan-bat-inventor/.

Block, David. *Baseball Before We Knew It: A Search for the Roots of the Game*. Lincoln: University of Nebraska Press, 2005.

Bollinger, Rhett. "Bat Rules Being Implemented for 2010." MLB.com, March 1, 2010.

Bondy, Filip. *The Pine Tar Game: The Kansas City Royals, the New York Yankees, and Baseball's Most Absurd and Entertaining Controversy*. New York: Scribner's, 2015.

Booth, Tim. "Get a Grip: Axe Bat Is Trying to Revolutionize Baseball Bats." *Associated Press*, April 25, 2018. https://www.denverpost.com/2018/04/25/axe-handle-bats-major-league-baseball/.

Boughton, David. "Derek Jeter's P72 to Become First Bat Model Retired by Louisville Slugger in 133 Years." *Sports Business Daily*, May 10, 2017. Accessed April 25, 2018. https://www.sportsbusinessdaily.com/Daily/Issues/2017/05/10/Marketing-and-Sponsorship/Louisville-Slugger-Jeter.aspx.

Bibliography

Bowyer, Jim L., Rubin Shmulsky, and John Haygreen. *Forest Products and Wood Science: An Introduction.* 5th ed. Ames, IA: Blackwell, 2007.

Boyt, Dave. "Invasive Bugs." *Sawmill & Woodlot,* May/June 2016.

Bratkovich, Stephen, et al. "Forests of the U.S." Dovetail Partners, March 20, 2012. Accessed March 25, 2018. www.dovetailinc.org/report_pdfs/2012/dovetailusforests0312.pdf.

"Bryce Harper's Bat." *Bat Digest,* Accessed September 1, 2018. https://www.batdigest.com/mlbbats.

Buckley, James. *America's Classic Ballparks.* San Diego: Thunder Bay Press, 2013.

Canella, Stephen. "Good Wood." *Sports Illustrated,* March 25, 2002. Accessed November 27, 2017. https://www.si.com/vault/issue/703412/108/2.

Davey, Monica. "Balmy Weather May Bench a Baseball Staple." *New York Times,* July 11, 2007. Accessed December 6, 2018. https://www.nytimes.com/2007/07/11/us/11ashbat.html.

_____. "Baseball: Ash to Ashes for Bat Makers." *New York Times,* July 12, 2007. Accessed December 6, 2018. https://www.nytimes.com/2007/07/12/sports/12iht-BATS.1.6626195.html.

Denig, Joseph. "Drying Hardwood Lumber." USDA, Department of Forestry. Accessed January 31, 2018. https://www.fpl.fs.fed.us/documnts/fplgtr/fplgtr118.pdf.

Diaz, George. "Player's Best Friend? How About His Bat?" *Chicago Tribune,* May 1, 1988. Accessed March 9, 2019. https://www.chicagotribune.com/news/ct-xpm-1988-05-01-8803130672-story.html .

"Differences Between Maple Bats and Birch Bats." Max Bats. January 5, 2015. Accessed February 2, 2017. https://www.maxbats.com/blog/differences-maple-bats-birch-bats/.

Dorsey, David. "Bat Makers Look to Hit Home Runs with Players." *News-Press/USA Today,* March 24, 2014. Accessed January 7, 2017. http://www.news-press.com/story/sports/mlb/2014/03/22/bat-makers-look-to-hit-home-runs-with-players/6723579/.

"Dover Man's Axe Bat Invention Gains Major League Following." *Poughkeepsie Journal,* April 25, 2018. Accessed November 21, 2018. https://www.poughkeepsiejournal.com/story/sports/recreational/2018/04/25/dover-mans-axe-bat-invention-gains-major-league-following/549446002/.

Drane, Patrick, James Sherwood, Renzo Colosimo, and David Kretschmann, "A Study of Wood Baseball Bat Breakage." *Science Direct* 34 (2012): 616–621. Accessed November 12, 2018. https://www.sciencedirect.com/science/article/pii/S1877705812017183.

Dzierzak, Lou. "Batter Up: Shattering Sticks Create Peril in MLB Ballparks." *Scientific American,* July 14, 2008. Accessed August 26, 2018. https://www.scientificamerican.com/article/baseball-bat-controversy.

Fei, Songlin. "Divergence of Species Responses to Climate Change." *Science Advances,* May 17, 2017. Accessed December 23, 2018. http://advances.sciencemag.org/content/3/5/e1603055.

Feinstein, John. *Open: Inside the Ropes at Bethpage Black.* Boston: Little, Brown, 2003.

Finley, Marty. "Wilson Sporting Goods Acquires Rights to Louisville Slugger." March 23, 2015. Accessed January 13, 2018. https://www.bizjournals.com/louisville/news/2015/03/23/wilson-sporting-goods-acquires-rights-to.html.

"Frequently Asked Questions About UNC History." University of North Carolina Press. Accessed March 13, 2019. https://museum.unc.edu/faqs.

Frisaro, Joe. "Lighter Bat Means Farther Homers for Stanton." MLB.com, September

18, 2013. Accessed February 6, 2019. https://www.mlb.com/news/lighter-bat-means-farther-homers-for-stanton/c-61118846.

Frost, Robert. "Stopping by Woods on a Snowy Evening." Poetry Foundation, 1995. Accessed March 25, 2018. https://www.poetryfoundation.org/poems/42891/stopping-by-woods-on-a-snowy-evening.

_____. "The Road Not Taken." Poetry Foundation, Accessed March 25, 2018. https://www.poetryfoundation.org/poems/44272/the-road-not-taken.

Gentille, Sean. "For $2.22 at a Goodwill, an Intern Bought a Hall of Famer's Baseball Bat." *Pittsburgh Post-Gazette*, August 11, 2017. Accessed January 4, 2018. http://www.post-gazette.com/sports/pirates/2017/08/11/pie-traynor-bat-mears-auctions-pirates-memorabilia/stories/201708110113.

Glor, Jeff. "Marucci Bats a Hit with Pro Baseball Players." CBS News, April 4, 2012. Accessed March 9, 2019. https://www.cbsnews.com/news/marucci-bats-a-hit-with-pro-baseball-players/ .

"The Grip—It Starts with the Hands." Be a Better Hitter, accessed November 21, 2018. https://www.beabetterhitter.com/the-grip-it-starts-with-the-hands/.

Gupta, Vijay. "Biomechanical Study of the New Axe Handle Baseball Bats and Comparison with Standard Round Knob Bats." Baden Sports. https://cdn.shopify.com/s/files/1/0134/8092/t/5/assets/AXE_Bat_Study_4_10_14.pdf.

Gutman, Dan. *Banana Bats & Ding-Dong Balls: A Century of Unique Baseball Inventions*. New York: Macmillan, 1995.

Haack, Robert, Yuri Baranchikov, Leah Bauer, and Therese Poland. "Emerald Ash Borer Biology and Invasion History." *Biology and Control of Emerald Ash Borer*. Roy G. Van Driesche and Richard C. Reardon, USDA Forest Service, Eds. Washington, D.C.: USDA Forest Service, 2015. 1-13. Accessed January 20, 2019. https://www.fs.fed.us/foresthealth/technology/pdfs/FHTET-2014-09_Biology_Control_EAB.pdf.

Harlow, William, and Ellwood Harrar. *Textbook of Dendrology, 5th Ed.* New York: McGraw-Hill, 1969.

Haugen, Dennis. Forest Entomologist, USDA Forest Service, St. Paul, Minnesota. Internet correspondence, March 3, 2017.

"Have You Ever Wondered What's Up with All That Gunk on Pablo Sandoval's Helmet?" MLB.com, April 9, 2013. Accessed March 15, 2019. https://mlblogsmoresplashhits.wordpress.com/2013/04/09/have-you-ever-wondered-what's-up-with-all-that-gunk-on-pablo-sandoval's-helmet/.

Hernandez, Roland. "Review of 2009 MLB Baseball Bat Regulations." *Woodbat*, January 2009. Accessed November 17, 2018. http://www.woodbat.org/woodbat.pdf.

Hill, Bob. *Crack of the Bat: The Louisville Slugger Story.* Champaign, IL: Sports Publishing, 2002.

Hilton, K. "How an Axe-Handle Bat Is Going to Take Over Baseball." *Popular Science,* 2016. Accessed November 21, 2018. https://www.popsci.com/how-an-axe-handled-bat-is-going-to-take-over-baseball.

Hise, Beth. *Swinging Away: How Cricket and Baseball Connect.* London: Scala Books, 2010.

Hoadley, Bruce. *Understanding Wood.* Newtown, CT: Taunton Press, 2000.

Hoch, Bryan. "Pineda Ejected for Having Pine Tar on Neck." MLB.com, April 24, 2014. Accessed March 15, 2019. https://www.mlb.com/news/yankees-right-hander-michael-pineda-ejected-for-having-pine-tar-on-neck/c-73145346.

Hornung, Chris. "Maker Spotlight: The History of Wright and Ditson." *Antique Foot-*

Bibliography

ball, November 24, 2015. Accessed September 20, 2017. http://www.antiquefootball. com/wright_ditson.htm.

Jaspersohn, William. *Bat, Ball, Glove: The Making of Major League Baseball Gear*. Boston: Little, Brown and Company, 1989.

Katovich, Steven. Forest Entomologist, USDA Forest Service, St. Paul, Minnesota. Internet correspondence, March 6, 2017.

Kingseed, Wyatt. "President William McKinley: Assassinated by an Anarchist." History Net, October 1, 2001. Accessed March 24, 2018. http://www.historynet.com/ president-william-mckinley-assassinated-by-an-anarchist.htm.

Kirst, Sean. "At World Series Time in Dolgeville: Baseball History Has Turned on Bats Made in This Plant." Syracuse.com, October 26, 2014. Accessed January 25, 2017. http://www.syracuse.com/kirst/index.ssf/2014/10/at_world_series_time_in_ dolgeville_baseball_history_has_turned_on_this_plant.html.

_____. "Cut from a Family Tree: Kren Bats Used by Baseball Legends, Once Made in Syracuse." *Syracuse Post-Standard*, October 25, 1995. Accessed November 13, 2017; also see https://www.krenbats.com/.

Lazzarino, Chris. "Inventor Hopes New Bat Hits Home Run for Safety." *Profile* 4 (2006). Accessed January 7, 2019. http://proxr.com/wp-content/uploads/2010/03/ KUAlumniGradyBatRevisedT.jpg.

Leerhsen, Charles. *Ty Cobb: A Terrible Beauty*. New York: Simon & Schuster, 2016.

Lemire, Joe. "Marucci Bats Got from Tool Shed to Clubhouse One Convert at a Time." *Sports Illustrated*, March 10, 2011. Accessed March 19, 2018. https://www. si.com/more-sports/2011/03/10/marucci-bats.

Lepperd, Tom, ed. *Official Baseball Rules*. New York: Office of the Commissioner of Baseball, 2018.

Leventhal, Josh. *A History of Baseball in 100 Objects: A Tour Through the Bats, Balls, Uniforms, Awards, Documents, and Other Artifacts That Tell the Story of the National Pastime*. New York: Black Dog & Leventhal, 2015.

"Louisiana Purchase, 1803." Department of State, Bureau of Public Affairs, Office of the Historian. Accessed January 12, 2018. https://history.state.gov/milestones/1801-1829/louisiana-purchase.

"Louisville Slugger Retires P72 Bat Model in Honor of Derek Jeter." MLB.com, September 24, 2014. Accessed August 25, 2017. https://www.mlb.com/news/louisville-slugger-retires-p72-bat-model-in-honor-of-derek-jeter/c-96195366.

MacCleery, Douglas. "Resiliency: The Trademark of American Forests." *Forest Products Journal* 45:1 (1995).

Magee, David, and Philip Shirley. *Sweet Spot: Years of Baseball and the Louisville Slugger*. Chicago: Triumph Books, 2009.

"Manny's Helmet Has a Story to Tell." *La Vida Baseball*, January 2019. Accessed March 5, 2019. https://www.lavidabaseball.com/manny-ramirez-helmet-hall-of-fame/.

McAuley, Grant. "Axe Handle Bat New Weapon of Choice for Braves' Swanson." 92.9 the Game, May 19, 2018. Accessed November 21, 2018. https://929thegame.radio. com/articles/axe-handle-bat-new-weapon-choice-braves-swanson.

McCaffrey, Jen. "Dustin Pedroia, Mookie Betts using Axe Bat to prevent injury, improve swing and offense." MassLive. 2016. Accessed November 21, 2018. https://www. masslive.com/redsox/index.ssf/2016/05/dustin_pedroia_mookie_betts_us.html.

McCarver, Tim, and Danny Peary. *Tim McCarver's Baseball for Brain Surgeons and Other Fans*. New York: Random House, 1998.

Millard, Candice. *The River of Doubt: Theodore Roosevelt's Darkest Journey*. New York: Broadway Books, 2006.

Bibliography

Miller, Stuart. *Good Wood: The Story of the Baseball Bat.* Chicago: ACTA, 2011.

Mittermeyer, Paul. "Eddie Collins." SABR BioProject, http://sabr.org/bioproj/person/c480756d.

"MLBPA Adopt Recommendations of Safety and Health Advisory Committee." MLB.com, December 9, 2008. Accessed October 11, 2018. http://www.mlb.com/pa/pdf/health_advisory_120908.pdf.

Morris, Peter. *A Game of Inches: The Story Behind the Innovations That Shaped Baseball.* Chicago: Ivan R. Dee, 2010.

Mueller, Rick. "Newly Discovered Gehrig Bat Sells for $436,970." *Sports Collectors Daily,* Accessed November 10, 2017. https://www.sportscollectorsdaily.com/new-gehrig-bat-uncovered-was-used-as-homeowners-protection/.

_____. "Peck and Snyder: The Company." *Sports Collectors Daily,* February 17, 2010. Accessed November 6, 2017. https://www.sportscollectorsdaily.com/peck-and-snyder-the-company/.

Mussill, Bernie. "The Baseball Bat: From the First Crack to the Clank." *Oldtyme Baseball News* 2 (1998): 21.

"Naval Stores." National Park Service, accessed March 13, 2019. https://www.nps.gov/mocr/learn/historyculture/upload/Naval-Stores.pdf.

Newcomb, Tim. "Facts About Floors: Detailing the Process Behind NBA Hardwood Courts." *Sports Illustrated,* December 2, 2015. Accessed June 26, 2017. https://www.si.com/nba/2015/12/02/nba-hardwood-floors-basketball-court-celtics-nets-magic-nuggets-hornets.

"NOAA Data Show 2016 Warmest Year on Record Globally." NASA, January 18, 2017. Accessed on December 26, 2018. https://www.giss.nasa.gov/research/news/20170118/

Norris, Jack. "Maruccci Sports Acquires Victus Sports." *Baseball America,* February 17, 2017. Accessed December 31, 2017. https://www.baseballamerica.com/business/marucci-sports-acquires-victus-sports/.

Odell, John, ed. *Baseball as America.* Washington, D.C.: National Geographic Society, 2002.

Oklahoma State University Extension Service. "Fundamental Aspects of Kiln Drying Lumber." Oklahoma State University Extension, March 2017. Accessed January 30, 2018. http://factsheets.okstate.edu/documents/fapc-146-fundamental-aspects-of-kiln-drying-lumber.

Panshin, A. J., and Carl de Zeeuw. *Textbook of Wood Technology.* Vol. 1. New York: McGraw-Hill, 1970.

Passan, Jeff. "New MLB Rules Cause Maple Bat Flap." Yahoo! Sports, January 19, 2009. Accessed October 19, 2018. https://www.yahoo.com/news/mlb-rules-cause-maple-bat-051500525--mlb.html.

Perez-Pena, Richard. "This Factory's Bats Are Going, Going, Gone; As Home of McGwire's 'Big Stick,' Struggling Upstate Town Gets a Life." *New York Times,* April 25, 1999. Accessed December 9, 2017. http://www.nytimes.com/1999/04/25/nyregion/this-factory-s-bats-are-going-going-gone-home-mcgwire-s-big-stick-struggling.html.

Petri, Josh. "What Is Pine Tar and Why Is It Illegal in Baseball?" Digg.com, April 24, 2014. Accessed February 15, 2019. https://digg.com/2014/what-is-pine-tar-and-why-is-it-illegal-in-baseball.

Pfeiffer, David. "Baseball Patents." National Archives, April 3, 2015. Accessed April 19, 2018. https://text-message.blogs.archives.gov/2015/04/03/baseball-patents/.

Bibliography

"Pontiac Turning Company Bat." Keyman Collectibles. Accessed November 7, 2017. http://keymancollectibles.com/bats/pontiacturningcobaseballbat.htm.

Pucci, Jacob. "29 Things You Probably Didn't Know Were Invented in Upstate New York." NYup.com, May 2016. Accessed December 4, 2017.

"Rawlings Holder Angry Over K2 Pact with Nintendo in Buyout." *Marketwatch*, Accessed March 18, 2018. https://www.markewtwatch.com/story/rawlings-holder-angry-over-k2-pact-nintendo-in-buyout .

Ritter, Lawrence. *The Story of Baseball*. 3d ed. New York: Morrow Junior Books, 1999.

Roberts, Quinn. "Growing Number of Hitters Ditching Batting Gloves." MLB.com, July 16, 2015. Accessed March 15, 2019. https://www.mlb.com/news/growing-number-of-hitters-ditch-batting-gloves/c-136913172.

_____. "Huge Strides Being Made in Reducing Broken Bats." MLB.com, August 3, 2012. https://www.mlb.com/news/c-36046676/print.

Rosenthal, Ken. "After Dropping the Ball on Pink Bats Last Year, MLB Moves to Get It Right." Fox Sports, May 7, 2014. Accessed May 16, 2018. https://www.foxsports.com/mlb/story/after-dropping-ball-on-pink-bats-last-year-mlb-moves-to-get-it-right-050714.

_____. "Maple Bat Problem Not Easy to Solve." Fox Sports, September 21, 2010. Accessed November 10, 2018. https://www.foxsports.com/mlb/story/ash-may-not-be-solution-to-baseballs-maple-bat-problem-092110.

"The Rundown—Maple vs. Ash." Marucci Sports, July 8, 2015. Accessed December 1, 2018. bats/https://rundown.maruccisports.com/2015/07/08/maple-vs-ash/.

Rushin, Steve. *The 34-Ton Bat*. New York: Little, Brown, 2013.

Schartman, Joe. "Wright & Ditson Tennis, Golf, Baseball and Sporting Goods." *Wood Tennis*, accessed September 20, 2017. http://www.woodtennis.com/WaD.html and http://www.antiquefootball.com/wright_ditson.htm.

Schmidt, Steve. "Zimmerman Manufacturing Company." Shiawassee History, accessed October 10, 2017. http://shiawasseehistory.com/zimmerman.html.

Sharp, John B. *Wood Identification: A Manual for the Non-professional*. Knoxville: University of Tennessee, Agricultural Extension Service Publication 1389, 1990.

"Should I Be Swinging an Axe Bat?" BaseballMonkey Blog, 2018. Accessed November 21, 2018. http://blog.baseballmonkey.com/should-i-be-swinging-an-axe-bat/.

Simons, Jessica. "The Emerald Ash Borer: A Pest, a Problem, and an Opportunity." *Sawmill & Woodlot*, December 2006 / January 2007.

"Slash Pine, Pinus Elliottii." ChasingTrees.net. March 16, 2018. Accessed March 13, 2019. https://chasingtrees.net/?tag=tar-and-pitch-from-pine-rosin-was-once-used-to-seal-ships.

Slutsky, Bruce. "The Pine Tar Game, July 24, 1983." SABR, Accessed March 10, 2019. https://sabr.org/gamesproj/game/july-24-1983-george-brett-pine-tar-game#_edn6.

Smith, Curt. *Storied Stadiums: Baseball's History Through Its Ballparks*. New York: Carroll & Graf, 2001.

Sparks, James. USDA, Forest Products Laboratory, Madison, Wisconsin. News release, July 12, 2013.

Stamp, Jimmy. "A Brief History of the Baseball." *Smithsonian*, June 28, 2013. Accessed March 9, 2019. https://www.smithsonianmag.com/arts-culture/a-brief-history-of-the-baseball-3685086/.

Sunder, Rashmi. "What Is a Rosin Bag and How Is It Used in Different Sports?" *Sports Aspire*, February 26, 2018. Accessed March 15, 2019. https://sportsaspire.com/what-is-a-rosin-bag-how-is-it-used-in-different-sports.

Bibliography

Swayne, Matt. "Invasion." *Penn State Ag Science* 18 (Fall/Winter 2016). https://agsci.psu.edu/magazine/articles/2016/fall-winter/invasion.

Thompson, Andrea. "The Science Behind Breaking Baseball Bats." Live Science, accessed October 18, 2018. https://www.livescience.com/2699-science-breaking-baseball-bats.html.

Thorn, John. *Baseball in the Garden of Eden: The Secret History of the Early Game.* New York: Simon & Schuster, 2011.

_____. "The Bat and Ball, a Distinct Game or a Generic Term." Our Game, November 27, 2012. Accessed April 11, 2017. https://ourgame.mlblogs.com/the-bat-and-ball-a-distinct-game-or-a-generic-term-ebfdc19df329.

_____. "A Peek Into the Pocket Book." MLB.com, April 19, 2016. Accessed May 1, 2017. https://ourgame.mlblogs.com/a-peek-into-the-pocket-book-a9bd03dfe31d.

Thurm, Wendy. "Breaking Maple Bats: Why Rookies Must Use Higher Density Bats This Season." *SBNation*, February 29, 2012. Accessed November 5, 2018. https://www.sbnation.com/2012/2/29/2829452/new-rule-rookies-maple-bat-density.

"Tudor England Contents." English History, Accessed February 10, 2019. https://englishhistory.net/tudor/.

U.S. Department of Agriculture. *Forest Service Agriculture Handbook. Utilization of the Southern Pines.* Volume 2. Washington, D.C.: USDA, 1972.

_____. "Plant Pest and Disease Programs." USDA, accessed January 31, 2017. https://www.aphis.usda.gov/plant_health/plant_pest_info/asian_lhb/downloads/response-guidelines.pdf.

U.S. Forest Service. "Study Suggests That Tree Ranges Are Already Shifting Due to Climate Change." Autumn 2010. Accessed December 26, 2018. https://www.fs.fed.us/nrs/news/review/review-vol11.pdf .

_____. "Forest Resources of the United States- Table 2." USDA Forest Service, accessed December 14, 2018. https://www.fia.fs.fed.us/program-features/rpa/docs/2017RPAFIATABLESFINAL_050918.pdf .

"Vacuum Kiln Plants." *American Wood Technology*, Accessed January 30, 2018. https://www.americanwoodtechnology.com/vacuum-kiln-plants/.

van Dyck, Dave. "Shattering Maple Bats Raise Concerns." *Chicago Tribune*, May 25, 2008. Accessed September 1, 2018. http://articles.chicagotribune.com/2008-05-25/sports/0805240422_1_maple-bats-major-league-baseball-darts/2.

Walker, Ben. "Properties of Baseball Bats." *Baseball Research Journal*, Summer 2010. Accessed May 16, 2018. http://sabr.org./research/properties-baseball-bats.

Watts, Robert, and A. Terry Bayhill. *Keep Your Eye on the Ball: The Science and Folklore of Baseball.* New York: W. H. Freeman, 1991.

Weintraub, Robert. "Two Who Did Not Return." *New York Times*, May 25, 2013. Accessed January 14, 2018. http://www.nytimes.com/2013/05/26/sports/baseball/remembering-the-major-leaguers-who-died-in-world-war-ii.html.

Wenger, Karl. *Forestry Handbook: Second Edition.* New York: John Wiley & Sons, 1984.

"What Is Pine Tar? Here's Everything You Need to Know." JustBats.com, November 1, 2017. Accessed February 15, 2019. https://blog.justbats.com/what-is-pine-tar-what-does-pine-tar-do.

"Who Owns America's Forests?" U.S. Endowment for Forestry and Communities, accessed December 14, 2018. https://www.fia.fs.fed.us/program-features/rpa/docs/2017RPAFIATABLESFINAL_050918.pdf.

"Whose MLB Baseball Bat You Looking For?" *Bat Digest*, Accessed December 6, 2018. https://www.batdigest.com/mlb-bats/ .

Williams, Ted, and Jim Prime. *Ted Williams' Hit List.* Toronto: Stoddart, 1996.

Bibliography

Williams, Ted, and John Underwood. *The Science of Hitting*. New York: Simon & Schuster, 1970.

Wolff, Rick. *The Baseball Encyclopedia*. 8th Ed. New York: Macmillan, 1990.

Woodall, C. W. "An Indicator of Tree Migration in Forests of the Eastern United States." *Forest Ecology and Management 257* (2009): 1434-1444. Accessed December 23, 2018. https://www.nrs.fs.fed.us/pubs/jrnl/2009/nrs_2009_woodall_001.pdf.

Wright, Frank Lloyd. "In the Cause of Architecture: Wood." *Architectural Record* 23, no. 3 (March 1908): 155-165. https://www.architecturalrecord.com/ext/resources/news/2016/01-Jan/InTheCause/Frank-Lloyd-Wright-In-the-Cause-of-Architecture-March-1908.pdf.

Zabarenko, Deborah. "Unshattered Record: Pro Baseball Bats Now Break 50 Percent Less, USDA Says." Reuters.com. July 12, 2013. Accessed October 29, 2018. https://www.reuters.com/article/us-usa-baseball-bats/unshattered-record-pro-baseball-bats-now-break-50-percent-less-usda-says-idUSBRE96B1132013071

Websites

Axe Bat. https://axebat.com.

Birch Bats. https://www.birchbats.com/why-swing-birch.php.

BWP Bats. https://bwpbats.com.

Chandler Bats. https://www.chandlerbats.com.

Don't Move Firewood. https://www.dontmovefirewood.org/about.

Goldin Auctions. www.goldinauctions.com.

Heritage Auctions. www.ha.com.

Leatherstocking Hand-Split Billet Company. http://www.leatherstockinghandsplits.com/about-us.aspx.

Marruci Sports. https://rundown.maruccisports.com/2015/07/08/maple-vs-ash/.

Max Bats. https://www.maxbats.com/blog/differences-maple-bats-birch-bats/.

PowerBilt. http://powerbilt.com/about-powerbilt-golf.

ProXR. https://proxr.com/about/.

Spalding Sporting Goods. http://www.spalding.com/about-spalding.html.

Trinity Bat Company. http://www.trinitybatco.com/wood-types/.

VacDry Kilns. http://www.vacdry.com.

Victus Sports. http://victussports.com.

Vintage Bats. https://www.vintagebats.com/feature_page-JoeMauer.htm.

Wright & Ditson. https://wrightanddison.com/history/.

Index

Index

Index

Index

Index

wicket 7, 8
wide-grain 62, 63
Williams, Ted 14, 25, 26, 27, 28, 29, 30, 36, 37, 63, 65, 68, 69, 70, 71, 92, 113, 124, 130, 132, 133, 134, 141, 142, 146
willow 15, 16, 41, 95, 104
Wilson Sporting Goods 46, 113
wood preservative 156
wood science 2, 3, 72, 75, 76
World Series 1, 3, 8, 16, 17, 28, 36, 41, 43, 48, 49, 50, 54, 57, 89, 92, 130, 136, 149, 161
Worth Company 51

Wright, Frank Lloyd 58
Wright, George 9, 39, 41, 44, 57, 63, 79, 88, 92, 130, 149, 157
Wright, Harry 9, 37, 38, 39, 58
Wright, Sam 39
Wright & Ditson 38, 39, 40, 41

Yahoo Sports 78
Yankee Stadium 43, 49
Yastremzski, Carl 63

Zimmerman Manufacturing Co. 41